# LET THERE BE LIGHT

## BY

## CLIFFORD A. GRACE

**UNRAVELING THE MYSTERIES OF THE BIBLE FROM GENESIS THROUGH REVELATION**

Copyright © 2011 by Clifford A Grace

*Let There Be Light*
*Unraveling The Mysteries of The Bible from Genesis Through Revelation*
by Clifford A Grace

Printed in the United States of America

ISBN 9781613797273

All rights reserved solely by the author. The author guarantees all contents are original and do not infringe upon the legal rights of any other person or work. No part of this book may be reproduced in any form without the permission of the author. The views expressed in this book are not necessarily those of the publisher.

Unless otherwise indicated, Bible quotations are taken from The Revised Standard Version of the Bible. Copyright © 1972 by Thomas Nelson Inc.

All Hebrew and Greek translations are taken from Strong's Exhaustive Concordance of the Bible by American Christian College Press.

www.xulonpress.com

This book is dedicated to the Lord, because without his grace it would not be possible to accomplish.

A special thanks to Linda Woolley for her writing skills and suggested input into this work.

Also

A special thank you to The Shepherd's Page for establishing precise critical dates for past Biblical events and an online calculator to compute different calendars and dates for future time-oriented prophecies that will take place.

# INTRODUCTION

If you have ever tried to put together a thousand piece puzzle, you have probably learned that it helps to have the cover of the box next to you. By doing so, you can see the big picture that will take shape from your work. You can separate the edge pieces and the different colored pieces of the interior into separate piles to draw from when needed. Time and frustration can be reduced, but each individual piece must still be dealt with to accomplish the task. Life on planet earth is no different. The millions of little pieces of the puzzle that make up our life must be dealt with and put into a proper perspective. For the Christian, all of the pieces of the puzzle are contained in the Word of God, the Bible. But without the Holy Spirit of God revealing the pieces to us, we will never understand the larger picture. The only way our life will come into the fullness, which God intended, is by sitting at the feet of Jesus in prayer and in the study of God's Word.

The purpose of *Let There Be Light* is to assist you in understanding the big picture in your relationship to God. This book is an overview from Genesis through Revelation. It unravels the mysteries of the Bible, clarifies the events that are now taking place, and explains the events that are to come. It is the culmination of thirty-nine years of sitting at the feet of Jesus and searching the Word of God. Without the call of God on my life and the revelation of the Spirit, this work would never have been accomplished. It has been a gift of God by grace through faith! Does that mean it is perfect in every detail? The answer is no. For that to happen, it would have to be a direct dictation from God to me as he did with Moses. While the main work is the revelation of the Spirit in my life, there are some issues where I have rendered opinions when the Scripture doesn't give us the information. Those issues can be clearly perceived by the manner of my statements. If Scripture does not balance from Genesis through Revelation, then error has occurred, and it is not with the Word of God! Problems can come from a poor translation from the Hebrew or Greek to our English Bibles. Or it can be derived from a limited understanding on a given issue on our part. It can also come through translating figurative terms into literal terms. Revelation 6:14 is a good example, "... and every mountain and island was removed from its place."

In the assembling of this material, I have used the Revised Standard Version of the Scriptures. I have only used the essential verses in support of the issues covered. In extracting the precise dating of events, I have used the research provided by The Shepherd's Page at www.abdicate.net for their "Chronology of Time According to Scripture." I also used their calendar converter for calculating the dates for future events based upon my understanding of Scripture. If I have made any miscalculations in the timing of events, fear not! The events recorded in the Bible are still going to take place for God has ordained them!

For those who have eyes to see and ears to hear in the words of Jesus, Matthew 13:11–17 sums up the issue of *Let There Be Light*.

> To you [the Christian] it has been given to know the secrets of the kingdom of heaven, but to them [unbelievers] it has not been given. (12) For to him who has [faith in Christ] will more be given, and he will have abundance; but from him who has not [faith in Christ], even what he has will be taken away. (13) This is why I speak to them in parables, because seeing they do not see, and hearing they do not hear, nor do they understand. (14) With them indeed is fulfilled the prophecy of Isaiah which says: "You shall indeed hear but never understand, and

you shall indeed see but never perceive. (15) For this people's heart has grown dull, and their ears are heavy of hearing, and their eyes they have closed, lest they should perceive with their eyes, and hear with their ears, and understand with their heart, and turn for me to heal them." (16) But blessed are your eyes, for they see, and your ears, for they hear. (17) Truly, I say to you, many prophets and righteous men longed to see what you see, and did not see it, and to hear what you hear, and did not hear it.

Because we are looking at the entire picture of Scripture from Genesis through Revelation, we need to grasp the issue of eternity. In Deuteronomy 33:27 it states: "The eternal God is your dwelling place, and underneath are the everlasting arms." God has no beginning and he has no end. He has no time structure that controls his existence or duration of life. He *IS*, always in the present tense! He is life, and he will always exist. He is eternity! Apart from what God creates, nothing else exists, because there is nothing else beyond God. God is eternal life, the focal point of everything. He is a person who's substance is spirit (John 4:24). John 17:3 sums up the purpose of our life on planet earth: "And this is eternal life, that they know thee the only true God, and Jesus Christ whom thou hast sent."

In dealing with Scripture, we are confronted with what God has done in the past, what he is doing now, and what he has already established for the future. In looking at the past, present, and future revealed in Scripture, we are confronted with three different creations. Because of these three major benchmarks in eternity, I am labeling them Eternity Past, Eternity Present, and Eternity Future. While God is the same yesterday, today, and forever, what he does in his creation will change. All changes are for the good of his created beings that love him and serve him in his state of holiness.

## ETERNITY PAST

The first creation is presented in Genesis 1:1: "In the beginning God created the heavens and the earth." It is a statement of fact, complete in and of itself. The details must be gleaned from the rest of the Bible. This creation consisted of two heavens and one earth. The outer heaven was God's throne. The inner heaven was the spiritual dimension of the angelic realm with an earth on which they lived. In Genesis 1:2 we have an explanation of what happened within that creation after it came into existence: "The earth was without form and void, and darkness was upon the face of the deep; and the Spirit of God was moving over the face of the waters." This passage must be reviewed from the Hebrew terms used and supported by other verses throughout the Bible to be understood. The English translation does not clearly give the meaning of the verse. What this verse describes is the rebellion of Lucifer, an angel who had great power and authority. Lucifer decided he wanted to be like God without God. One-third of the angels followed Lucifer in his rebellion. In Genesis 1:3–5, God makes a proclamation to deal with the situation: "And God said, 'Let there be light' and there was light. (4) And God saw that the light was good; and God separated the light from the darkness. (5) God called the light Day, and the darkness he called Night. And there was evening and there was morning, one day."

**ETERNITY PRESENT**

The second creation begins with God's proclamation, "Let there be light." God separated the faithful angels from the unfaithful. He then expands his creation and creates a new heaven in the center of the existing two heavens. He restructures the angelic earth and places it into the new heaven along with the creation of the sun, moon, and stars. He creates new life-forms upon the earth and creates mankind. And this is where we live now. God does all of this in seven stages called days. The new creation is then subjected to God's "light" and Lucifer's rebellion, "darkness." These two issues of "light" and "darkness" will become an educational program, for all creation to come to a clear-cut understanding of why God's created beings cannot live without God's holy sovereign control. Using the created time system of this new creation, it will run for a period of seven thousand years. In the first creation of the angelic realm, there is no measurement of time using day and night. There is only the continuous light derived from the presence of God. No rest is needed in that dimension because of the eternal energy coming from God, and there was no death in any form. Since there is no time measurement in that dimension, it is impossible to determine how long it existed before the rebellion of Lucifer and the creation of our system. The other major change from the first creation to ours is that God created every angelic form of life individually, compared to the procreation process of this creation.

## ETERNITY FUTURE

The third creation will begin at the end of the seven thousand years of our creation. The educational program for all creation that God has undertaken will be complete. This earth and the heaven around it, plus the angelic heaven, will be destroyed. Every angel that was not part of the rebellion will be assembled before the throne of God. Every human from the time of Adam and Eve will also be assembled there. All humans who were not part of the rapture of Jesus will stand before the judgment seat of God. All those who refused to believe and follow God in his light will be separated and thrown into the lake of fire, which is eternal damnation. God will then create another new heaven and a new earth for all of his created beings. It will be the same order of Genesis 1:1, two heavens and one earth, and it will exist in an even greater manifestation of God's glory due to God's educational program. This segment is covered in Revelation 20:11–22:21.

There are three different calendars used in this document concerning our creation, Eternity Present. The first is the astrological time count beginning with the creation of our universe as year 0 and labeled "Creation Year." In the use of this time count, I am using only the number of the year, not the days. The second time count is labeled "Western," using the Gregorian calendar. It begins with the year 3977 BC and counts backwards to what was believed to be (but is not), the year of the birth of Christ AD 1. So the Creation Year 0 and the Western year 3977 BC begin at the same point. If this creation terminates at the exact end of seven thousand years, it will be Creation 7000 or January 1, AD 3025. The third time system used is the Jewish calendar. It is critical in calculating the prophetic events based upon the ceremonial laws, primarily the feasts. Their calendar does not begin until Creation Year 216, and it uses twelve lunar months of 29 and 30 days. The time loss is made up every third year by adding an additional month to the calendar called Adar II. It is placed between the months of Adar I and Nisan. At the end of the three years, the total will average 365.2468 days per year.

The month of Nisan begins the religious part of their calendar. It runs for seven months through the month of Tishri. Tishri 1 is the beginning of the Jewish New Year. Their New Year falls during the Western calendar months of September and October. So we have the following equation: Creation Year 216 equals the Jewish month Tishri 1, year 1, which equals the Western month September 7, 3761 BC.

Since this earth did exist in the first creation of Genesis 1:1, our earth may well be millions of years old, or billions, if measured accurately by our time system. What must be taken into consideration when establishing scientific theory is that there was a major restructuring of this earth when God moved it into the new heaven. Also, at the time of Noah's flood, there had to be major changes to the landscape of this earth that need to be calculated into the equation. According to the Word of God, for our new creation, we are just short of six thousand years old! In consideration of the dinosaurs, there is nothing noted in Scripture. But that does not disqualify God from enlarging any of the species of animals he created at the beginning before the flood of Noah. When we look at man in the Old Testament, there are numerous verses that refer to giants. 1 Chronicles 20:8 states: "These were descended *from the giants in Gath*; and they fell by the hand of David and by the hand of his servants" (italics added). While God created all of the species that have the "breath of life" to produce after their kind, it does not prohibit God from making alterations to the size or color of a species at any point in time. While it is indicated that full-grown dinosaurs were not on the ark, the miniature may have been there but did not enlarge after being released because of the multiple changes in the environment. The entire issue of the ark reveals the power of God to save and destroy as he wills. God does perform miracles!

God has given us a complete perspective of the past, present, and future of our creation. One of the future miracles that will take place on May 14, AD 2014, will be the sun turning black as sackcloth and the moon turning to blood. For seven 24 hours days there will be darkness around the entire world. The heat of the sun will not stop, but the light will. God will not freeze our planet. That is not the purpose of the event, and God is not bound by the natural order that he established. On the eighth day, May 21, AD 2014, the sky will be rolled back like a scroll, and the entire world will be able to look into the throne room of God! This will take place in a moment of time. Since God's throne room is two heavens beyond our galaxy, the event will have to exceed the speed of light. But God is not bound by the speed of light! It is only a part of our creation. God is bound by the promises he has made to us in Scripture, and these events will take place, even if I have miscalculated the date.

The judgments of God are coming upon the earth at this point in time to destroy the greed, corruption, and evil that governs our lives. True repentance by every man, woman, and child on the face of the earth, concerning our sins against God, is the only solution to stop the judgments. But that is not going to happen. So the plan of Scripture that God has revealed to us, in his timing, will take place. So those who do repent and commit their lives to Christ will be saved.

I believe the Bible is the infallible Word of God and does not contradict itself. While errors have entered into Scripture through translation, the work of the Holy Spirit leads us into all truth, provided we are searching for it. As a foundation for our search, we do need to understand that when God gave to man the Old Testament, he was speaking to spiritually dead people. He, therefore, used objects of the natural order to identify things in the spiritual realm. For example, we know water quenches the thirst of the body. The living water of Christ quenches the thirst of the soul. It is the enlightenment of God. The sea refers to the ocean in the natural; it also refers to the peoples, nations, and tongues; the spiritual tidal flow of humanity. A mountain can be literal or represent a king or government, depicting an elevated position. Mount Zion in the spirit is the government of God with Christ as king. These are simple illustrations of how the language of the Old Testament translates into the spiritual. The Ritual Law given to Moses is a picture of the work that Christ would fulfill when he came.

Discernment is needed in applying the spiritual. This must come from God through the Holy Spirit since he is the author of the Bible. Under the New Covenant, we are no longer in bondage to the form and ritual of the old Covenant of Law. That does not mean the law is null and void. It is fulfilled in Christ. For example, the Feast of Passover is the ritual of our salvation. Today, when we believe that Jesus is the Son of God and paid the price for the forgiveness of our sins, through the enlightening work of the Holy Spirit, we accept what is revealed to us and accept Jesus as our savior! In doing this, we have fulfilled the Feast of Passover under the New Covenant. The Spirit of God then comes to live in us and reveal the Word and will of God. Spiritual rebirth takes place and we have a personal relationship with God. We don't have to do this every year as in the Old Testament.

When we see the command that says we should not covet, but cannot stop from coveting, we ask forgiveness from the Lord and his help for us to overcome the condition. We don't have to offer an animal as a sacrificial offering to cover the problem. The shed blood of Jesus covers all our sins—past present, and future—but we must repent and confess to the Lord our failure and seek his help by changing our life. This is what he will do in time as we draw closer in our relationship with him. It's like lifting weights to become stronger. If we do it every day, we will accomplish the goal. If we only do it once a month, there will be very little change. The freer we want to become from our fallen sinful nature and the sins that are destroying our life, the more time we must spend with Jesus in prayer and bible study. He will bring it to pass. The Covenant of Law did not deliver man from his sinful nature; it showed us the standard of God and pointed out the sin in us. But through following God's laws, with animal sacrifice in repentance, God protected and blessed his people. Today, God wants to transform the lives of his people in Christ through the power of the Holy Spirit. That is the difference between the Old and New Covenant. We have the glory of a personal relationship with God in Christ. Nothing on this earth can compare to the joy of knowing and serving him. And this is what eternal life is all about! Living apart from him is degradation and death.

# CONTENTS

INTRODUCTION .................................................................... vii

CHAPTER 1   IN THE BEGINNING ........................................ 25
TIME FRAME: Eternity Past—The creation of the angelic realm

CHAPTER 2   A NEW CREATION ........................................ 38
TIME FRAME: Eternity Present—The creation of our heaven and earth

CHAPTER 3   FATHER, SON, AND HOLY SPIRIT ............... 55
TIME FRAME: Eternity Present—The creation of our heaven and earth

CHAPTER 4   MAN IN THE IMAGE OF GOD ..................... 68
TIME FRAME: Eternity Present—Creation 0, Western 3977 BC

CHAPTER 5   THE FIRST PHASE OF GOD'S EDUCATIONAL PROGRAM .................................................. 87
TIME FRAME: Eternity Present—Creation 0, Western 3977 BC

CHAPTER 6   LIFE OUTSIDE OF PARADISE ................... 100
TIME FRAME: Eternity Present—Creation 5, Western 3972 BC

xxi

CHAPTER 7   TOTAL DEGENERATION OF LIFE ON
EARTH .................................................................... 107
TIME FRAME: Eternity Present—Creation 1657, Jewish
1441, Western 2320 BC

CHAPTER 8   THE SECOND PHASE OF GOD'S
EDUCATIONAL PROGRAM ................................ 117
TIME FRAME: Eternity Present—Creation 1657, Jewish
1441, Western 2320 BC

CHAPTER 9   THE THIRD PHASE OF GOD'S
EDUCATIONAL PROGRAM ................................ 129
TIME FRAME: Eternity Present—Creation 2453, Jewish
15 Nisan 2237, Western
March 27, 1524 BC

CHAPTER 10   THE FOURTH PHASE OF GOD'S
EDUCATIONAL PROGRAM ................................ 148
TIME FRAME: Eternity Present—Creation 3971, Jewish
15 Tishri 3755, Western
October 6, 7 BC

CHAPTER 11   INTRODUCTION TO THE GREAT
TRIBULATION PERIOD ........................................ 171

CHAPTER 12   THE FIRST SEAL—THE FIRST RIDER OF
THE APOCALYPSE ................................................ 181
TIME FRAME: Eternity Present—Creation 5962, Jewish
5746, Western AD 1986 TO
Creation 5993, Jewish 1 Kislev 5778, Western November 19, AD 2017

CHAPTER 13   THE SECOND SEAL—THE SECOND
RIDER OF THE APOCALYPSE ............................. 199
TIME FRAME: Eternity Present—Creation 5962, Jewish

5746, Western AD 1986 TO
Creation 5993, Jewish 1 Kislev 5778, Western November 19,
AD 2017

CHAPTER 14  THE THIRD SEAL—THE THIRD RIDER
OF THE APOCALYPSE .......................................................... 207
TIME FRAME: Eternity Present—Creation 5962, Jewish
5746, Western AD 1986 TO
Creation 5993, Jewish 1 Kislev 5778, Western November 19,
AD 2017

CHAPTER 15  THE FOURTH SEAL—THE FOURTH
RIDER OF THE APOCALYPSE ............................................. 213
TIME FRAME: Eternity Present—Creation 5962, Jewish
5746, Western AD 1986 TO
Creation 5993, Jewish 1 Kislev 5778, Western November 19,
AD 2017

CHAPTER 16  THE FIFTH SEAL—MARTYRDOM OF
THE SAINTS ........................................................................... 218
TIME FRAME: Eternity Present—Creation 5962, Jewish
5746, Western AD 1986 TO
Creation 5997, Jewish 9 Sivan 5781, Western May 20, AD 2021

CHAPTER 17  THE SIXTH SEAL ......................................... 232
TIME FRAME: Eternity Present—Creation 5990, Jewish
14 Iyyar 5774, Western May 14,
AD 2014

CHAPTER 18  THE SEVENTH SEAL—FIRST HALF
OF THE SEVENTIETH WEEK .............................................. 243
TIME FRAME: Eternity Present—Creation 5990, Jewish
21 Iyyar 5774, Western May 21,
AD 2014 TO Creation 5993, Jewish 1 Kislev 5778, Western
November 19, AD 2017

# Let There Be Light

CHAPTER 19  THE LAST HALF OF THE SEVENTIETH WEEK AND ARMAGEDDON ............ 275
TIME FRAME: Eternity Present—Creation 5993, Jewish 1 Kislev 5578, Western November 19, AD 2017 TO Creation 5997, Jewish 24 Tammuz 5781, Western July 4, AD 2021

CHAPTER 20  THE SEVEN BOWLS OF WRATH ............ 288
TIME FRAME: Eternity Present—Creation 5993, Jewish 1 Kislev 5778, Western November 19, AD 2017 TO Creation 5997, Jewish 19 Iyyar 5778, Western May 1, AD 2021

CHAPTER 21  THE RETURN OF JESUS TO THE EARTH ............ 308
TIME FRAME: Eternity Present—Creation 5997, Jewish 9 Sivan 5781, Western Thursday May 20, AD 2021 TO Creation 5998, Jewish 1 Tishri 5783, Western Monday September 26, AD 2022

CHAPTER 22  THE FIFTH PHASE OF GOD'S EDUCATIONAL PROGRAM ............ 327
TIME FRAME: Eternity Present—Creation 5998, Jewish 1 Tishri 5783, Western Monday September 26, AD 2022 TO Creation 5998, Jewish 15 Tishri 5783, Western Thursday October 10, AD 2022

CHAPTER 23  THE FINAL JUDGMENT ............ 347
TIME FRAME: Eternity Future

TIMETABLE OF EVENTS FROM GENESIS THROUGH REVELATION ............ 365

ENDNOTES ............ 371

# CHAPTER 1

# IN THE BEGINNING

**EVENT: The first creation**
**TIME FRAME: Eternity Past—The creation of the angelic realm**
**INTRODUCTION NARRATIVE:** *God's first creation was the angelic realm. Time as we know it in our solar system did not exist. Because of God's presence throughout his creation, there was pure light all of the time filled with energy. Sleeping to restore energy was not necessary. All of God's created beings had eternal life with God. There was no reality of death in God. How long this creation existed in that state cannot be calculated. What caused a major change to this creation was the rebellion of Lucifer who wanted to be like God, set up his own kingdom, and rule over others.*

*He convinced one-third of the angels to follow in his path. This became a major problem for God to resolve in a clear perspective concerning all of his created beings with free will. The central issue is: Why created beings of God with free will and limited ability in wisdom, knowledge, and power cannot function without God's master plan, power, and control over all creation in a state of holiness and love. This problem is dealt with through his educational program called "Let there be light."*

As we undertake our search for God's light, comparing the Word with the Word, let us start from the beginning. Genesis 1:1 (RSV) states: "In the beginning God created the heavens and the earth." Here we have a simple statement. There are no in-depth details. Still we can derive a great deal from the verse. First, God already was before creation. Creation was not an accident. That means the creator must be intelligent and have great power. Second, the creation consisted of heavens and an earth. "Heavens" is plural, more than one dimension. "Earth" is singular. The term "created" is in the past tense. This means the creation was operating according to the design of God. The statement is complete in and of itself.

When we read Genesis 1:2 we see that: "The earth was without form and void, and darkness was upon the face of the deep; and the Spirit of God was moving over the face of the waters." The standard view of this passage is that it is a continuation of the creation process. But, in examination of the terms used, it really describes an event that happened to an already existing creation. The statement, "without form and void," is found only one other time in Scripture, Jeremiah 4:23. The term "without form" in the Hebrew means: "to lay waste, a desolation, confusion, vain, vanity waste." The Hebrew definition for the term "void" is: "to be empty, a vacuity, i.e., an undistinguishable ruin; -emptiness." As Jeremiah the prophet uses this statement, it is concerning the downfall of Jerusalem and the nation of Jews. They had been rebellious against the will of God. Jeremiah sees them in confusion and ruin. The meanings of the terms are the same when presented in Genesis 1:2. The context deals with a spiritual downfall from an established system. Thus, the creation entered a state of spiritual chaos. It does not mean that it was not there in materiel shape and form.

Let us look at the second issue of Genesis 1:2. "Darkness was upon the face of the deep." The Hebrew term for "darkness" translates into: (literal) darkness; (figurative) misery,

27

destruction, death, ignorance, sorrow, wickedness. Using the figurative meaning, all six of the terms describe rebellion against God. In looking at the term "face of the deep," it refers to a surface area of something that has great depth. That surface was the known or exposed will of God for his creation. To make it simple, let's retranslate that verse for clarity: The known will of God and his plan for creation were confronted with rebellion! In the rest of the statement, "and the Spirit of God was moving over the face of the waters," the term "moving" translates in the Hebrew as "brooding" over what had transpired. The waters here represent "peoples and multitudes and nations and tongues" as translated in Revelation 17:15. This is a viewing of the condition by the Holy Spirit concerning the spiritual tide of rebellion.

After the Spirit of God viewed the condition, there is a proclamation. Genesis 1:3: "And God said, 'Let there be light'; and there was light." In 2 Corinthians 4:6, Paul the Apostle refers to this proclamation when he says, "for it is the God who said, 'Let light shine out of darkness,' who has shown in our hearts to give the light of the knowledge of the glory of God in the face of Christ." This statement, "Let light shine out of darkness," gives us better clarity of God's intention. That intention is to use the rebellion (i.e. darkness, misery, destruction, death, ignorance, sorrow, wickedness) in his creation for the education and benefit of those he created and will create.

At this point, we need to ask: who is rebelling and what is the issue of the rebellion? The creation of Genesis 1:1 is dealing with the angelic realm. This was the first order of God's creation. The rebellion is that of Lucifer the angel. And the "waters" of that passage represents the spiritual flow of the multitudes of the angelic realm. The Bible gives us some information concerning this realm. We are informed there are archangels, angels, cherubim, seraphim, and even horses populating that dimension. The government is a theocracy. Each angel was created, not birthed as we are. They do not marry, and they can move between the different dimensions of creation. These are a few of the facts.

In the book of Ezekiel 28:11–19, we receive insight through the prophet concerning the background and fall of Lucifer:

> Moreover the word of the LORD came to me: (12) "Son of man, raise a lamentation over the king of Tyre, and say to him, 'Thus says the Lord GOD: You were the signet of perfection, full of wisdom and perfect in beauty. (13) You were in Eden, the garden of God; every precious stone was your covering, carnelian, topaz, and jasper, chrysolite, beryl, and onyx, sapphire, carbuncle, and emerald; and wrought in gold were your settings and your engravings. On the day that *you were created* they were prepared. (14) With an anointed guardian cherub I placed

you; you were on the holy mountain of God; in the midst of the stones of fire you walked. (15) You were blameless in your ways from the day *you were created*, till iniquity was found in you. (16) In the abundance of your trade you were filled with violence, and you sinned; so I cast you as a profane thing from the mountain of God, and the guardian cherub drove you out from the midst of the stones of fire. (17) *Your heart was proud because of your beauty; you corrupted your wisdom for the sake of your splendor.* I cast you to the ground; I exposed you before kings, to feast their eyes on you. (18) By the multitude of your iniquities, in the unrighteousness of your trade you profaned your sanctuaries; so I brought forth fire from the midst of you; it consumed you, and I turned you to ashes upon the earth in the sight of all who saw you. (19) All who know you among the peoples are appalled at you; you have come to a dreadful end and shall be no more for ever.'" (italics added)

While God, through the prophet Ezekiel, is addressing the King of Tyre, who reigned about 550 BC, Bible scholars agree the language denotes the fall of Lucifer. Let us go through a simplified translation of these verses. Eden is a reference to the paradise of God. Lucifer had great wisdom and beauty. The stones represent the gifts of God (individual talents) set in gold (the divine nature of God). His purpose was clear from the "engravings." He was created for a specific task. He held a high position in God's government (the holy mountain of God) with a guardian cherub. He walked among the holy and pure angelic beings (stones of fire). He was perfect in every way. Then he became proud because of his beauty. His self-centered esteem corrupted his wisdom. He placed more value in his beauty and ability than God or anyone else. In his glorious position with a self-centered attitude, he was filled with violence and sinned. His iniquity multiplied through his position and work. God exposed him, but he would not be corrected. He lost his position.

The Prophet Isaiah also gives us insight into the fall of Lucifer. Isaiah 14:12–14, "How you are fallen from heaven, O Day Star, son of Dawn! How you are cut down to the ground, you who laid the nations low! (13) You said in your heart, '*I will ascend to heaven*; above the stars of God. *I will set my throne on high; I will sit on the mount of assembly in the far north;* (14) *I will ascend above the heights of the clouds, I will make myself like the Most High*'" (italics added). In the KJV, "O Day Star" translates "Lucifer." Day Star and son of Dawn denote great illumination. Then we receive five reasons for his fall. "I will ascend to heaven," means that I don't accept where God has placed me. I am going to elevate myself. "Above the stars of God I will set my throne on high," means he will be over everyone and establish and independent kingdom. "I will sit on the mount of assembly," means that others will gather unto him, and he will make the decisions concerning what is to be done. "I will ascend above the heights of the clouds," is a statement of self glorification. "I will make myself like the Most

High," means that he will play the part of God. These five "I will's" form the foundation of rebellion against God.

There is no information concerning how many angelic beings existed when Lucifer rebelled. We do know from Revelation 12:4 that Lucifer's actions caused one-third of the angelic population to follow him. This was no small conflict with God. It was a major confrontation. It affected the entire plan of God. "Darkness was upon the face of the deep." The condition had to be dealt with. Destruction and desolation were now active in a system that had only known light, goodness, love, joy, peace, productivity, and fulfillment—individually and collectively.

At this point we might ask the question: Why doesn't God just destroy the rebellious group and continue? Why should God put up with rebellion in his creation? To answer these questions, we need to look at some of God's principles in Scripture. First, God creates his creatures in love. Psalms 149:4 says, "For the Lord takes pleasure in his people." God is the only one who has everything. He creates individuals with free will, not as puppets, to partake of what he is and has to offer. God gives himself to his crated life-forms. Their acceptance and response in love and obedience completes the purpose of life in a continuous cycle of growth and development that will never end. The essence of our life in God is love.

Second, there is a sovereign principle given to us in Romans 8:28. "We know that in everything God works for good with those who love him, who are called according to his purpose." The principle is that God works for good in everything. He doesn't say that everything is good in this verse. It was until the rebellion. And it always will be for those who trust and follow him. If God had instantly terminated one-third of the angels when the rebellion took place, a tremendous fear would have developed in those who remained. The love relationship of the faithful would have been greatly impaired. God does not want his creatures to live in fear but in love and faith, with insight and understanding. Therefore, his created must be educated about Lucifer's alternate lifestyle!

When God said, "Let there be light," he was saying: Let light shine out of the darkness that has come into creation, so everyone can know and understand why my authority and way must prevail. The Scripture goes on to say, "and there was light." An educational program was formed in the mind of God to resolve the problem. Two-thirds of the angelic population had remained faithful to God's position. In Genesis

1:4 it states: "And God saw that the light was good [his plan of education]; and God separated the light from the darkness." God sees those who want to live in the light (God's way) and those who want to live in darkness (the destructive act of rebellion) and separates the two groups. This separation is no small issue. The rebellious are placed into "pits of nether gloom to be kept until the judgment" (2 Peter 2:4). This new condition for the rebellious is void of the loving illumination of God's presence and direction. This separation was an act of eternal punishment, not termination. The condition is called "death" because you are cut off from the spiritual life-flow from God. Hell is the place where those who live and remain in a state of death go! Final judgment for the fallen angels is withheld until God's educational process is complete.

In Genesis 1:5 we see that, "God called the light Day, and the darkness he called Night. And there was evening and there was morning one day." The terms "Day" and "Night" now represent two established position in God's creation. Those who live in faithfulness, love, obedience, spiritual enlightenment, and productivity verses those who live in the rebellion of misery, wickedness, destruction, ignorance, sorrow, death, and punishment. The terms "evening" and "morning" define the *direction* of the two positions. In parallel with our evening and morning, evening is the beginning of darkness going into greater darkness. Morning is the beginning of light going into greater light or enlightenment. The term "one day" marks the beginning of a new dimension and time period in God's creation which I call Eternity Present. It will last for a period of seven thousand years in accordance with our solar time system. At the end of this time period, God will take us into another new dimension of his creation which I have labeled Eternity Future. God is always the same, he never changes! What did change from Eternity Past is the spiritual condition and physical material makeup of God's creation. At the end of the seven thousand years of Eternity Present there will be another major change in the spiritual and physical material creation which will mark the beginning of Eternity Future.

**POINTS TO REMEMBER:**

1. God created the heavens and the earth; they did not evolve.

2. In the first creation, there were two heavens and one earth.

3. God created the angelic realm first.

4. God created all life-forms individually, and they do not reproduce on their own. They were given eternal life with God. There was no death.

5. God governed and controlled the activities and productivity of all life in righteousness and love.

6. After a long period of time, Lucifer—an angel with great power, ability and authority—allowed pride to rise up in his heart. He then wanted to be god, independent of God.

7. Lucifer led a rebellion against God and sold his ideas to one-third of the angels. It was the beginning of the spiritual darkness upon the angelic earth.

8. God sees the rebellion and decides to use it as an educational program for all creation to come to a full realization of why his crated children with free will cannot live lives with limited knowledge, truth, understanding, and wisdom apart from God, without destroying the quality of life God provides.

9. God separates the faithful angels from the rebellious. He places the rebellious into "pits of nether gloom." They are cut off from the divine life-flow of God. God is going to use them to reveal the depth of evil, degradation, pain, suffering, misery, despair that will take place without God's holy governing control.

10. God uses the term "evenings and morning one day" to define the beginning of a new condition in his creation. The term "day" and "night" do not deal with the issue of time as we translate it. They present the spiritual condition of the faithful and rebellious angels.

# CHAPTER 2
# A NEW CREATION

**EVENT:** Creation of Mankind

**TIME FRAME:** Eternity Present—The creation of our heaven and earth

**INTRODUCTION NARRATIVE:** *Because of Lucifer's rebellion and God's proclamation, "Let there be light," along with the separation of the faithful and rebellious angels, God expands his first creation. He creates a new heaven in the center of the two existing heavens. Then he restructures the angelic earth and places it into the new heaven. God establishes boundaries for the conduct of the fallen angels relative to the new creation. Then he creates the sun, moon, and stars of our solar system, and he creates new life-forms upon* *the earth. Then man is created in his image and likeness to rule over the earth under his guidance. With the completion of the new creation, God blesses what he has established. We now have three heavens and one earth. It is like having a balloon within a balloon within another balloon. The outer balloon is the heaven of God's throne. The next inner balloon is the heaven of the angelic realm. The center balloon with the earth is the creation where we live.*

With the rebellion of Lucifer and the separation of the angelic realm into two different camps of "Day" and "Night," God continues his new educational program. Genesis 1:6 states: "And God said, 'Let there be a firmament in the midst of the waters, and let it separate the waters from the waters.'" The "firmament" is to be a new dimension in an already existing creation. It will divide the material waters from the spiritual waters and again divide the spiritual waters of "Day" and "Night." It will be a central dividing point of the two camps of evening and morning, darkness and light, and their inherent lifestyles. It will become the focal point and main issue of God's educational program.

Genesis 1:7: "And God made the firmament and separated the waters which were under the firmament from the waters which were above the firmament. And it was so." The "waters under the firmament," are the physical material realm of creation. The "waters which were above" represent the spiritual realm. The creation of this new heaven, I believe, is what scientists have labeled "The Big Bang Theory." In the book of Isaiah 45:12, the prophet speaks of this event. "*I made the earth, and created man upon it; it was my hands that stretched out the heavens and I commanded all their host*" (italics added). God and scientists have two different views on this issue!

Genesis 1:8 states: "And God called the firmament Heaven. And there was evening and there was morning, a second day." Only three heavens are mentioned in Scripture after the creation of this new "Heaven." Paul states in 2 Corinthians 12:2–4, "I know a man in Christ who fourteen years ago was caught up to the *third heaven*—whether in the body or out of the body I do not know, God knows. (3) And I know that this man was caught up into Paradise—whether in the body or out of the body I do not know, God knows—(4) and he heard things that cannot be told, which man may not utter" (italics added). If this new heaven makes a total of three, *then there were two heavens in Genesis 1:1*. The third heaven counting upward from our earth is the throne of God.

The second heaven is the angelic realm. The new heaven is the dimension we live in on the earth. The angels have access to all three heavens as seen in Job 1:6–7. We are confined to this dimension unless God takes us into the other two.

"There was evening and morning a second day." Evening and morning refer to the two types of angelic beings: the rebellious and the faithful that are part of the new creation in its development. "A second day" refers to the new condition added to the rebellion, proclamation, and separation of the "first day." The term "day" encompasses the event and result. The "second day" is a new dimension, heaven, added to an existing creation.

Genesis 1:9: "And God said, 'Let the waters under the heavens be gathered together into one place, and let the dry land appear.' And it was so." The term "waters" refer to the physical material dimension of creation in this verse. "Under the heavens" is a positional reference. Material substance is on a lower plain compared to spiritual waters. With the rebellion that took place, there was a contamination of the physical material elements (also called waters) of the earth of Genesis 1:1. With the relocation of the angelic earth into the new heaven, there was a cleansing process and a reconfiguration that took place in preparation for a new species called "mankind." "And it was so" means that it was completed!

Genesis 1:10–13:

> God called the dry land Earth, and the waters that were gathered together he called Seas. And God saw that it was good. [God gives us terms for two main components of the material planet. He calls them "earth" and "sea."] (11) And God said, "Let the earth put forth vegetation, plants yielding seed, and fruit trees bearing fruit in which is their seed, each according to its kind, upon the earth." And it was so. (12) The earth brought forth vegetation, plants yielding seed according to their own kinds, and trees bearing fruit in which is their seed, each according to its kind. And God saw that it was good [It should be noted here that everything produces after its kind. Apple trees will not produce walnuts and vice versa. It is a fixed law of this creation, contrary to the Theory of Evolution.]. (13) And there was evening and there was morning a third day.

This new event is added to and incorporated into the first two events and is classified as the "third day."

Genesis 1:14–15: "And God said, 'Let there be lights in the firmament of the heavens to separate the day from the night; (15) and let them be lights in the heavens to give light upon the earth.' And it was so." When we read this verse, we automatically think that God is referring to the literal stars being placed in the firmament. But he is not telling us that! He is telling us about the assignment of his holy, faithful angels to render spiritual light to this new creation and restrain the darkness and the fallen angels as he commands.

To clarify this issue, let us start with Job 38:1–11:

> Then the LORD answered Job out of the whirlwind: (2) "Who is this that darkens counsel by words without knowledge? (3) Gird up your loins like a man, I will questions you, and you shall declare to me. (4) *Where were you when I laid the foundation of the earth?* Tell me, if you have understanding. (5) Who determined its measurements—surely you know! Or who stretched the line upon it? (6) *On what were its bases sunk, or who laid its cornerstone,* (7) *when the morning stars sang together, and all of the sons of God shouted for joy?* (8) Or who shut in the sea with doors, when it burst forth from the womb, (9) when I made clouds its garment, and thick darkness its swaddling band, (10) and prescribed bounds for it, and set bars and doors, (11) and said, '*Thus far shall you come, and no farther, and here shall your proud waves be stayed.*'" (italics added)

"Morning stars" is a figurative term for the holy faithful angels that rejoiced at God's intervention in Lucifer's rebellion, and the term "sons of God," is their positional relationship with God. Verse 8 is the rebellion when it broke fourth from the secure position under God's protection symbolized by "the womb." Verses 9-11 define in figurative terms that God has control over the rebellion of Lucifer and has set up a confinement with boundaries for his activities. Satan and his followers are on a leash in spiritual darkness doomed for eternal destruction!

In Daniel 9:20–23 we have an example of how God uses his holy angels to bring us spiritual light:

> While I was speaking and praying, confessing my sin and the sin of my people Israel, and presenting my supplication before

the LORD my God for the holy hill of my God; (21) while I was speaking in prayer, the man Gabriel, whom I had seen in the vision at the first, came to me in swift flight at the time of the evening sacrifice. (22) He came and he said to me, "O Daniel, I have now come out to give you wisdom and understanding. (23) At the beginning of your supplications a word went forth, and I have come to tell it to you, for you are greatly beloved; therefore consider the word and understand the vision."

Then in Revelation 12:7–9 we see the authority of God's holy angels over the fallen angels:

> Now war arose in heaven, Michael and his angels fighting against the dragon; and the dragon and his angels fought, (8) but they were defeated *and there was no longer any place for them in heaven.* (9) And the great dragon was thrown down, that ancient serpent, who is called the Devil and Satan, the deceiver of the whole world—he was thrown down to the earth, and his angels were thrown down with him. (italics added)

This event will take place several years before the Battle of Armageddon. It verifies how God established and uses the angelic realm in his new creation.

At the end of Genesis 1:15 it states: "And it was so." That means that the authority structure of the angelic realm, relative to the new creation, was established. Then, in continuation of the development of the new heaven around the restructured earth, Genesis 1:16–19 states: "And God made the two great lights, the greater light to rule the day, and the lesser light to rule the night; he made the stars also. [Now, God establishes the material sun, moon, and stars.] (17) And

God set them in the firmament of the heavens to give light upon the earth, (18) to rule over the day and over the night, and to separate the light from the darkness. And God saw that it was good. (19) And there was evening and there was morning, a fourth day." First God establishes the angelic authority in the new heaven, then he establishes the physical material ruling structure in the heaven, and he does this in a parallel to the spiritual issue.

The sun is a symbol of the Word of God and the Son of God, Jesus, who will rule over the earth giving spiritual light. The "lesser light," which is the moon, is a symbol of the ruling authority of mankind over the earth in its spiritual conduct. The moon has no light of its own, it only reflects the light of the sun, and it regulates the tidal flow of the seas. The literal seas are a symbol of the spiritual flow of humanity in Scripture. If the moon is not reflecting the light of the sun in its movement around the earth, then there will be greater darkness covering the earth. In a 24 hour day, light and darkness are upon the earth reflecting the fact that this creation is subjected to good and evil

God also placed the stars in the heaven as symbols of the angels, even to the extent that stars can fall from their positions and burn out. Also, there are black holes that can suck stars into them. The design of this new creation reflects the spiritual issues that mankind must deal with. That is the power of light and the power of darkness.

These events are added to the first three days. With the completion of the fourth day, time as we count it, begins on this earth as year 0 in our astrological time system. When the Gregorian calendar was developed several thousand years later, this date was labeled January 1, 3977 BC. For our purpose, it is called Western Time Count. In the process of this creation, the singular term "day" takes on different meanings. The term "day" can refer to the spiritual light of God or the literal time. It must be discerned in the context of its usage throughout the Scripture.

The new creation continues in Genesis 1:20–23:

> And God said, "Let the waters bring forth swarms of living creatures, and let birds fly above the earth across the firmament of the heavens." (21) God created the great sea monsters and every living creature that moves, with which the waters swarm, according to their kinds, and every winged bird according to its kind. And God saw that it was good. (22) And God blessed them, saying, "Be fruitful and multiply and fill the waters in the seas, and let birds multiply on the earth." (23) And there was evening and there was morning, a fifth day.

God creates lower forms of life in the fish of the sea and the birds of the air. There are great varieties, each according to its kind. This, again, precludes the evolutionary process of a lower life form mutating to a higher form. When God blessed them and said, "Be fruitful and multiply. . ." it meant that they each had a productive part to play according to their individual design. Their corporate activity would harmonize, blend, and balance for the mutual benefit of the whole earth. "And multiply" means they should increase in number. The spiritual issue of "evening and morning" still prevails with the addition of these events, and it was called the "fifth day."

Genesis 1:24–25:

> And God said, "Let the earth bring forth living creatures according to their kinds: cattle and creeping things and beasts of the earth according their kinds." And it was so. (25) *And God made* the beasts of the earth according to their kinds and the cattle according to their kinds, and everything that creeps upon the ground according to its kind. And God saw that it was good. (italics added)

In verse 24 God creates cattle and creeping things and beasts of the earth and finishes with, "It was so," meaning that it was accomplished. Then in verse 25 the issue is repeated but the term "made" is used. This refers to a structuring of what is already created. God programmed every creature he created! Every animal including the insects were given divine orientation and purpose. "And God saw that it was good."

After the lower life-forms are created, God undertakes the highest life-form to be placed upon the earth, man.

Genesis 1:26: "Then God said, '*Let us make man in our image, after our likeness; and let them have dominion over the fish of the sea, and over the birds of the air, and over the cattle, and over all the earth, and over every creeping thing that creeps upon the earth*'" (italics added). Because of the depth of man in the image and likeness of God, we will deal with the issue in chapter 4. What we need to understand at this point in the creation structure, is that man has dominion over *all life* on earth. Created after the image of God, he has superior intelligence, power, authority, ability, and position. He doesn't mutate up the ladder of evolution through millions of years of ignorance before arriving at the top. He is at the top in the beginning, programmed to grow and expand his God-given abilities.

Genesis 1:27–28:

> So God created man in his own image, in the image of God he created him; male and female he created them. (28) And God blessed them, and God said to them, "Be fruitful and multiple, and fill the earth and subdue it; and have dominion over the fish of the sea and over the birds of the air and over every living thing that moves upon the earth."

Male and female both were created in the image of God. They have instruction to be fruitful and multiply. To be fruitful, means that you grow in knowledge, understanding, and wisdom and produce with your mind and your hands beneficial projects under God's direction for your welfare and enjoyment, and the welfare and benefit of others. To multiply means to bear children. To "fill the earth and subdue it" is a divine task that is set before mankind. Mankind's principle function is to learn from God, be obedient to his directions, bear children, be productive, and rule over the earth. The most important aspect is a love relationship with God first, then spouse, children, and the rest of mankind. This will produce a glorious life in all that God created.

Every living creature that God created with the breath of life has total sustenance. Genesis 1:29–30:

> And God said, "Behold, I have given you every plant yielding seed which is upon the face of the all the earth, and every tree with seed in its fruit; you shall have them for food. (30) And to every beast of the earth, and to every bird of the air, and to everything that creeps on the earth, everything that has the breath of life, I have given every green plant for food." And it was so.

There was no laboring for food; it was part of the natural system. All life species were non-carnivorous. Everything that was needed to sustain life for man, animals, fish, birds, and insects were provided by God. There was no time clock to punch, union dues, insurance policies, medical programs, advertising, disease, famine, war, or death. Everything and everyone would live forever by the governing control and sustenance of God in productive activity in an environment of love. "And it was so."

Genesis 2:1–3:

> Thus the heavens and the earth were finished, and all the host of them. (2) And on the seventh day God finished his work which he had done, and he rested on the seventh day from all his work which he had done. (3) So God blessed the seventh day and hallowed it, because on it God rested from all his work which he had done in creation.

The term "heavens" is plural. While there was only one new heaven created, there was a restructuring of the angelic heaven in between the heaven of the throne of God and the new heaven. Now, all of the new life-forms in the new creation are functioning according to divine impartation. The "seventh day" condition, the blessing and rest, allowed the creation to function under God's divine plan. This was holy. The earth would continue to be fruitful day in and day out, year in and year out, century in and century out, under the seventh day condition of rest with God in control. But the continued blessing of the seventh day was dependant on obedience by the free will of man to follow God's direction. Thus, all of man's activities would be successful in an atmosphere of love, joy, and peace. He did not have to earn a living because he would always be sustained by God. There would never be a shortage of supply of anything, nor the need for money. God would provide the spiritual light for man to grow and develop and govern the earth. It would not be a struggle or laboring process with destruction, failure, or death. It would be a fun, enjoyable, rewarding, productive process. *That was the blessing of the seventh day of rest!*

In Genesis 2:4 it states: "These are the generations of the heavens and the earth when they were created." The term "generations" clarifies the progression of events called days. Each new event proceeded from the previous condition. This verse should actually end chapter 1 of Genesis. In the original writing in the Hebrew language, the chapter and verse markings were not there. They were added later when it was translated. Verse 4 continues on, "In the day that the LORD God made the earth and the heavens..." In the RSV, this part of the verse beings a new paragraph. In the KJV a comma separates the two verses. This is a problem in translation. Yet, God enlightens us. In close analyses of the verse, we will see major changes in the use of terms. It is the beginning of many revelations concerning the union of God and man during the sixth day of creation. As we look at these issues in depth, they will untangle the confusion between Genesis chapter 1 and 2.

## POINTS TO REMEMBER

1. God expands his creation and creates a new heaven within the two existing heavens. This event is labeled a "second day" because it is added to the purpose of the first day of his education program called, "Let there be light."

2. God takes the existing earth of the angelic realm and restructures it to accommodate his education program and places it in the new heaven. This event is added to the first two "days" and is called the "third day."

3. God establishes the boundaries of conduct for both the holy angels and the fallen angels concerning their relationship to this new creation. Then God creates the material sun, moon, and stars in the new heaven. They are a visual picture of the spiritual condition of light and darkness (good and evil) that now exists. It presents the continual night and day activity concerning life on planet earth for as long as it will exist. This event is called the "fourth day," and it marks the beginning of our astrological time count for which all of our different calendars must be synchronized.

4. God creates new life-forms upon the reconditioned earth in the new heaven and called it the "fifth day."

5. God creates man from the dust of the earth and breaths into him the breath of life. Man is given authority under God over the earth, to fill the earth and subdue it. This becomes the "sixth day" of God's new creation.

6. With the completion of the "six days," God blesses what he has created concerning the new heaven and earth and all of the life forms upon the earth. The "seventh day blessing" is a pure condition that will continue to function in a state of God's holiness as long as mankind remains faithful to the will of God. The activity of Lucifer's rebellion is confined and cannot be activated on earth without the free will choice of man to partake of Lucifer's lifestyle. So God rests on the "seventh day" condition, which is not a 24 hour period. It is the totality of what God has created in love. Participation with God or participation with Lucifer will be a life and death educational program for all creation, angels and humans, to reveal every aspect of every conceivable condition that can possibly take place, concerning why God's free will

life-forms must remain in harmony with God's perfect will throughout his creation.

## CHAPTER 3

# FATHER, SON, AND HOLY SPIRIT

**EVENT: The reality of the Trinity**
**TIME FRAME: Eternity Present—The creation of our heaven and earth**

**INTRODUCTION NARRATIVE**: *There are three persons called God in Scripture. Their substance is spirit. There are seven spiritual facets that make up each person of the Trinity—God the Father, God the Son, and God the Holy Spirit. The only difference between the three is their positional function in all the activity of creation. They are one in substance and unity. It has always been that way, and it will never change because there is no higher form of reality* *apart from them. There is one God, three persons in unity, harmony, and glory with all power. Nothing is above them, everything is below them.*

In Genesis 1:26 when God says, "Let us make man in our image after our likeness," the "us" refers to the Trinity. There are three persons under one God-head. A reality that is hard to comprehend with the human finite mind. Still, if we are going to understand the composition of man and understand our relationship with God, we need to have a simple knowledge of the Trinity.

The first person of the Trinity is God the Father, who is the same person of Genesis 1:1 who created the heavens and the earth. The second person is the Son, Jesus. The Gospel of John 1:1 calls him the Word of God. Then the third person is the Holy Spirit. He is first identified in Genesis 1:2 while "moving over the face of the waters." As labeled, the Son of God and the Spirit of God are both God. Three very distinct persons, yet Scripture declares only one God (Galatians 3:20). Since we have one God and three persons, the substance has to be the same; only the form and activity are different. An example is water. It can be a pool, vapor, mist, rain, snow, or a block of ice. In each form it is still water. The substance remains constant.

What then is the substance of the Trinity? John 4:24 says: "God is spirit, and those who worship him must worship in spirit and truth." *Spirit is the substance.* Going through the RSV Bible, the term "spirit" appears some 566 times. There are four Hebrew terms and two Greek terms used to define the English word. There are a variety of meanings. After doing an exhaustive study on the words' variable usage, I discovered a common denominator. It always expresses a form of activity. Spirit is not a dormant substance. It carries life, activity, and energy.

In Revelation 1:4–5, the Apostle John gives greeting to the churches and refers to the Trinity. "John to the seven churches that are in Asia: Grace to you and peace from him who is and who was and who is to come, and from *the seven spirits who* are before his throne, (5) and from Jesus Christ the faithful witness, the first-born of the dead, and the ruler of the kings on earth" (italics added). The first person he gives reference to is God the Father. The second person is the Holy Spirit, and then the Son, Jesus Christ. Here the Holy Spirit consists of "seven spirits who are before his throne." This means that there are seven different forms of life, activity, and energy making up the one Holy Spirit.

What are the seven spirits of God before his throne? The first one is the "breath of life." In Genesis 2:7 when God created Adam, he "breathed into his nostrils the breath of life." The Hebrew word *neshawmaw* for the term "spirit" translates breath (i.e. spirit of life). This is the basic element of the life on earth for man, beast, bird, or fish. Without it, we do not have life. Malachi 2:15 says, "Has not the one God made and sustained for us the spirit of life?" Life is the first activity of God.

The next four spirits are found in Isaiah 11:2. "And the Spirit of the LORD shall rest upon him, the spirit of *wisdom* and *understanding*, the spirit of *counsel* and might, the spirit of *knowledge* and the fear of the LORD" (italics added). This passage refers to the earthly ministry of Jesus, with the anointing of the Holy Spirit upon him. The basic activity of the spirit of life must be developed. Its development comes through the spirit of knowledge. This constitutes the acquisition of facts and information. Our lives are dependent upon knowledge. The more we know, the stronger we become, and with it, our ability to function expands. All knowledge is in God, and the Holy Spirit is all knowing. The spirit of knowledge is the second of the seven.

The third spirit, in order of importance and sequence, is the spirit of understanding. This also comes from Isaiah 11:2. Understanding is the ability to relate facts and information and put them into proper perspective. I can have a great amount of knowledge, but if I cannot understand how it relates to me and living in this world, it is of no value. Each activity of the seven spirits is dependent upon every other one. I cannot understand unless I have knowledge. I cannot have knowledge until I have life. Only God understands everything.

To find the fourth spirit, we need to look at John 16:13–15.

> When the *Spirit of truth* comes, he will guide you into all the truth; for he will not speak on his own authority, but whatever he hears he will speak, and he will declare to you the things that are to come. (14) He will glorify me, for he will take what is mine and declare it to you. (15) All that the Father has is mine; therefore I said that he will take what is mine and declare it to you. (italics added)

Jesus is speaking to his disciples just before his death. He refers to the Holy Spirit of truth. The "spirit of truth" is an essential part of the sevenfold composition. The truth is the absolute reality of God's creation in every detail. Truth is something we can accept by faith or by learning it the hard way. Parents teach their children not to touch pots on the stove because they can get burned. Some of us learn the truth the hard way, but we learn, and hopefully, it doesn't kill us in the process!

Jesus declares in John 14:6, "I am the way, *and the truth*, and the life; no one comes to the Father, but by me" (italics added). Only God can declare that he is the truth. I can tell you that I know the truth, but only *God is the truth*. If I have knowledge that is not of the truth, I have nothing, and it will create confusion and chaos in my life. The first three spirits are dependent upon the *spirit of truth*. *Jesus is the truth*, and it is the person of the *Holy Spirit that gives us the truth* to bring our lives into alignment with God the Father.

In looking at Isaiah 11:2 we do not see the spirit of truth listed. The reason for this is the Scripture covers the anointing of the Holy Spirit upon the earthly life and ministry of Jesus. Jesus is the truth. What we see in Isaiah 11:2 is the "spirit of might." Jesus didn't have deception in his life. He was in perfect harmony with God the Father. He knew who he was and his purpose on earth in clarity. With the Holy Spirit upon him, he walked in a spirit (activity) of might (the universal power of God). This is a product of the interacting seven spirits of God. From the seven basic spirits of God, all other forms of activity come about. In parallel, our colors of red, green, blue produce an infinite spectrum of color.

Isaiah 11:2 lists the fifth item of activity. It is the spirit of wisdom. Wisdom is the application of what we know and understand in the light of truth. It is the best and right way to accomplish a given task. If you have ever purchased an unassembled product from a store, wisdom is reading the instructions first and then following them. Each of us has our own way of doing things which quite often creates a mess. The wisdom of God is the best way to do anything. Wisdom is the path to the desired end. It is dependent upon life, knowledge, understanding, and truth, and they are dependent on wisdom for application.

Number six on the list also comes from Isaiah 11:2. It is the spirit of counsel. This is the ability to reason. Through this activity facts can be sorted and then understood. A conclusion can be reached and then applied in wisdom. It is this attribute that separates humans from other life-forms. People can look at their past and present condition and then plan for the future. However, to do this without consulting God for his plan for your future is an exercise in foolishness and that is where most of the world is today. God has already made his plans for mankind, the angelic realm, and the entire physical material creation.

The seventh spirit on the list deals with free will. In Luke 1:16–17 we have a reference to John the Baptist concerning his will and purpose. "And he will turn many of the sons of Israel to the Lord their God, (17) and he will go before him *in the spirit and power of Elijah*, to turn the hearts of the fathers to the children, and the disobedient to the wisdom of the just, to make ready for the Lord a people prepared" (italics added). The context of the term "spirit" means his will and purpose. John received the call of God to prepare the way of the Lord. Like Elijah, John was of the *will* and *purpose* to *serve God* under God's anointing. When we say that we are of "one spirit," it means unity in will and purpose.

In Isaiah 11:2 "spirit" is referred to as the "spirit of fear of the Lord." Fear, in this context, is a holy reverence for the will of God. In Isaiah 11:3 it states: "And his delight shall be in the fear of the LORD." The focal point of the life of Jesus was to do the will of God the Father, and it was a "delight." In John 5:30, Jesus states: "I can do nothing on my own authority; as I hear, I judge; and my judgment is just, because *I seek not my own will but the will of him who sent me*" (italics added). When God created us, he gave us the free will to choose, so when we use the term the "spirit of man," we are referring to his will and purpose, be it good or bad. This activity is dependent upon the other six spirits to make free will decisions. The other six spirits are dependent upon the free will to determine their purpose.

The seven basic activities of life are the substance of God. Being active means there is energy in seven forms. This energy is total intelligence with free will. What becomes incomprehensible to the finite mind is that God has no beginning and no end. He always existed and will continue to do so. He is sufficient unto himself. In the study of physics, we know that energy can be converted into matter, and matter into energy. The two are interchangeable and nothing is ever lost. Out of the energy of God's spiritual being, he creates all matter and forms all life. Simultaneously, he is independent of what he creates and forms. Everything exists within him. Nothing exists outside of him, and he is omnipresent throughout his creation. Creation was not an accidental evolution that took billions of years to formulate. It is intelligent design by God through his power in a very short time span.

In looking at the Trinity, God the Father is the absolute reality that always has been and always will be. The Word of God is the formulated reality of the will and purpose of God the Father, in spirit. The Word manifest what God is. He is the statement of God's being. The Word is separate from God the Father and simultaneously is God. As John 1:1–3 states: "In the beginning was the Word, and *the Word was with God*, and *the Word was God*. (2) He was in the beginning with God; (3) *all things were made through him*, and *without him was not anything made that was made*" (italics added). The Word is the spiritual blueprint of God the Father's creation, his will and purpose! Hebrews 1:1–3 clearly states: "In many and various ways God spoke of old to our fathers by the prophets; (2) but in these last days he has spoken to us by *a Son, whom he appointed the heir of all things, through whom also he created the world*. (3) *He reflects the glory of God and bears the very stamp of his nature, upholding the universe by his word of power*" (italics added).

The third person of the Trinity that is presented throughout Scripture, from Genesis through Revelation, is the Holy Spirit. In Revelation 1:4–5 he is presented as "the seven spirits before the throne." In Genesis 1:2 he is "the Spirit of God" moving over the surface of the waters. Jesus presents him in John 26:25–26: "These things I have spoken to you, while I am still with you. (26) *But the Counselor, the Holy Spirit, whom the Father will send in my name, he will teach you all things, and bring to your remembrance all that I have said to you*" (italics added). In short, the Holy Spirit is the *administrator* of the Word of God in all seven spirits that make up one holy God. The Holy Spirit is the same substance and reality of God. So there are three persons, yet one God. The three will always be in harmony because there is no higher form of life to go to.

While we can look at the substance and composition of God in Scripture, what is truly important to see and understand is the character of God. He is a person. The following Scriptures reveal this issue to us (italics added):

> Psalm 73:1: "Truly God *is good* to the upright, to those who are pure in heart."
>
> Psalm 19:8 "...the commandment of the LORD *is pure*, enlightening the eyes."
>
> Psalm 99:9: "Extol the LORD our God, and worship at his holy mountain; for the LORD *our God is holy!*"
>
> Daniel 9:14: "Therefore the LORD has kept ready the calamity and has brought it upon us; for the LORD our God *is righteous* in all works which he has done, and we have not obeyed his voice."

Psalm 145:17: "The LORD *is just in all his ways*, and kind in all his doings."

1 Corinthians 10:13: "God *is faithful*, and he will not let you be tempted beyond your strength, but with the temptation will also provide the way of escape, that you may be able to endure it."

1 John 4:16: "God is *love*, and he who abides in love abides in God, and God abides in him."

**POINTS TO REMEMBER**

1. There are three persons who are called God in Scripture: God the Father, God the Son, and God the Holy Spirit.

2. The substance is the same in all three, being spirit.

3. Spirit contains life, energy, power, and intelligent activity.

4. There are seven spiritual facets that make up each person of the Trinity.

5. The seven spirits are: the spirit of life, the spirit of knowledge, the spirit of truth, the spirit of understanding, the spirit of wisdom, the spirit of counsel, the spirit of God (which is God's free will and purpose).

6. The seven spirits of God are eternal. They have no beginning and no end, and they cannot be destroyed. They make up the sum total of the person of God the Father, God the Son, and God the Holy Spirit.

7. The three persons of the Trinity carry out three different functions. The Father determines and governs what is to be in every aspect of creation. The Son, who is the Word of God, is the living reality of everything that the Father establishes. The Holy Spirit is the administrator of the will of the Father through the Son. The three are in perfect harmony. They always have been, and always will be!

8. Included in the seven spiritual facets of God is a character factor that is spelled out in Scripture: God is good, God is pure, God is holy, and God is righteous, God is just, God is kind, God is faithful, and God is *love!*

## CHAPTER 4

# MAN IN THE IMAGE OF GOD

**EVENT:** The sixth day
**TIME FRAME:** Eternity Present—Creation 0, Western 3977 BC[1]

**INTRODUCETION NARRATIVE:** *In understanding our heritage, the second chapter of Genesis gives us some major insights. The first issue, and most important, concerns the structure of our relationship with God. The second issue concerns our union as husband and wife.*

As noted earlier, the real beginning of chapter 2 should start halfway though verse 4: "In the day that the Lord God made the earth and the heavens…" At this point in

Scripture there is a major transition. Without understanding this shift, Genesis chapter 2 will appear to contradict Genesis chapter 1. The first thing that we need to take note of is the term "day." It is singular. It deals exclusively with the sixth day of creation described in Genesis 1, the creation of man. Chapter 2 expounds upon the limited details already given.

The next change that needs to be observed is the term "Lord God." Throughout chapter 1, only the term "God" is used. In the Hebrew, "God" is "Elohim." It is used with special reference to his power and might. "Lord" in Hebrew is "Jehovah," meaning "self-existent" or "eternal." When the two terms are used together they define the sovereign governing control of his might and power. God will always be God. But being Lord involves his personal ongoing governing participation in the lives of his people. Thus, in chapter 2 his personal relationship with creation is presented. If he is not the "Lord" of your life, then you will not receive his blessings and protection.

The third item of importance is the change from "heavens and earth" to "earth and heavens," which is preceded by the term "made" not "created." The term "made" in Hebrew means to "appoint, bestow, have the charge of." The result of these changes explains to us God's sovereign plan. In the sixth day of creation he is establishing a divine governing structure upon the earth. It will be in direct union with the heavens over which he is Lord, not just God. The focal point of this governing structure is man. The system is spiritual.

Let us look at verse 4 again with verse 5–6 in Genesis 2.

> In the day that the LORD God made the earth and heavens, (5) when no plant of the field was yet in the earth and no herb of the field had yet sprung up—for the LORD God had not caused it to rain upon the earth, and there was no man to till the ground; (6) but a mist went up from the earth and watered the whole face of the ground.

When we read verse 5 and apply the term "day" of verse 4 to mean the sixth day of creation, we have a problem. According to Genesis 1, plant life came about in the third day of creation. Thus the Lord is not talking about material plants and herbs but spiritual. Using the natural order to identify the spiritual (which is used throughout Scripture), the plants and herbs are ideas, concepts, inspiration, and direction. It is a spiritual planning of the Lord, which man is to till and keep. The spiritual plants will unite the natural order with the heavenly order of God. When cultivated by man they will produce the will of God in, through, and for the benefit of man in a productive life. On the spiritual side, the fruit of these activities will cause love, joy, peace, patience, kindness, faithfulness, goodness, self control, and gentleness to develop in man's relationship to others (Galatians 5:22). The "seed" is the Word of God (Mark 4:14).

The second issue to be understood is the rain. It is also spiritual. There are four components that make up spiritual water. They are knowledge, truth, understanding, and wisdom. The watering process causes the idea, concept, inspiration, and direction to grow and produce. This is the governing relationship between earth and heaven in the realm of the spirit. At this point in creation, God has not caused it to "rain" spiritually because man was not created. "But a mist went up from the earth and watered the whole face of the ground." The "mist" spoken of here is the natural rain. It is the process of evaporation, condensation, and rain of the material waters. This process started in the fourth day of creation when the sun, moon, and stars were placed in the heaven.

In Genesis 2:7, man is made. "The LORD God formed man of dust from the ground, and breathed into his nostrils the breath of life; and man became a living being." Here we see the physical body of man is from the earth. The second component is spiritual, the "breath of life," i.e. "spirit of life." The result is a living soul. The soul in this context is the total person. It encompasses the total makeup of man, physical and spiritual. In the New Testament the term "soul" in the Greek is "psyche." The meaning covers the spiritual composition of man and includes the spirit of man, which in this context, is man's free will and purpose.

Genesis chapter 1 told us that man is made in the image and likeness of God. "Image means a representative figure. "Likeness" means to fashion in manor. Therefore, man is designed with the same attributes of God and is to function like him. The main difference between the image, man, and the real thing, God, is a functional limitation. Here, God will always have total control and power, while man has limited control and power. God will never be under anyone and will always be subject to himself. Man will always be under God and subject to him. Man in the image of God is only a reflection, not God. But through obedience to God, he is called a son of God and can function like God. For example, if God directs me to lay my hands on a dying person and say, "In the name of Jesus be healed!" and God heals that person instantly, then I have functioned like a son of God in his will and purpose, but without God, the healing would not have taken place. In obedience, I get great joy and pleasure based upon what has taken place, and God gets the glory. With God, anything is possible. Without God, I am very limited.

Within the physical makeup of mankind, there are small differences in the size and shape of our individual parts. These differences make each individual a unique person unto God with no two people being exactly alike. These variations in size and structure determine our ability and limitations. For example, a person who is of a slight build weighing 120 pounds standing 5´0´´ will not have the strength of a person who is 6´6´´ with a large build and weighs 250 pounds. Variation in vocal cords and lung capacity determine our ability to sing. The result of our physical makeup determines in great measure the kind of work in life we will undertake. Men will never be mothers. Blind people will not be cab drivers. The mentally challenged will not be lawyers or physicians.

While there are physical differences between everyone and biological differences between male and female, what is it that makes men and women in the image of God? The answer lies in the spiritual composition. We have the same seven spiritual attributes of God the Father, God the Son, and God the Holy Spirit. When God breathed into man the spirit of life, man received the basic life force of God. With the physical deigns of the human body, the spirit of life develops in union with the other six spirits.

The spirit of knowledge comes through our five senses that God designed in our body and is activated by the spirit of life. The spirit of understanding comes through the spirit of counsel, which is our ability to reason due to the design of our brain. The spirit of man, that is, man's free will and purpose, began when the spirit of life entered into man's body, making it a living soul. The spirit of truth develops in us through education, growth and maturity, trial and error in the natural order. Truth is hindered through deception from the demonic order but can be overcome through the direct revelations of God to each of us. The spirit of wisdom develops from applying what we know and understand in the light of truth. Our individual personality and education develops through the uniqueness of our body coupled with spiritual activity and the decisions we make. It is drawn from our environment with the parents that raise us and the schools we attend. There are billions of variables to the persons we become. Continual growth and maturity increase our ability to function in the image of God. The only difference between a newborn baby and one who has just been conceived is the stage of development. Both are real people! Today, that same spirit of life that was given to Adam is passed through the male sperm to connect with the egg of the woman, and at the moment of contact, we have a new living soul. The only difference is the stage of development, but all of the components are inherent in that union.

There are two separate avenues of learning knowledge, understanding, truth, and wisdom. The first avenue is that which is derived from life in the natural order of this world through our five senses and educational system learning from one another. The second avenue is that which is given to you directly from the Spirit God. Both are essential for a complete life upon this earth because it is impossible for any human being to have all knowledge, understanding, truth, and wisdom and function correctly in every situation without damaging or destroying our life or the life of some other person.

When God said, "Let us make man in our image after our likeness," there are two facets to this statement. The first facet is the "image" which we have covered in our spiritual composition. The second facet is the "likeness." Man, with his deigns in the image of God, has the ability to grow and mature independent of God. However, without having the "likeness of God," there is a major problem because it deals with the holiness and morality of God in every aspect of conduct. Without this ingredient, people will turn into wild beasts and life becomes a living hell instead of a paradise with God. Morality is like the oil in the crankcase of a car that keeps everything running smoothly, without which the engine would grind to a halt due to friction. While a person can mechanically learn to build a house, what is their relationship with co-workers? 1 John 4:16 states: "God is love, and he who abides in love abides in God, and God abides in him."

At the age of nineteen when I was an atheist and received a vision from God, I was specially told that, "Love is the essence of life!" I know today that God is that "essence," and without that essence of God in our lives and our submission to him, our selfishness destroys true love to one another in our fallen state. We have a multitude of moral laws that we are not able to keep. "Thou shall not covet," is just one example. True love embodies every aspect of God's standard of morality.

*Here is a composite of the spiritual makeup of man and terms in Scripture:*

| COMPONENT | FUNCTION | BIBLICAL TERM |
|---|---|---|
| 7. Spirit of man | Man's free will and purpose | |
| 6. Spirit of counsel | Man's ability to reason | #6 + #7 = heart of man |
| 5. Spirit of wisdom | Man's ability to apply what he knows | |
| 4. Spirit of understanding | Man's ability to comprehend facts and issues | |
| 3. Spirit of truth | Man's relationship to reality | |
| 2. Spirit of knowledge | Man's ability to acquire information | #2–#5 = living water |
| 1. Spirit of life | Man's life force | #1 = breath of life |

For the above system to work perfectly, truth must always be present in the process. Truth is the absolute reality that God has established in creation, both visible and invisible. If a lie is used in the process of reasoning, we will come to a flawed conclusion, which acted upon, will produce an exercise in futility. Only God has all truth about every issue.

In Genesis 2:8–9 it states: "And the LORD God planted a garden in Eden, in the east; and there he put the man whom he had formed. (9) And out of the ground the LORD God made to grow every tree that is pleasant to the sight and good for food, the tree of life also in the midst of the garden, and the tree of the knowledge of good and evil." The Garden of Eden was the home for man. It was the paradise of God on earth. Its location in the east was symbolic for the rising of light. The garden was both spiritual and material in composition. The two trees represented the two kingdoms: the kingdom of Light (God) and kingdom of Darkness (Lucifer in rebellion). Because God caused them to grow, there was a structuring of both systems relative to man on earth. God predetermined the boundaries for Lucifer to operate in his state of rebellion (Job 38:4–11). The names of the two trees describe the systems. Only the Tree of Life carries the divine life force with purpose and direction in a holy state of activity. The Tree of Knowledge of Good and Evil only uses knowledge of good and evil. This becomes a floating vale system when it is not related to a holy master plan.

For example, I buy a piece of property and want to build a housing project to house the poor who live on the streets. Based upon today's need, we would call the plan good. But when I consult with the city planning department to construct the project, I discover that my property is in the path of a planned freeway that will serve multitudes of people. I cannot build my project. As an independent plan it was good. In relationship to the master plan, it was not acceptable. To build my project without approval would create chaos and futility. In life, without a master plan and absolute authority in holiness, good and evil take on relative values. The philosophy of "nothing is good or bad, but thinking makes it so" could not be further from the truth in God's creation.

Genesis 2:10–14:

> A river flowed of out Eden to water the garden, and there it divided and became four rivers. (11) The name of the first is Pishon; it is the one which flows around the whole land of Havilah, where there is gold; (12) and the gold of that land is good; bdellium and onyx stone are there. (13) The name of the second river is Gihon; it is the one which flows around the whole land of Cush. (14) And the name of the third river is Tigris, which flows east of Assyria. And the fourth river is the Euphrates.

The river that flowed out of the Garden of Eden was a literal spring of water branching out into four parts. This natural flow would carry the development of God's garden paradise out into the rest of the undeveloped world. With this natural river, there is also the spiritual counterpart, "living waters." It comes from one source, God, and it is divided into the four spiritual building blocks of knowledge, truth, understanding, and wisdom and causes life to develop in the plan of God.

Genesis 2:15–17:

> The LORD God took the man and put him in the Garden of Eden to till it and keep it. (16) And the LORD God commanded the man, saying, "You may freely eat of every tree of the garden; (17) but of the tree of the knowledge of good and evil you shall not eat, for in the day that you eat of it you shall die."

In Genesis 2:8 man is placed in the garden and God causes everything to grow up around him. Now, in Genesis 2:15 the man is placed in the garden a second time. Why? Because there are two gardens! The first is the natural, and the second is the spiritual. It is the spiritual garden that mankind is told to "till it and keep it." From our five senses, man is able to learn from the natural order about its development, but it is from the spiritual enlightened direction from God that we must till and keep! God provides the natural food for the sustenance of the material man. God also provides the spiritual sustenance for man to feed upon, and he is free to help himself at all times. The only tree that he is told not to partake of is the Tree of Knowledge of Good and Evil. It has a natural form, but produces a spiritual substance called disobedience to God, which is sin, because every tree produces after its own kind. For mankind, it will produce "death," which is separation from God and his divine sustenance that allows mankind to live forever in his paradise existence.

Genesis 2:18–20:

> Then the LORD God said, "It is not good that the man should be alone; I will make him a helper fit for him." (19) So out of the ground the LORD God formed every beast of the field and every bird of the air, and brought them to the man to see what he would call them; and whatever the man called every living creature, that was its name. (20) The man gave names to all cattle, and to the birds of the air, and to every beast of the field; but for the man there was not found a helper fit for him.

Adam is getting and education through the natural order and the spiritual order form God, and it is very extensive! God wants to bring a helpmate for Adam, but Adam needed to be educated first. In Genesis 1 on the fifth day, God created sea life and the birds of the air. On the sixth day, God created the cattle, creeping things, and beasts of the earth, and then he creates man. The animal population is on the earth before man. In Genesis 2 we are presented with greater clarification of the sixth day of creation. So, when the Scripture says: "So out of the ground the LORD God formed every beast of the field and every bird of the air, and brought them to the man to see what he would call them," God is not creating the animals. The term "formed" is used. What God had created, he gives a purpose in life. Here, he is revealing to Adam the creation and purpose of the animals in a vision form of each individual species to the mind of Adam without parading the literal animal through the garden.

My first major encounter with God came at the age of nineteen in the form of a vision that took place in my life. It appeared in a moment of time with thousands of pieces of a puzzle assembling before my eyes, presenting the past, present, and part of the future of my life in meticulous detail. It was visual, and it was audible, and it was the truth! And it changed the whole course of my life. John the Apostle received the Book of Revelation in an audible and visionary form. I believe this method was part of the educational process that was given to Adam before Eve was created. Adam was certainly no dumb caveman when God finished the process!

Genesis 2:21–23:

> So the LORD God caused a deep sleep to fall upon the man, and while he slept took one of his ribs and closed up its place with flesh; (22) and the rib which the LORD God had taken from the man he made into a woman and brought her to the man (23) Then the man said, "this at last is bone of my bones and flesh of my flesh; she shall be called woman, because she was taken out of Man."

With the creation and presentation of women by God to man, there is an immediate understanding of the unity and purpose of the relationship. How much of an education the woman received before the time of her presentation is not given. Since she was a composite from the rib of man, there may have been a transfer from the spiritual side also, just as we can transfer information from one computer to another. Whatever the scenario, there had to be sufficient education in both man and woman before God could enter into the seventh day of rest. In that seventh day condition, the creation would function according to its design, being productive and fruitful in God's governing flow through all life.

In looking at Genesis 2:24–25 there is a projected plan of God for man. "Therefore a man leaves his father and his mother and cleaves to his wife, and they become one flesh. (25) And the man and his wife were both naked, and were not ashamed." In the reproduction process of mankind, there is a bonding of two hearts, minds, and souls in the husband and wife relationship. It is a deep communion of two people with a unity of purpose and direction, separating from the parents. This is the meaning of becoming "one flesh." If the purpose and direction are from God, the relationship is fruitful. We are not alone! "The man and his wife were both naked, and were not ashamed." The standard of life was established by God. The man and the woman were designed and enlightened to function according to that standard. By living their lives in accordance with the life flow of God, there would never be any shame, just fruitful activity in love.

## POINTS TO REMEMBER

1. Time as we know it came into existence on the *fourth day* of our creation.

2. The seventh day blessing by God of our creation became a fixed condition concerning God's relationship with this creation in a state of holiness. It would continue every day of every year until the sin of man would impact God's relationship with mankind.

3. Chapter 2 of Genesis gives us more detail of the sixth day of our creation concerning God's personal involvement with mankind.

4. There are parallels between the design of the natural order of our creation and the spiritual order. The natural order

gives us a visual picture of the issue of light and darkness in the spiritual dimension concerning the rebellion of Lucifer. God uses the natural order throughout Scripture to identify the spiritual.

5. Man is made up of two components: the dust of the earth and the spirit of God. Man is material and spiritual.

6. God will always rule over people. People will never be capable of ruling over God.

7. Mankind grows in knowledge, truth, understanding, and wisdom through the natural and spiritual order.

8. While mankind was made in the image of God (man's ability to function with the seven spirits of God), mankind must maintain the likeness of God, which deals with his moral character. Without that factor, mankind will damage and destroy one another.

9. Mankind was subjected to two systems of life in the Garden of Eden: the Tree of Life (the system of God), and the Tree of Knowledge of Good and Evil (the rebellion of

Lucifer). The first one is a lifestyle of being totally centered on God. The second is a lifestyle being totally centered on self. The first system brings abundant life, the second system brings death. A mixture of the two makes a mess!

10. There were two gardens in Eden: a natural garden and a spiritual garden. It was the spiritual garden that Adam was told to till and keep.

11. Adam was given an education by God before Eve was made from the rib of Adam.

## CHAPTER 5

# THE FIRST PHASE OF GOD'S EDUCATIONAL PROGRAM

**EVENT:** The seventh day
**TIME FRAME:** Eternity Present—Creation 0, Western 3977 BC (?)[2]

**INTRODUCTION NARRATIVE:** *Lucifer's deception in the angelic creation brought chaos into the pure and holy state of God's creation. With the new creation, God allows the evil of Lucifer's rebellion to be presented to mankind. People will have the free will choice to either walk with God or the Devil. It is an educational program for all creation to view the results. While mankind will come into bondage* *to sin, each person will have the opportunity, through the grace of God to be redeemed into fellowship with God for eternal life. Lucifer and all of the angels that followed him do not have the opportunity for redemption. At the end of this creation, they will all be thrown into the lake of fire, which is eternal damnation. Every human that rejects the grace of God during the seven thousand year period of our creation will also spend eternity in the lake of fire. Each person at an age of accountability, before their death, must make that decision! At the end of seven thousand years, all creation will fully understand why we cannot live our lives independent of God's control!*

## Genesis 3:17:

> Now the serpent was more subtle than any other wild creature that the LORD God had made. He said to the woman, "Did God say, 'You shall not eat of any tree of the garden?' (2) And the woman said to the serpent, "We may eat of the fruit of the trees of the garden; (3) but God said, 'You shall not eat of the fruit of the tree which is in the midst of the garden, neither shall you touch it, lest you die.'" (4) But the serpent said to the woman, "You will not die. (5) For God knows that when you eat of it your eyes will be opened, and you will be like God, knowing good and evil." (6) So when the woman saw that the tree was good for food, and that it was a delight to the eyes, and that the tree was to be desired to make one wise, she took of its fruit and ate; and she also gave some to her husband, and he ate. (7) Then the eyes of both were opened, and they knew that they were naked; and they sewed fig leaves together and made themselves aprons.

Satan presents himself through a serpent with the subtle deception in questioning the character and reliability of God and what he said. Then the outright lie is presented in verse 4 and 5. A simple paraphrase would be: "You don't need God. He's holding out on you. You can be God without God." Adam and Eve partook of the fruit and exchanged the spirit of truth for a lie. At that point deception became an integral part of mankind's lifestyle. The pure spiritual system of man's ability to reason with clear-cut knowledge and direction by the light of God was lost to him. The first state of death became a reality. Man became separated from God spiritually. The development of the earth was now cursed with a system of deception that would erode the life of mankind into toil, degradation, and physical death. In verse 7, their eyes were opened, and they clearly saw that they had entered into evil, and they were no longer under the protective covering of God's Word. They were "naked." Physically, they were just as naked before the sin as they were after the fact. But they know from the education of God that everything produces after its own kind! So they tied fig leaves together to cover their reproductive organs in an effort to hide their unholy state of being. They experienced shame and fear. Their protective spiritual covering from God was gone.

Genesis 3:8–13:

> And they heard the sound of the LORD God walking the garden in the cool of the day, and the man and his wife hid themselves from the presence of the LORD God among the trees of the garden. (9) But the LORD God called to the man, and said to him, "Where are you?" (10) And he said, "I heard the sound of thee in the garden, and I was afraid, because I was naked; and I hid myself." (11) He said, "Who told you that you were naked? Have you eaten of the tree of which I commanded you not to eat?" (12) The man said, "The woman whom thou gavest to be with me, she gave me fruit of the tree, and I ate." (13) Then the LORD God said to the woman, "What is this that you have done?" The woman said, "The serpent beguiled me, and I ate."

When we know what is right and do what is wrong, we enter into a state of shame for what we have done. Then the next thing that takes place is the fear of discovery. A peaceful and loving union with God and others is the way God designed life to be in his creation. In violating God's standard, the fear of being discovered and punished enters our heart. We don't want to face the consequences of our action, so we will try a system of self-justification rather than face the truth of the issue. This is how sin works in our lives. Adam blames God and the woman. The woman blames the serpent. And God knows the truth of the entire situation and pronounces his disciplinary action. God will not have deception and self-justification or self-glorification in his kingdom no more than you would allow the garbage collector to drop a load of garbage in your living room! God lives in a pure, holy state of existence and wants us to live in that state of being also.

Genesis 3:14–19:

> The LORD God said to the serpent, "Because you have done this, cursed are you above all cattle, and above all wild animals; upon your belly you shall go, and dust you shall eat all the days of your life. (15) I will put enmity between you and the woman, and between your seed and her seed; he shall bruise your head, and you shall bruise his heel." (16) To the woman he said, "I will greatly multiply your pain in childbearing; in pain you shall bring forth children, yet your desire shall be for your husband, and he shall rule over you." (17) And to Adam he said, "Because you have listened to the voice of your wife, and have eaten of the tree of which I commanded you, 'You shall not eat of it,' cursed is the ground because of you; in toil you shall eat of it all the days of your life; (18) thorns and thistles it shall bring forth to you and you shall eat the plants of the field. (19) In the sweat of your face you shall eat bread till you return to the ground, for out of it you were taken; you are dust, and to dust you shall return."

In verse 14 judgment begins with Lucifer. His life, relative to this earth, is cursed. He will not be successful in his endeavors, and eternal damnation will be his reward. He will only be able to feed upon the natural things of the earth. He will not be able to partake of the spiritual life and glory of the Lord. In verse 15, there will be hatred between the Devil and the woman. (The woman here is a reference to the "bride of Christ" that is everyone who will come forth from woman and walk with God on the earth as noted in Revelation 19:7). There will be hatred between the "seed" of the Devil (those who will follow him) and the seed of the woman which is Jesus, the Son of God taking on human flesh from the woman. "He [Jesus] shall bruise your head, and you shall bruise his heel." This refers to the battle that will play out between the righteousness of God in Christ and the evil of Lucifer, the Devil, Satan, the serpent, upon this earth.

Then in verse 16 comes the judgment upon the woman. Childbearing shall be painful for the woman. There are two kinds of pain. There is the physical pain, and there is the spiritual pain of bringing a child into a war zone between good and evil with the knowledge of all the problems the child will be confronted with during his or her life and that death can come at any time. At the same time, the woman will have a desire for her husband, and he will rule over her. A structure of authority is established between the two of them. The man will rule over the woman. Prior to the sin, both were equally submitted to the authority of God. Now, if the man is not walking with God, the woman will suffer. Also, if the woman is not walking with God, the man will suffer. In addition, if the children do not walk with God, the parents will suffer and vice versa.

Then in verse 17, the judgment falls upon Adam. Because Adam listened to his wife and acted upon her desire instead of being obedient to the instructions given by God, "cursed is the ground because of you; in toil you shall eat of it all the days of your life." Blight has come upon the earth. The deception of Lucifer was confined to the Tree of Knowledge of Good and Evil. The only way he had access to the new world system was through the participation of mankind partaking of the fruit of the tree in disobedience to God. With the participation of man and woman, mankind's ability to reason became tainted with deception. Deception was now free to grow in every person because mankind was separated from God's divine covering that would keep humanity in a state of purity in mind and body.

In verse 18, "thorns and thistles it shall bring forth to you; and you shall eat the plants of the field." Now, seeds of deception will be planted in the minds of people by the Devil and will become "thorns and thistles." Mankind will reap everything that they sow. People will no longer know what to do and when to do it by the direction of God, and their desires shall be self-centered instead of God-centered.

"In the sweat of your face you shall eat bread till you return to the ground." The natural earth is also cursed with thorns and thistles that will have to be dealt with in the process of farming. In the spiritual system of government, the thorns and thistles of greed and corruption will be evident. Life on earth is now going to be one miserable struggle in toil with a physical death sentence attached!

Genesis 3:20–21: "The man called his wife's name Eve, because she was the mother of all living. (21) And the LORD God made for Adam and for his wife garments of skins, and clothed them." The term "Eve" is translated in the Hebrew as "lifegiver" and "the first woman:—Eve." There are two issues here. The first is that Eve was the first of mankind to sin and that sinful nature would be passed down to all generations. This is in keeping with the design of creation; everything produces after its own kind "because she was the mother of all living." The second issue of the name Eve is taken from a root word in Hebrew that has a very positive outlook: "To live, have life, remain alive, sustain life, live prosperously, live for ever, be quickened, be alive, be restored to life or to continue in life, remain alive, to sustain life, to live on or upon, to live (prosperously), to revive, be quickened, from sickness, from discouragement, from faintness, from death." This is a direct reference to the fact that through the woman God would bring to us our redeemer, Jesus the Christ, the son of God! In support of this issue, "the LORD God made for Adam and for his wife garments of skins and clothed them." Through the killing of animals, the bodies of Adam and Eve were covered from their nakedness. God performs a substitution death to cover the physical nakedness of mankind brought into view through spiritual disobedience. It is a symbolic picture that points us to the woman, a virgin, giving birth to the Son of God, Jesus. He would die on a cross on our behalf to cover our sins and restore us to our relationship with God as it was before sin. Faith in the sacrificial offering prescribed by God would keep mankind covered until the perfect sacrifice, Jesus could be offered.

Genesis 3:22–24:

> Then the LORD God said, "Behold, the man has become like one of us, knowing good and evil; and now, lest he put forth his hand and take also of the tree of life, and eat, and live for ever"—(23) therefore the LORD God sent him forth from the garden of Eden, to till the ground from which he was taken. (24) He drove out the man; and at the east of the Garden of Eden he placed the cherubim, and a flaming sword which turned every way, to guard the way to the tree of life.

Before Adam and Eve sinned, they only knew and experienced good. With their partaking of the forbidden fruit, they experienced evil and came to know what it was all about. When God said, "Behold, the man has become like one of us, knowing good an evil" he is referring to the Trinity. The Trinity experienced and knew what evil was because of the rebellion of Lucifer and its destructive results, but they had never become evil. Adam and Even entered into it. Now for mankind to come out of sin, they must eat of the Tree of Life. But the Tree of Life is denied to them. Man was driven from the Garden of Eden and would have to till the ground from which he came from. Now he would have to earn a living. The spiritual garden that he was to "till and keep" was no longer available. He was driven out of the two gardens, the natural and the spiritual, that gave total sustenance. The condition of the seventh day rest of God was broken, and a new day of rest would not be given to man by God until he established a Covenant of Law with Moses for the Jews. But their state of rest would only be a symbolic form when God took them into the Promised Land where they would set up their tabernacle in Shiloh in 1479 BC. And this state of rest was totally dependent upon the Jews trusting in the Word of God and being obedient. The substance of that rest would not be equivalent to the rest in the Garden of Eden.

In verses 24, when God drove man out of the garden, he placed cherubim at the east of the garden with "a flaming sword that turned every way" that would guard the way back to the tree of life. The "flaming sword" is a symbol of the Word of God. Hebrews 4:12 states: "For the word of God is living and active, sharper than any two edged sword, piercing to the division of soul and spirit, of joints and marrow, and discerning the thoughts and intentions of the heart. (13) And before him no creature is hidden, but all are open and laid bare to the eyes of him with whom we have to do." Since the Tree of Life is hidden from us, how do we partake of its fruit? As we shall see, it will come by God's grace through faith as a gift during God's educational program over a period of seven thousand years.

From this point on, if someone wanted God to control their life, they would have to make sacrificial offerings as prescribed by God. It was no longer free. There was a sin barrier between God and man. Man was no longer pure and holy like God. People will now have to exercise faith in God's promise for redemption through prescribed sacrificial offerings. It will be the only avenue open for man with a death sentence upon his life. Spiritual death, which is separation from God's constant divine flow into the life of humanity, became a reality to all the descendants of Adam and Eve in every generation because God designed everything to produce after its own kind. (Genesis 1:24–25). So we are birthed into the world without the loving presence of God in our life, even though we are designed in his image. The central purpose of each person is to come to know him, or life on earth will be an exercise in futility, and we will be eternally separated from God. To walk with God is a free will choice. The only thing that you posses that is precious to God is your free will choice to trust him to govern your life, and that is faith! *"And without faith it is impossible to please him"* (Hebrews 11:6; italics added).

## POINTS TO REMEMBER

1. Deception by Lucifer brought about the rebellion and the fall of one-third of the angels. Now mankind is trapped by the same ploy: we can be gods without God!

2. Without God's protective covering, deception and self-justification become a lifestyle of futility.

3. Without God's protective covering, life becomes a constant struggle for survival with physical pain and spiritual torment. Hatred, wars, famine, pestilence, and death are all part of life outside of the kingdom of God.

4. God foreknew the fall of mankind and prepared a plan for our redemption to enter into his kingdom and live under his protection. But God will not take away our free will choice in making that decision. The return path is filled with difficulties in every walk of life, through every time period during the seven thousand years of this creation. The purpose is to develop our faith in God for every issue that confronts us during our lifetime on this earth. He holds the answer for every problem we face. So long as we think we can handle life without God, we are not a candidate for his guidance and power to deliver us from our fallen condition.

5. With the fall from the Garden of Eden, man is required to offer prescribed sacrificial offerings unto God to receive his favor. It is no longer free!

## CHAPTER 6

# LIFE OUTSIDE OF PARADISE

**EVENT:** Life outside of Eden
**TIME FRAME:** Eternity Present—Creation 5, Western 3972 (?)[3]

**INTRODUCTION NARRATIVE:** *The first 1,656 year period after the fall of Adam and Eve is a history lesson in compounding depravity in the heart of man separated from God without constraint. In the garden, humans had everything supplied to them in the natural and spiritual order with a close personal relationship with God. Outside the garden relationship, humans would have to struggle to survive all the days of their life on earth with the end results of a grave as their reward. Eternal life with God no longer belonged to them. If they wanted God's* *favor and blessing upon their life, they would have to render sacrificial offerings according to God's requirements. The life of mankind was now plagued with deception and ignorance. Truth and wisdom belonged to God. The Sabbath day of rest was destroyed through disobedience called sin.*

Genesis 4:1–6:

> Now Adam knew Eve his wife, and she conceived and bore Cain, saying, "I have gotten a man with the help of the LORD." (2) And again, she bore his brother Abel. Now Abel was a keeper of sheep, and Cain a tiller of the ground. (3) In the course of time Cain brought to the LORD an offering of the fruit of the ground, (4) and Abel brought of the firstlings of his flock and of their fat portions. And the LORD had regard for Abel and his offering, (5) but for Cain and his offering he had no regard. So Cain was very angry, and his countenance fell. (6) The LORD said to Cain, "Why are you angry, and why has your countenance fallen? (7) If you do well, will you not be accepted? And if you do not do well, sin is couching at the door; its desire is for you, but you must master it."

With the birth of Cain, there is an indication by the way it is stated, "... help of the Lord," that Eve may have given birth to two or three girls before Cain. Because the male is the dominant figure over the household, the births of women are not recorded in Scripture concerning the genealogy of mankind. Abel is the second male child. Cain and Abel each rendered offerings unto God. Abel had a sincere heart to walk with God, and his offering was accepted. Cain's offering was rejected because of a corrupt heart. He offered the sacrifice out of obedience. It was not what he offered; it was the attitude in which he offered it. His offering did not come from the first fruits of his field as required. God was not the priority of his life. So Cain got angry because his sin was exposed. God assured him that if he did "well" (not what is perfect because it is impossible for humans to be perfect with a sinful nature), he would be accepted. God deals with Cain's heart condition. And God states the reason, "sin is couching at the door; its desire is for you." Sin, like a recumbent animal, is waiting for the right moment to do what is evil, and we must master it, or it will totally take over our lives. Having the right attitude comes when your heart is set to please God, in every aspect of your life. *Then you will do well.* We will never be perfect until God delivers us out from our human flesh with its sinful nature.

**EVENT: Degeneration of life in sin**
**TIME FRAME: Eternity Present—Creation 36, Western 3941 BC[4]**

Genesis 4:8–16:
> Cain said to Abel his brother, "Let us go out to the field." And when they were in the field, Cain rose up against his brother

Abel, and killed him. (9) Then the LORD said to Cain, "Where is Abel your brother?" He said, "I do not know; am I my brother's keeper?" (10) And the LORD said, "What have you done? The voice of your brother's blood is crying to me from the ground. (11) And now you are cursed from the ground, which has opened its mouth to receive your brother's blood from your hand. (12) When you till the ground, it shall no longer yield to you its strength; you shall be a fugitive and wanderer on the earth." (13) Cain said to the LORD, "My punishment is greater than I can bear. (14) Behold, thou hast driven me this day away from the ground; and from thy face I shall be hidden; and I shall be a fugitive and away from the ground; and from thy face I shall be hidden; and I shall be a fugitive and a wanderer on the earth, and whoever finds me will slay me." (15) Then the LORD said to him, "Not so! If anyone slays Cain, vengeance shall be taken on him sevenfold." And the Lord put a mark on Cain, lest any who came upon him should kill him. (16) Then Cain went away from the presence of the LORD, and dwelt in the land of Nod, east of Eden.

When God inquires of Cain concerning his brother, Cain lies to God. The progression of sin compounds. While Abel was killed, he is still alive unto God in the earth and crying out. His voice is heard because of his obedient faith in God, yet he is still separated from God. It would be a four thousand year separation until Jesus paid the redemptive cost for the sins of mankind on a cross. Then the departed saints could enter into heaven and the Spirit of God could enter into people again to personally govern their life. Cain's degenerate behavior brings further separation from God and from the rest of the family. At this point, God does not allow the retribution of someone else to kill another for their crime.

Further separation from God was the punishment along with the consequences it would bring. Cain takes a sister for his wife and leaves to develop a self-centered lifestyle and is no longer able to see God or hear his voice. Now, he is totally on his own.

Genesis 4:17–34:

> Cain knew his wife, and she conceived and bore Enoch; and he built a city, and called the name of the city after the name of his son, Enoch. (18) To Enoch was born Irad; and Irad was the father of Mehuja-el, and Mehuja-el the father of Methusha-el, and Methusha-el the father of Lamech. (19) And Lamech took two wives; the name of the one was Adah, and the name of the other Zillah. (20) Adah bore Jabal; he was the father of those who dwell in tents and have cattle. (21) His brother's name was Jubal; he was the father of all those who play the lyre and pipe. (22) Zillah bore Tubal-cain; he was the forger of all instruments of bronze and iron. The sister of Tubal-cain was Naamah. (23) Lamech said to his wives: "Adah and Zillah hear my voice; you wives of Lamech, hearken to what I say: *I have slain a man for wounding me, a young man for striking me.* (24) If Cain is avenged sevenfold, truly Lamech seventy-sevenfold." (italics added)

Taking a sister for a wife or having two wives was not a violation of the law until the population increased and the law was given by God against it. Six generations downstream from Cain, there is boasting concerning the killing of one another in verses 23–24. The depravity of sin multiplies in the family of Cain.

**EVENT: Continuation of life in righteousness**
**TIME FRAME: Eternity Present—Creation 130, Western 3847 BC**

Genesis 4: 25–26: "And Adam knew his wife again, and she bore a son and called his name Seth, for she said, 'God has appointed for me another child instead of Abel, for Cain slew him.' (26) To Seth also a son was born, and he called his name Enosh. At that time men began to call upon the name of the LORD." Another son is born to Adam and Eve named Seth. He also had a heart for God, and his descendants all walked with God. Now we have two different types of people on earth. Those who walk in the darkness of sin, descendants from the heritage of Cain, and those who walk in the light of God's righteousness through the descendants of Seth.

**POINTS TO REMEMBER**

1. Sacrificial offerings to entreat God's blessing must come from a sincere heart wanting to know him and live in his light. Ritual activity without a love for God will not produce God's favor.

2. The faith of Abel during his life preserved his life with God, even in his death. While the sins of his brother Cain increased, the separation from God became greater until Cain lived a life of depravity without God and produced descendants who walked without God.

3. From the godless lifestyles of Cain, his descendants morally declined into fighting and killing one another, and boasting about it.

4. Adam and Eve gave birth to another son called Seth. He loved God and produced descendants who loved and walked with God and were blessed by him.

# CHAPTER 7

# TOTAL DEGENERATION OF LIFE ON EARTH

**EVENT:** The decline of righteousness

**TIME FRAME:** Eternity Present—Creation 1536, Jewish 1130, Western 2441 BC

**INTRODUCTION NARRATIVE:** *With the sin nature of mankind, those who walk without God become progressively degenerate. With the passing of time, those who walked with God became attracted to the women without God and married them. Slowly, they adapted to the lifestyle of the ungodly until wickedness and evil dominated the world. Noah and his family, a total of eight, remained faithful to God. So God* *destroyed the world with a flood, but he saved Noah and his family.*

Genesis 6:1–4:

> When men began to multiply on the face of the ground, and the daughters were born to them, (2) the sons of God saw that the daughters of men were fair; and they took to wife such of them as they chose. (3) Then the LORD said, "My spirit shall not abide in man for ever, for he is flesh, but his days shall be a hundred and twenty years." (4) The Nephilim were on the earth in those days, and also afterward, *when the sons of God came in to the daughter of men, and they bore children to them.* These were the mighty men that were of old, the men of renown. (italics added)

The righteous line of the descendants of Seth who walked with God, are called the "sons of God." They began to mingle with the unrighteous descendants of Cain and married their daughters. In doing so, they took on their lifestyles and became wicked. In verse 3, God foresees the falling away of the righteous and proclaims that it will be one hundred and twenty years when he will put a stop to the corruption and wickedness upon the face of the earth. The Nephilim were giants in the land that were highly esteemed by men.

Genesis 6:5–22:

> *The LORD saw that the wickedness of man was great in the earth, and that every imagination of the thoughts of his heart*

## Let There Be Light

*was only evil continually.* (6) And the LORD was sorry that he had made man on the earth, and it grieved him to his heart. (7) So the LORD said, "I will blot out man whom I have created from the face of the ground, man and beast and creeping things and birds of the air, for I am sorry that I have made them." (8) But Noah found favor in the eyes of the LORD. [Noah is 480 years old at this point in time and is faithful to God.] (9) These are the generations of Noah. Noah was a righteous man, blameless in his generation; Noah walked with God. (10) And Noah had three sons, Shem Ham, and Japheth. (11) Now the earth was corrupt in God's sight, *and the earth was filled with violence.* (12) And God saw the earth, and behold, it was corrupt; for all flesh had corrupted their way upon the earth. (13) And God said to Noah, "I have determined to make an end of all flesh; for the earth is filled with violence through them; behold, I will destroy them with the earth. (14) Make yourself an ark of gopher wood; make rooms in the ark, and cover it inside and out with pitch. (15) This is how you are to make it: the length of the ark three hundred cubits, its breadth fifty cubits, and its height thirty cubits. (16) Make a roof for the ark, and finish it to a cubit above; and set the door of the ark in its side; make it with lower, second, and third decks. (17) For behold, I will bring a flood of waters upon the earth, to destroy all flesh in which is the breath of life from under heaven; everything that is on the earth shall die. (18) But I will establish my covenant with you; and you shall come into the ark, you, your sons, your wife, and your sons' wives with you. (19) And of every living thing of all flesh, you shall bring two of every sort into the ark, to keep them alive with you; they shall be male and female. (20) Of the birds according to their kinds, and of the animals according to their kinds, of every creeping thing of the ground according to its kind, two of every sort shall come in to you, to keep them alive. (21) Also take with you every sort of food that is eaten, and store it up; and it shall serve as food for you and for them." (22) Noah did this; he did all that God commanded him. (italics added)

Noah and his sons have one hundred and twenty years to build the ark and gather the animals that God has selected, before God destroys everything upon the earth and starts over again. And Noah accomplishes the task in verse 22.

**EVENT: The flood of Noah**
**TIME FRAME: Eternity Present—Creation 1656, Jewish 1440, Western 2321 BC**

Genesis 7:1–5:

> Then the LORD said to Noah, "Go into the ark, you and all your household, for I have seen that you are righteous before me in this generation. (2) Take with you seven pairs of all clean animals, the male and his mate; and a pair of the animals that are not clean, the male and his mate; (3) and seven pairs of the birds of the air also, male and female, to keep their kind alive upon the face of all the earth. (4) For in seven days I will send rain upon the earth forty days and forty nights; and every living thing that I have made I will blot out from the face of the ground." (5) And Noah did all that the LORD had commanded him.

Because Noah was obedient to the voice of God throughout his life to this point, he and his family, a total of eight, will be spared from the destruction coming upon the whole world. Mankind, left without restraint under the demonic leading of Lucifer, degenerated into a system of total destructive wickedness. This becomes the first major history lesson of why God's created beings cannot live outside of God's sovereign control.

Genesis 7:11–16:

> In the six hundredth year of Noah's life, in the second month, on the seventeenth day of the month, *on that day all the fountains of the great deep burst forth*, and the windows of the heavens were opened. (12) *And rain fell upon the earth forty days and forty nights.* (13) On the very same day Noah and his sons, Shem and Ham and Japheth, and Noah's wife and the three wives of his sons with them entered the ark, (14) they and every beast according to its kind, and all the cattle according to their kinds, and every creeping thing that creeps on the earth according to its kind, every bird according to its kind, every bird of every sort. (15) They went into the ark with Noah, two and two of all flesh in which there was the breath of life. (16) And they that entered, male and female of all flesh, went in as God had commanded him; *and the LORD shut him in.* (italics added)

Noah was six hundred years old when the flood took place. The life span of humans before the flood would go for hundreds of years with the longest life span recorded of 969 years for Methuselah in Genesis 5:27. After the flood, man's life span would slowly diminish to an average age of seventy years. With the flood came major changes to the earth. It states in verse 11, that "all the fountains of the great deep burst forth." It was more than just forty days and nights of rain! There was a cataclysmic change. Some scientists believe that the earth before the flood had a canopy over it to create a hot house environment. But with the flood came an instant freezing of the North and South Pole and a removal of the protective canopy. Before the flood began, verse 16 states, "the LORD shut him in" the ark. Noah, his family, and all of the animals were secure under the divine protection of the Lord God!

Genesis 7:17–24:

> The flood continued forty days upon the earth; and the waters increased, and bore up the ark, and it rose high above the earth. (18) The waters prevailed and increased greatly upon the earth; and the ark floated on the face of the waters. (19) And the waters prevailed so mightily upon the earth that all the high mountains under the whole heaven were covered; (20) the waters prevailed above the mountains, *covering them fifteen cubits deep.* (21) And all flesh died that moved upon the earth, birds, cattle, beasts, all swarming creatures that swarm upon the earth, and every man; (22) *everything on the dry land in whose nostrils was the breath of life died.* (23) He blotted out every living thing that was upon the face of the ground, man and animals and creeping things and birds of the air; they were blotted out from the earth. Only Noah was left, and those that were with him in the ark. (24) And the waters prevailed upon the earth a hundred and fifty days. (italics added)

In accordance with verse 19, all of the mountains were covered with water, leaving the world as one solid ocean. Only the sea life remained alive.

Genesis 8:13–19:

> In the six hundred and first year [of Noah's life], in the first month, the first day of the month, the waters were dried from off the earth; and Noah removed the covering of the ark, and behold, the face of the ground was dry. (14) In the second month, on the twenty-seventh day of the month, the earth was dry. (15) Then God said to Noah, (16) "Go forth from the ark, you and your wife, and your sons and your sons' wives with you. (17) Bring forth with you every living thing that is with you of all flesh—birds and animals and every creeping thing that creeps

on the earth." (18) So Noah went forth, and his sons and his wife and his sons' wives with him. (19) And every beast, every creeping thing, and every bird, everything that moves upon the earth, went forth by families out of the ark.

It is one year and ten days that Noah and his family spent in the ark. Everyone is alive and healthy, including the animals. God is able to do the miraculous on our behalf if we are willing to make him Lord over our life and be obedient.

Genesis 8:20–22:

> Then Noah built an alter to the LORD, and took of every clean animal and of every clean bird, and offered burnt offerings on the altar. (21) And when the LORD smelled the pleasing odor, the LORD said in his heart, "I will never again curse the ground because of man, *for the imagination of man's heart is evil from his youth*; neither will I ever again destroy every living creature as I have done. (22) *While the earth remains*, seedtime and harvest, cold and heat, summer and winter, day and night, shall not cease." (italics added)

Noah makes a sacrificial offering by fire of the clean animals and birds. Because of the sin separation between humanity and God, God uses the characteristics of animals to identify to mankind what is acceptable and unacceptable behavior using the terms "clean" and "unclean." A lamb is a clean animal, willing to follow his master in a state of innocence. A pig was classified as unclean because it eats garbage and wallows in the mud. At this point in time, the legal commandments of the law were not part of God's relationship to humanity. Yet a holy sacrifice was to be offered if someone wanted God's protection and enlightenment. There is no detailed information present on the issue of sacrificing at this point in time in Scripture, only the evidence of it. By deduction, God imparted the information to Adam and Even when he drove them out of the Garden of Eden.

There is detailed information given to us concerning clean and unclean animals when Moses receives the Covenant of Law from God, which is covered in Leviticus 11:1–47. With the offering of Noah, the Lord promises to "never again curse the ground because of man." This does not stop God from bringing his judgments upon segments of land due to man's wickedness, but he will not destroy the whole earth as in the flood. There will always be productive harvests. That is a one-way covenant by God to mankind, regardless of what we do. However, this does not prohibit God from killing large segments of the population on earth if they will not repent of their wickedness.

## POINTS TO REMEMBER

1. Two lifestyles developed upon the earth after the separation of Cain: those who walked with God and those who rejected God.

2. In the process of time, those who walked with God stated to marry those who rejected God. The ungodly corrupted the righteous, and they became one in doing evil in the sight of God.

3. God saw what was taking place and gave them one hundred and twenty years before he would destroy the earth with a flood.

4. God saw that Noah and his family remained faithful and chose Noah to build an ark of protection against the forthcoming flood.

5. God preserves Noah, his family, and each species of the animal population to repopulate the earth after the flood.

6. God promises never to destroy the earth with another flood, but he will continue to bring destructive judgments when wickedness reaches an intolerable position, in his educational program.

## CHAPTER 8

# THE SECOND PHASE OF GOD'S EDUCATIONAL PROGRAM

**EVENT:** Changes in the creation

**TIME FRAME:** Eternity Present—Creation 1657, Jewish 1441, Western 2320 BC

**INTRODUCTION NARRATIVE:** *With the destruction of the world, God changes the conditions upon the earth. Man and animals become carnivorous. It is a hostile environment. Mankind will be held accountable to one another for sins that are committed. God will not allow the world to become totally corrupt again. With the repopulation of* *the world in the process of time, God calls upon Abraham and makes a covenant with him. God blesses Abraham and his descendants and makes them into a holy nation before him. He promises to give the land of Canaan to Abraham's descendants. Through them, God reveals to the world the blessing that comes to a nation of people who are willing to follow God and be obedient to his laws. Abraham agreed, and through him, God brings forth the Jewish nation.*

Genesis 9:1–7:

> And God blessed Noah and his sons, and said to them, "be fruitful and multiply, and fill the earth. (2) The fear of you and the dread of you shall be upon every beast of the earth, and upon every bird of the air, upon everything thing that creeps on the ground and all the fish of the sea; into your hand they are delivered. (3) Every moving thing that lives shall be food for you; and as I gave you the green plants, I give you everything. (4) Only you shall not eat of flesh with its life, that is, its blood. (5) For your lifeblood I will surely require a reckoning; of every beast I will require it and of man; of every man's brother I will require the life of man. (6) Whoever sheds the blood of man, by man shall his blood be shed; for God made man in his own image. (7) And you, be fruitful and multiply, bring forth abundantly on the earth and multiply in it.

With a new beginning Noah and his sons are blessed by God and instructed to be fruitful and multiply. Fruitful is dealing with the spiritual side of man in God's image. That is, being productive in his creative activities and in his relationship through love, peace, joy, patience, and kindness. They are also to multiply in repopulating the world. But in this new setting, there are changes. The animals have been given a spirit of fear towards mankind. And man is no longer a vegetarian. He may eat the fish of the sea, the birds of the air, the beasts of the earth, and everything that creeps upon the ground. The wildlife is also carnivorous. It is a hostile environment, and mankind is given dominion over everything. While man is allowed to feed upon the flesh of the wildlife, he is not allowed to partake of the blood because it represents the life of the animal. In short, man is to emulate the life of God, not lower life-forms. This becomes a central issue throughout Scripture. The life of man is in his blood. Everything that man does while he lives on earth, he will be held accountable to God for judgment. It is not a free ride to do what we want, when we want, how we want, without a standard of accountability. Whoever sheds the blood of man, mankind will shed his blood. God will not allow mankind to degenerate into total wickedness again. With a hostile environment and accountability to God and others, coupled with a sin producing nature, man will have to be careful how he lives. While the world was cleansed of evil people, the angelic realm, both good and

## Let There Be Light

evil, did not change. They still have a part to play in the development of our creation.

Genesis 9:18-27:

> The sons of Noah who went forth from the ark were Shem, Ham, and Japheth. Ham was the father of Canaan. (19) These three were the sons of Noah; and from these the whole earth was peopled.
> (20) Noah was the first tiller of the soil. He planted a vineyard; (21) and he drank of the wine, and became drunk, and lay uncovered in his tent. (22) And Ham, the father of Canaan, saw the nakedness of his father, and told his two brothers outside. (23) Then Shem and Japheth took a garment, laid it upon both their shoulders, and waked backward and covered the nakedness of their father; their faces were turned away, and they did not see their father's nakedness. (24) When Noah awoke from his wine and knew what his youngest son had done to him, (25) he said, "Cursed be Canaan; a slave of slaves shall he be to his brothers." (26) He also said, "Blessed by the LORD my God be Shem; and let Canaan be his slave. (27) God enlarge Japheth, and let him dwell in the tents of Shem; and let Canaan be his slave."

In the process of time, Noah's family brought forth offspring, and Noah plants a vineyard. After the harvest, he made wind and got drunk. While he is passed out in his tent, his grandson Canaan, through his son Ham, had sexual relations with Noah's wife.[5] Ham saw what was taking place. He tells his brothers, Shem and Japheth. They do not want to look upon the evil, so they walk backward with a blanket to cover the sin. When Noah awakened and became aware of what took place, he cursed Canaan, and a new line of degenerates began. The greater the sins of a person, the more degrading their life becomes. To be a slave, in bondage to a person, is degrading. To be a "slave of slaves" is to become the scum of the earth in degradation. Sickness, disease, poverty, suffering, death are all the conditions brought about through disobedience to God. Returning to God is the only way out of this condition. While Canaan is cursed, Shem and Japheth are to be blessed by God for what they did.

Genesis 9:28-29: "After the flood Noah lived three hundred and fifty years. (29) All the days of Noah were nine hundred and fifty years; and he died." Because of Noah's faithfulness to God, even though he was a sinner, his life was fruitful and productive, blessed by God.

The command to Noah and his sons when they got off of the ark was to, "Be fruitful and multiply, and fill the earth." In obedience, the family began to multiply and expand out into the world. In the second generation downstream from Canaan, Nimrod was born and Genesis 10:8 states: "... he was the first on earth to be a mighty man." Then in Genesis 10:10-12 it states: "The beginning of his kingdom was Babel, Erech, and Accad, all of them in the land of Shinar. (11) From that land he went into Assyria, and built Nineveh,

Rehoboth-Ir, Calah, and (12) Resen between Nineveh and Calah; that is the great city."

The story of Nimrod's disobedience against God is summed up in Genesis 11:1-9:

> Now the whole earth had one language and few words. (2) And as men migrated from the east, they found a plain in the land of Shinar and settled there. (2) And they said to one another, "Come, let us make bricks, and burn them thoroughly." And they had brick for stone, and bitumen for mortar. (4) Then they said, "Come, let us build ourselves a city, and a tower with its top in the heavens, *and let us make a name for ourselves,* lest we be scattered abroad upon the face of the whole earth." (5) And the LORD came down to see the city and the tower, which the sons of men had built. (6) And the LORD said, "Behold, they are one people, and they have all one language; and this is only the beginning of what they will do; and nothing that they propose to do will now be impossible for them. (7) Come, let us go down, and there confuse their language, that they may not understand one another's speech." (8) So the LORD scattered them abroad from there over the face of all the earth, and they left off building the city. (9) Therefore its name was called Babel, because there the LORD confused the language of all the earth; and from there the LORD scattered them abroad over the face of all the earth. (italics added)

God's educational plan to develop the world will not be stopped by the rebellious acts of mankind. Today, the Plains of Shinar are part of Iraq. It is where the Babylonians built the city of Babylon, which decayed over the centuries after the territory was taken over by the Media-Persian Empire. This same city will be reconstructed in our day.

**EVENT: The birth of Abram**
**TIME FRAME: Eternity Present—Creation 1948, Jewish 1732, Western 2029 BC**

This date, 2029 BC, marks the birth of Abram (his name is later changed to Abraham) 1,948 years after the creation of Adam and Eve. God began a new work through Abram in the second phase of his educational program. When Abram was seventy-five years old, he was called by God to leave his land and kindred and go to a land that God would show him. It was the land of Canaan, the degenerates. God was going to use Abram as an example of the blessings that would come forth for those who would trust God with their lives. God made promises to Abram. Abram believed God and acted in obedience, like Noah, to God's directions. One of the promises to Abram was that his descendants would be as many as the stars of heaven. Abram was childless and his wife was beyond her childbearing years. In an effort to have children, Abram's wife Sahai gives Abram her Egyptian maid Hagar to bear a child for them. Hagar conceived and bore a son named Ishmael. Abram was eighty-six years old at the time.

When Abram was ninety-nine years old, the Lord appeared to him and said:

"I am God Almighty; walk before me, and be blameless. (2) And I will make my covenant between me and you, and will multiply you exceedingly." (3) Then Abram fell on his face; and God said to him, (4) "Behold, my covenant is with you, and you shall be the father of a multitude of nations. (5) No longer shall your name be Abram, but your name shall be Abraham; *for I have made you the father of a multitude of nations.* (6) I will make you exceedingly fruitful; and *I will make nations of you, and kings shall come forth from you.* (7) And *I will establish my covenant between me and you and your descendants after you throughout their generations for an everlasting covenant, to be God to you and to your descendants after you.* (8) And *I will give to you, and to your descendants after you, the land of your sojourning, all the land of Canaan,* for an everlasting possession; and I will be their God." (Genesis 17:1–8; italics added)

### Then in Genesis 17:15–21 God states:

"As for Sarai your wife, you shall not call her name Sarai, but Sarah shall be her name. (16) I will bless her, and moreover I will give you a son by her; I will bless her, and she shall be a mother of nations; kings of people shall come from her." (17) Then Abraham fell on his face and laughed, and said to himself, "Shall a child be born to a man who is a hundred years old? Shall Sarah, who is ninety years old, bear a child?" (18) And Abraham said to God, "O that Ishmael might live in thy sight!" (19) God said, "No, but Sarah your wife shall bear you a son, and *you shall call his name Isaac. I will establish my covenant with him as an everlasting covenant for his descendants after him.* (20) As for Ishmael, I have heard you; behold, I will bless him and make him fruitful and multiply him exceedingly; he shall be the father of twelve princes, and I will make him a great nation. (21) *But I will establish my covenant with Isaac,* whom Sarah shall bear to you at this season next year." (italics added)

This is an extremely important issue in Scripture. The covenant made with Abraham will not pass through his son

Ishmael, conceived through Hagar. It will pass through the miraculous birth of Abraham's next son from Sarah. He is called Isaac. A few years after the birth of Isaac, Hagar and Ishmael depart from Abraham. From Ishmael comes forth twelve tribes that makeup the Arab nations. There is hatred between the Arabs and the Jews throughout history all the way to the Battle of Armageddon. In AD 626, after Jesus established the New Covenant with the Jewish nation, Mohammad, a descendant of Ishmael called a prophet by his people, establishes the religion of Islam. It is through Islam that the Antichrist will rise and dominate the world for a period of three and a half years before Armageddon takes place, and then Islam will be destroyed. The world will then be ruled by Jesus for a thousand years.

To Isaac was born Jacob, and Jacob had twelve sons. The twelve sons multiplied and became the twelve tribes of Israel. The nation of Jews is developed by God to be a light to the rest of the world through God's blessings based upon the faith and obedience of the people. As they began to develop as sojourners in the land of Canaan, God orchestrated their move to Egypt. In the process of time, they grew in number but became slaves to the Egyptians.

## POINTS TO REMEMBER

1. With a new beginning for the earth, God changes some of the conditions: (A) The fear of man is instilled into the animals. (B) The animals become carnivorous. (C) Man is no longer a vegetarian, he can eat the animals. (D) The earth now has a hostile environment. Man will be held accountable by people for the sins committed against one another on earth. (E) God is not going to allow the earth to degenerate into total corruption again until the rapture of the church.

2. Noah's grandson had intercourse with Noah's wife while Noah had passed out from too much alcohol. When Noah discovered what his grandson had done, he curses Canaan. Canaan and his descendants suffer the consequences becoming slaves of slaves in their degenerate condition.

3. Noah blesses Shem and Japheth, and they are rewarded for their conduct concerning Canaan's behavior.

4. Those that walk in obedience with God will be rewarded, and those who walk contrary will suffer loss, according to their degree of disobedience. Galatians 6:7 suns up the issue:

"Do not be deceived; God is not mocked, for whatever a man sows, that he will also reap."

5. Nimrod violate the known will of God by gathering the people to himself and building a tower unto heaven and setting up their own religion. God breaks it up by confusing their ability to communicate and scatters them abroad.

6. With the scattering of people around the world and the development of different countries, God called Abraham to become a holy nation of people unto God. They will be an example to the world concerning the blessings of God to those who will be governed directly by God, individually and collectively. Abraham accepts God's call upon his life.

7. Abraham has two sons. One son came through his wife's handmaiden, Hagar. The son's name is Ishmael. The other son is born through his wife Sarah. His name is Isaac, and all of the promises that God made to Abraham are passed through him, to his son Jacob, and his twelve sons that will multiply and become the nation of Israel. God promises are not passed through Ishmael. The totality of the prom-

ises made to the Jews, are ultimately to be fulfilled in and through Jesus Christ to all who commit their life to follow him, both Jew and gentile.

## CHAPTER 9

# THE THIRD PHASE OF GOD'S EDUCATIONAL PROGRAM

**EVENT:** The exodus from Egypt

**TIME FRAME:** Eternity Present—Creation 2453, Jewish 15 Nisan 2237, Western March 27, 1524 BC

**INTRODUCTION NARRATIVE:** *In the process of time, the Jews multiplied but became enslaved to the Egyptians. God delivers the Jews from bondage and makes a Covenant of Law with them in the wilderness. Then God takes them into the land of Canaan in fulfillment of his promise to Abraham. The success or failure of the nation was always dependent upon the free will choice of the people to follow the known will of God, as he led them.*

# Let There Be Light

Five hundred and five years after the birth of Abraham, God used a descendant of Abraham, Moses, to lead the Jews out of their bondage to Egypt. They now numbered in the millions. It was God's time for the Jews to take the land that God has promised to Abraham. Before they left Egypt, God established a ceremonial law called the Feast of Passover.

Exodus 12:1-13:

> The LORD said to Moses and Aaron in the land of Egypt, (2) "This month shall be for you the beginning of months; it shall be the first month of the year for you.[6] (3) Tell all the congregation of Israel that on the tenth day of this month[7] they shall take every man a lamb according to their fathers' houses, a lamb for a household; (4) and if the household is too small for a lamb, then a man and his neighbor next to his house shall take according to the number of persons; according to what each can eat you shall make your count for the lamb.[8] (5) Your lamb shall be without blemish, a male a year old; you shall take it from the sheep or from the goats; (6) and you shall keep it until the fourteenth day of this month, when the whole assembly of the congregation of Israel shall kill their lambs in the evening.[9] (7) Then they shall take some of the blood, and put it on the two doorposts and the lintel of the houses in which they eat them.[10] (8) They shall eat the flesh that night, roasted;[11] with unleavened bread[12] and bitter herbs they shall eat it.[13] (9) Do not eat any of it raw or boiled with water, but roasted, its head with its legs and its inner parts.[14] (10) And you shall let none of it remain until the morning, anything that remains until the morning you shall burn.[15] (11) In this manner you shall eat it: your loins girded, you sandals on your feet, and your staff in your hand; and you shall eat it in haste.[16] It is the LORD'S Passover.[17] (12) For I will pass through the land of Egypt that night, and I will smite all the first-born in the land of Egypt, both man and beast; and on all the gods of Egypt I will execute judgments: I am the

LORD. (13) The blood shall be a sign for you, upon the houses where you are; and when I see the blood, I will pass over you, and no plague shall fall upon you to destroy you, when I smite the land of Egypt."

God's judgments fell upon the unrepentant sinners when God delivered the Jews from the sinful estate of Egypt. *This same situation will take place when God delivers his saints from the evil of this world*, just before the rapture, when he kills one-third of the world's population in Revelation 9:13–15.

Through miraculous sings and wonders, God delivered his people and took them out into the wilderness en route to Canaan. There he established a Covenant of Law to govern their conduct in relationship to himself and to one another. Through their faith in God, exercised in obedience to the Covenant of Law (moral, civil, and ceremonial), God would bless and protect them against all enemies. God would verify to the people and the world of his sovereign ability to fulfill whatever he promised! But because of unbelief and rebellion in the ranks, and God's disciplinary actions, it took forty years to get them into the Promised Land. Only two people, Joshua and Caleb, out of that generation of adults that left Egypt were able to go into the land. The rest of that generation missed the blessing because of their unbelief in God's power and ability and their refusal to walk in God's statues.

Before the death of Moses and the entrance into the Promised Land, Moses proclaimed that another prophet would come forth from their brethren after the order of his ministry to speak to the Jews as he had done in representing God.

Deuteronomy 18:15–19:

> The LORD your God will raise up for you a prophet like me from among you, from your brethren—him you shall heed— (16) just as you desired of the LORD your God at Horeb on the day of the assembly, when you said, "Let me not hear again the voice of the LORD my God, or see this great fire any more, lest I die." (17) And the LORD said to me, "They have rightly said all that they have spoken. (18) *I will raise up for them a prophet like you from among their brethren; and I will put my words in his mouth, and he shall speak to them all that I command him.* (19) *And whoever will not give heed to my words which he shall speak in my name, I myself will require it of him.*"

The prophet would establish the New Covenant. This would be the Son of God, Jesus. But this would not take place for some 1,500 years in the future.

**EVENT: The entrance into the Promised Land**
**TIME FRAME: Eternity Present—Creation 2493, Jewish 2277, Western 1484 BC**

The new generation of Jews, who grew up under the Mosaic Covenant during the wilderness journey, entered into the

Promised Land. Only Joshua and Caleb from the adult population that left Egypt were allowed to enter. The new generation crossed the river Jordan on 11 Nisan 2277 and the Jews partook of the Passover Lamb on 15 Nisan, which was Saturday March 13, 1484 BC, in the Promised Land forty years after leaving Egypt.

During the next five years they had to do battle with the occupants of the land, and God gave them victory. It was during the fifth year of battle that God gave them rest in the Promised Land in fulfillment of God's promise to Abraham. With God, they had become a mighty nation, and their enemies feared them. They set up their tabernacle in Shiloh and made it their capitol city. This year becomes a major benchmark date in the history of the Jews because it marks the beginning of three prophetic time periods in the design of the tabernacle of Moses. They are: one-thousand-five-hundred years dispensation of law, two-thousand years for the church age period, and one-thousand years for the millennial reign of Christ. The total number of years is four-thousand-five-hundred. The beginning date of these three time periods is: Creation 2498, Jewish 2282, and Western 1479 BC.

The success or failure of the Jewish nation depended upon one issue: their obedience to God. In Leviticus 26:1–13

God proclaims the blessing that he will maintain for them through obedience:

> You shall make for yourselves no idols and erect no graven image or pillar, and you shall not set up a figured stone in your land, to bow down to them; for I am the LORD your God. (2) You shall keep my Sabbaths and reverence my sanctuary: I am the LORD.
>
> (3) If you walk in my statues and observe my commandments and do them, (4) then I will give you your rains in their season, and the land shall yield its increase, and the trees of the field shall yield their fruit. (5) And your threshing shall last to the time of vintage, and the vintage shall last to the time for sowing; and you shall eat your bread to the full, and dwell in your land securely. (6) *And I will give peace in the land, and you shall lie down, and no one shall make you afraid; and I will remove evil beasts from the land, and the sword shall not go through your land. (7) And you shall chase your enemies, and they shall fall before you by the sword. (8) Five of you shall chase a hundred, and a hundred of you shall chase ten thousand; and your enemies shall fall before you by the sword.* (9) And I will have regard for you and make you fruitful and multiply you, and will confirm my covenant with you. (10) And you shall eat old store long kept, and you shall clear out the old to make way for the new. (11) And I will make my abode among you, and my soul shall not abhor you. (12) And I will walk among you, and will be your God, and you shall be my people. (13) *I am the LORD your God, who brought you forth out of the land of Egypt, that you should not be their slaves; and I have broken the bars of your yoke and made you walk erect.*
> (italics added)

In Leviticus 26:14–46, God renders the judgments that he will bring upon them for their disobedience in five sequential forms. If they repent of their disobedience, the judgments will stop and restoration will begin. Without quoting the entire Scripture, I am listing the judgments in the order they are given.

First:

"I will appoint over you sudden terror, consumption and fever that waste the eyes and cause life to pine away. And you shall sow your seed in vain, for your enemies shall eat it; I will set my face against you, and you shall be smitten before your enemies; those who hate you shall rule over you, and you shall flee when none pursues you." (verse 17)

Second:

"I will break the pride of your power, and I will make your heavens like iron and your earth like brass; and your strength shall be spent in vain, for your land shall not yield its increase, and the trees of the land shall not yield their fruit." (verse 19)

Third:

"I will let loose the wild beasts among you, which shall rob you of your children, and destroy your cattle, and make you few in number, so that your ways shall become desolate." (verse 22)

Fourth:

"I will bring a sword upon you, that shall execute vengeance for the covenant; and if you gather within your cities I will send pestilence among you, and you shall be delivered into the hand of the enemy. When I break your staff of bread, ten women shall bake your bread in one oven, and shall deliver your bread again by weight; and you shall eat, and not be satisfied." (verse 24)

Fifth:

You shall eat the flesh of your sons, and you shall eat the flesh of your daughters. (30) And I will destroy your high places, and cut down your incense altars, and cast your dead bodies upon

> the dead bodies of your idols; and my soul will abhor you. (31) And I will lay your cities waste, and will make your sanctuaries desolate, and I will not smell your pleasing odors. (32) And I will devastate the land, so that your enemies who settle in it shall be astonished at it. (33) And I will scatter you among the nations, and I will unsheathe the sword after you; and your land shall be desolation, and your cities shall be a waste. (verses 29-33)

From the beginning of the conquest of the Promised Land through the leadership of Joshua, God ruled his people as a theocracy. The priesthood governed their walk with God in righteousness through the moral, civil, and ceremonial laws. The prophets rendered directives and warnings of punishments from God. And God appointed judges from their midst like Joshua, to give leadership to the people. This system was carried out for 415 years. Around 1064 BC, the people wanted a king to rule over them like the other nations. God warned them through the Prophet Samuel of the consequences it would bring.

1 Samuel 8:10–18:

> So Samuel told all the words of the LORD to the people who were asking a king from him. (11) He said, "These will be the ways of the king who will reign over you: he will take your sons and appoint them to his chariots and to be his horsemen, and to run before his chariots; (12) and he will appoint for himself commanders of thousands and commanders of fifties, and some to plot his ground and to reap his harvest, and to make his implements of war and the equipment of his chariots. (13) He will take your daughters to be perfumers and cooks and bakers. (14) He will take the best of your fields and vineyards and olive

orchards and give them to his servants. (15) He will take the tenth of your grain and of your vineyards and give it to his officers and to his servants. (16) He will take your menservants and maidservants, and the best of your cattle and your asses, and put them to his work. (17) He will take the tenth of your flocks, and you shall be his slaves. (18) And in that day you will cry out because of your king, whom you have chosen for yourselves; *but the LORD will not answer you in that day.*" (italics added)

They wanted a king. God allowed them to have a king and picked Saul for the job, and Samuel anointed and installed him to that office (1 Samuel 10:17–27). From that point on, the quality of the king that ruled over the nation led the way for either the blessing or curse that would fall upon the people. King Saul was the first failure when pride and arrogance rose to the surface. King David was the second king to take office. While his shortcomings became evident, David always repented of his sins and remained faithful to God during his lifetime. He brought the nation to the pinnacle of greatness.

At the end of David's rule, his son Solomon became King. He was given great wisdom by God to rule the nation. But King Solomon liked "foreign women," and he developed a harem of seven hundred wives and three hundred concubines. During his forty-year reign, he added a new wife on an average of every three weeks! Most of his wives were heathen women who embraced false gods. He violated the law of God by marrying outside of the faith. In his desire to please his wives, he set up altars and temples to heathen gods inside the territory of the Promised Land, and his own heart was turned from God. This became a major stumbling block for the people and angered God (1 Kings 11:1–14).

After the death of Solomon in 963 BC, the nation was split into two separate bodies. Ten tribes were known as Israel, and they occupied the northern territory. Two tribes were known as Judah. They occupied the southern territory around Jerusalem and the temple. With the division, each body has its own king. Civil war erupted. For the next thousand years, idolatry and unbelief eroded the stability of God's blessing upon the Jewish nation. In 721 BC, God used Assyria to punish Israel, and the Jews began to be taken into captivity as punishment for their idolatry and disobedience. In 716 BC, the conquest by the Assyrians was complete. From that point forward, the ten tribes called Israel no longer had their own king to rule over them. Bondage to a foreign power became a permanent condition because of their refusal to submit to God.

In 625 BC, the Babylonian Empire under King Nabopolassar conquered the Assyrians Empire. The captive Jews then became the property of the Babylonian

Empire. In 606 BC, God punished Judah because of their idolatry and disobedience. He sent the new Babylonian King Nebuchadnezzar to conquer Judah. The Prophet Jeremiah prophesied that their captivity would be for a seventy-year period (Jeremiah 25:11). At the beginning of the conquest, only some of the Jews from Judah were taken into Babylon. The rest were allowed to remain, providing they submitted to Babylonian authority. Now, the entire nation, Israel and Judah, was under the rule of a foreign power because of their disobedience to God.

In 593 BC, the prophet Ezekiel, who was in Babylonian captivity, received an additional prophetic judgment against Israel and Judah.

Ezekiel 4:1–8:

> And you, O son of man, take a brick and lay it before you, and portray upon it a city, even Jerusalem; (2) and put siege works against it, and build a siege wall against it, and cast up a mound against it; set camps also against it, and plant battering rams against it round about. (3) And take an iron plate, and place it as an iron wall between you and the city; and set your face toward it, and let it be in a state of siege, and press the siege against it. This is a sign for the house of Israel.
> (4) Then lie upon your left side, and I will lay the punishment of the house of Israel upon you; for the number of the days that you lie upon it, you shall bear their punishment. (5) *For I assign to you a number of days, three hundred and ninety days, equal to the number of the years of their punishment; so long shall you bear the punishment of the house of Israel.* (6) And when you have completed these, you shall lie down a second time, but on your right side, *and bear the punishment of the*

*house of Judah; forty days I assign you, a day for each year.* (7) And you shall set your face toward the siege of Jerusalem, with your arm bared; and you shall prophesy against the city. (8) And behold, I will put cords upon you, so that you cannot turn from one side to the other, till you have completed the days of your siege. (italics added)

From the beginning of the Assyrian conquest of Israel in 721 to 593 BC, a period of 128 years, there was no repentance in the lives of the Jews as a nation. After thirteen years of Judah's Babylonian captivity, God saw further rebellion in the hearts of his people dwelling in Jerusalem. God rendered two separate judgments. For the people in Jerusalem who had rebelled against the Babylonian authority, a stage-five judgment against the city would take place. The city and temple would be destroyed along with the slaughter of the people. For the people of Israel who were in Assyrian captivity and moved to Babylonian captivity, a stage-four judgment was pronounced, adding 390 years to their punishment. For the people of Judah who were taken to Babylon, forty more years would be added to their captivity. The combined years for Israel and Judah came to 430 years of punishment under foreign control. Ezekiel chapters 5–7 give a complete picture of the evil conduct within the nation of Jews who were in rebellion to God.

The siege of Jerusalem began in 589 BC by King Nebuchadnezzar. This marked the beginning of Ezekiel's prophecy against Jerusalem. The city was taken in 588 BC. The temple and walls of the city were destroyed in 587 BC. War, famine, pestilence, and wild beasts devoured the Jews. Only a small number were spared from death.

During the Jews captivity in Babylon, the Media-Persian Empire conquered the Babylonian Empire in 538 BC just before the completion of Judah's seventy-year punishment. In Daniel 9:24, Daniel reads the prophecy of Jeremiah concerning the "seventy years of captivity" at the end of the judgment. He prayed to God for understanding about the "end of the desolations of Jerusalem." He confessed the sins of the nation, along with the fact that they had still not repented of their idolatry. The angel Gabriel was sent to Daniel with a message from God in answer to his prayer. It would take another "seventy weeks of years" (490 years) to turn the nation to righteousness.

Daniel 9:24:

> Seventy weeks of years are decreed concerning your people and your holy city, to finish the transgression [the evil behavior of God's people], to put an end to sin [the violation of God's Law], and to atone for iniquity [to cover people's sin through the shed blood of Jesus on the cross], to bring in everlasting righteousness [God's righteousness in the reign of Jesus over the entire earth, which will begin when Jesus returns to the

earth on the last day of the seventieth week], to seal both vision and prophet [to secure all that God has revealed through vision and prophecy], and to anoint a most holy place [the continual blessing of God upon the hearts of people, which is their spirit and their ability to reason in a close personal union with God].

The additional time of punishment is added to, and entwined with, the previous judgments. This prophecy of Daniel would begin with a proclamation by King Artaxerxes of the Media-Persian Empire to rebuild the city of Jerusalem, and set up the government of the people. The date: Creation 3520, Jewish 1 Nisan 2204, Western March 26, 457 BC.

While God had allowed sin to take root in the life of mankind as an educational process for all creation, there was a line which he had drawn that would not be exceeded. At that point, evil is stopped with a stage-five exercise of his wrath. In Exodus 20:4–6, the second commandment dealt with the issue of idolatry in graven images:

> "You shall not make for yourself a graven image, or any likeness of anything that is in heaven above, or that is in the earth beneath, or that is in the water under the earth; (5) you shall not bow down to them or serve them; for I the LORD your God am a jealous God, *visiting the iniquity of the fathers upon the children to the third and fourth generation of those who hate me, (6) but showing steadfast love to thousands of those who love me and keep my commandments.*" (italics added)

When God said he is visiting the iniquity of the fathers upon the children to the third and the fourth generation of those who hate him, it is with disciplinary action designed to bring about repentance beginning at stage one and progressing to stage five. If there was no repentance and degeneration got progressively worse, it would end with their destruction. When God's wrath comes, God protects those who love him and walk in righteousness. Ezekiel 14:12–14 clarifies the issue:

> And the word of the LORD came to me: (13) "Son of man, when a land sins against me by acting faithlessly, and I stretch out my hand against it, and break its staff of bread and send famine upon it, and cut off from it man and beast, (14) even if these three men, Noah, Daniel, and Job, were in it, they would deliver but their own lives by their righteousness, says the Lord GOD."

While Jeremiah prophesied seventy years of captivity under Babylonian authority, he also prophesied their return to Jerusalem.

Jeremiah 29:10–14:

> For thus says the LORD: "When seventy years are completed for Babylon, I will visit you, and I will fulfill to you my promise and bring you back to this place. (11) *For I know the plans I have for you, says the LORD, plans for welfare and not for evil, to give you a future and a hope.* (12) Then you will call upon me and come and pray to me, and I will hear you. (13) *You will seek me and find me; when you seek me with all your heart,* (14) *I will be found by you, says the LORD, and I will restore your fortunes and gather you from all the nations and all the places where I have driven you, says the LORD, and I will bring you back to the place from which I sent you into exile.*" (italics added)

With all of the other extended judgments upon the nation, in 536 BC a remnant of Jews were allowed to return to Jerusalem and rebuild the temple and walls. But they were not released from the heathen authority ruling over them. Down through the years of their disciplinary punishment, their captivity would change from the Media-Persian Empire to the Grecian Empire and then to the Roman Empire. While the prophecy begins in 536 BC, the total fulfillment of Jeremiah's prophecy will not take place until October 10, AD 2022, at the entrance into the millennium reign of Jesus under the new Covenant.

**SUMMARY**

Under the first three phases of God's educational program for all creation, three issues become very clear. In the first phase, God shows us what happens to mankind living under the bondage of sin without restraint. The result is a progressive deterioration into total wickedness. In the second phase, mankind in bondage to sin is confronted with a hostile environment and a death penalty for killing one another. The result, mankind will still rebel against the known will of God and band together. They will establish their own values and standard to live by and will set up their own false gods to worship. In the third phase, God multiplies the descendants of Abraham, who are committed to serving him by faith. He allows them to be taken into captivity, and then releases them from their bondage and makes them a great nation through their faith and his complete Covenant of Law. They are an example to the world concerning the power of God to elevate a people and bless them, even with a sinful nature that prohibits them from walking in perfect accord with his Covenant of Law. As long as they continue to humble themselves and repent when they sin, in accordance with the sacrificial offering he established to cover the sin of his people, God continues to bless them as a nation. But when they enter into sin and refuse to repent, God exercise his progressive judgments upon them until there is true repentance.

**POINTS TO REMEMBER**

1. God increases the descendants of Abraham through Isaac over a period of five hundred years.

2. During this time the Jews become slaves to Egypt.

3. God elevates Moses to deliver the Jews from bondage and take them to the Promised Land of Canaan that God promised to Abraham. This is parallel in the natural order to the coming of the kingdom of God in the spiritual order when Jesus will deliver mankind from bondage to sin. Jesus will fulfill all of God's promises to everyone who will follow him by faith in a close personal relationship through the power of the Holy Spirit that will dwell in each believer.

4. God establishes the first ceremonial law of the Mosaic Covenant with the Jews in Egypt called the Feast of Passover. It is a portrayal of what Jesus will do when he dies on a cross for the sins of mankind to set us free from sin.

5. The journey from Egypt into the Promised Land took forty years. During that time, God established the complete Mosaic Covenant of Law with his chosen people.

6. After the Jews entered into the Promised Land, they had to conquer the people who occupied the territory. During the fifth year of battle, God gave them rest in the land.

7. The success or failure of the Jews was dependent upon their faith and obedience to God. Failure to obey God's commands brought disciplinary action. Obedience brought blessings.

8. The government of the Jews is a theocracy. Later, the Jews wanted a king to rule over them like other nations. So God gave them kings, and they suffered the consequences.

9. Through disobedience without repentance, the Jews went into captivity under the Assyrians, Babylonians, Media Persona, Grecians, and Romans as a disciplinary action from God.

10. The Covenant of law proved one thing: mankind with a sinful nature is not capable of keeping all of God's laws.

# CHAPTER 10

# THE FOURTH PHASE OF GOD'S EDUCATIONAL PROGRAM

**EVENT: The birth of Jesus, the Son of God**
**TIME FRAME: Eternity Present—Creation 3971, Jewish 15 Tishri 3755, Western October 6, 7 BC**

**INTRODUCTION NARRATIVE**: *With the history of the Jewish nation under a Covenant of Law, it was proven to mankind that humans, with a sinful nature, are not capable of keeping God's laws. Now God will bring forth his son Jesus to perfectly fulfill all of the laws of God the Father. Jesus will become the perfect sin offering to atone for the sins of humans by laying his life down for everyone under* *a New Covenant of grace. Everyone, Jew and Gentile, will be able to have a personal relationship with God the Father through the person of Jesus with the Holy Spirit taking up residence in each person. The doorway to become a child of God, as in the Garden of Eden, will be to make Jesus Lord of your life as a free will choice through faith in him.*

John 1:1–5:

> In the beginning was the Word, and the Word was with God, and the Word was God. (2) He was in the beginning with God; (3) all things were made through him, and without him was not anything made that was made. (4) In him was life, and the life was the light of men. (5) The light shines in the darkness, and the darkness has not overcome it.

Jesus is the Word of God. He is the absolute spiritual reality of every aspect of God the Father's creation. He is the total illumination that deception has not and cannot overcome.

John 1:6–8:

> There was a man sent from God, whose name was John. (7) He came for testimony, to bear witness to the light, that all might believe through him. (8) He was not the light, but came to bear witness to the light.

John the Baptist is a cousin of Jesus through their mothers, Elizabeth and Mary (Luke 1:36–38). John is a descendant of Aaron, the first high priest that governed the Mosaic Covenant. By birth, John was a priest and a prophet with the anointing of the Holy Spirit upon him to prepare the way of the Lord. John was six months older than Jesus.

John 1:9–13:

> The true light that enlightens every man was coming into the world. (10) He was in the world, and the world was made through him, yet the world knew him not. (11) He came to his own home, and his own people received him not. (12) But to all who received him, who believed in his name, he gave power to become children of God; (13) who were born, not of blood nor of the will of the flesh nor of the will of man, but of God.

Jesus was conceived in the womb of the Virgin Mary by the Holy Spirit. The pure spirit of God was not contaminated by the sinful nature that is passed through man from generation to generation. In order for Jesus to become a sinner, he would have to accept the lie of Satin for himself, and being God and knowing the truth that was not going to happen! Because his legal father on earth was Joseph, a direct descendant of King David through the tribe of Judah, Jesus held legal entitlement to be king. In his position with God the Father and the establishment of the New Covenant upon his death and resurrection, he became our high priest and king. For those who believe in him, they will have forgiveness, spiritual rebirth, and power to overcome their sinful nature and walk with God in righteousness. Our sinful nature is not taken away; it is overcome while we are on this earth, through our faith and God's transforming power. The two must work together.

John 1:14–18:

> And the Word became flesh and dwelt among us, full of grace and truth; we have beheld his glory, glory as of the only Son from the Father. (15) John bore witness to him, and cried, "This was he of whom I said, 'He who comes after me ranks before me, for he was before me.' (16) And from his fullness have we all received, grace upon grace. (17) For the law was given through Moses; grace and truth came through Jesus Christ. (18) No one has ever seen God; the only son, who is in the bosom of the Father, he has made him known."

Before the ministry of Jesus began at age thirty, God sent John the Baptist with a message to the entire nation of Jews: "Repent for the kingdom of heaven is at hand." It was the introduction to the New Covenant that God had promised to his people through the prophets beginning with Moses. The New Covenant would fulfill all of the laws of righteousness (moral, civil, and ceremonial) through God's son Jesus by the power of the Holy Spirit. The Spirit of God would be given to all who believed in Jesus, repented of their sins, and accepted him as Lord and Savior of their life. It was not limited to Jews.

During this period, God the Father bore witness to his Son's life, death, and resurrection. With the sacrificial offering of Jesus upon the cross for those who would believe in and follow Jesus through the power of the Holy Spirit, the barrier between mankind and God was removed. As humans walked in the garden with God before the fall in a close personal relationship, through Jesus humans could enter into that relationship again. All ceremonial laws and temple sacrificial offerings ended (Hebrews 10:1–10). People became the temple of the living God through the person of the Holy Spirit living in them. With the individual submitting himself to the will of God, the Holy Spirit would transform the mind and heart. People, simply placing their trust in Jesus every day and continually seeking God's will, would bring about the transformation in their life in overcoming the bondage to sin and demonic control. The power of the Holy Spirit of God working within them would accomplish the job. Failure to seek the Lord daily would diminish the transformation and the blessings. Our free will choice is not taken away! We cannot overcome our sinful nature without the revelation and power of the Word of God through the ministry of the Holy Spirit in us and upon us. In us from the day Jesus was resurrected, and then upon us from the day of Pentecost.

John the Baptist started preaching repentance and using water baptism as a symbol of the cleansing process of the soul six months before Jesus began his ministry. Jesus taught

*Let There Be Light*

the Word of God and performed many miracles. As a result, many of the Jews repented of their sins and accepted Jesus as their promised Messiah. But the religious hierarchy of the nation rejected Jesus. He was a threat to their conduct and positions of leadership over the people. They were not walking with God, and there was no repentance. For their hard-hearted condition, God placed a veil over their eyes as a judgment so they could not recognize Jesus as their Messiah and be delivered from their sins (Isaiah 6:6–13; Matthew 13:10–16).

At the end of the ministry of Jesus, he entered into Jerusalem on 10 Nisan 3787, which was 3 April, AD 27, riding on a colt. Jesus was proclaimed King of the Jews by the people who believed in him just before he was crucified by the leaders of the nation who hated him. It was Palm Saturday, not Sunday. Four hundred and eighty three years had been completed on 1 Nisan of that year, out of the 490 year period of the Jewish disciplinary judgment given in Daniel 9:24. The time clock stopped, due to the inauguration of the New Covenant with the death and resurrection of Jesus, their promised Messiah. Jesus came to bring forgiveness, healing, power, and authority to the people. *The fulfillment of the final week of Daniel's prophecy will not take place until the end of this fourth phase of God's educational program.* At that point, God will redeem the nation of Jews and bring them into the New Covenant with faith in Jesus. Then, the final thousand year phase of God's program will begin. Jesus will rule over the entire world from Jerusalem for one thousand years.

The month of Nisan in the Jewish calendar is the time of the Feast of Passover established by God to give us a symbolic picture of God's deliverance for mankind from the bondage of sin. It is first portrayed in the exodus of the Jews from bondage to Egypt. The fulfillment of its true reality is played out in AD 27 when Jesus goes to the cross. The time sequence is precise in the following display of dates and time:

> **FIRST EVENT**: Jesus rides into Jerusalem on a colt and is proclaimed King of the Jews on the beginning of Passover (Matthew 21:1–11). Jesus is the "lamb" that was to be picked on 10 Nisan by the Jews, and would be killed on 14 Nisan.
> **TIME FRAME**: Eternity Present—Creation 4003, Jewish 10 Nisan 3787, Western Saturday April 3, AD 27
>
> **SECOND EVENT**: Jesus is crucified (Matthew 26:17–27:61). Jesus goes to the cross at 9:00 a.m. and dies at 3:00 p.m. Jesus is placed in the tomb just before 6:00 p.m. on Wednesday. 6:00 p.m. Jewish time is the beginning of their new day. He comes out of the tomb after 6:00 p.m. three nights and three days later, which is the beginning of Sunday Jewish time. It is still Saturday in Western time.
> **TIME FRAME**: Eternity Present—Creation 4003, Jewish 14 Nisan 3787, Western Wednesday April 7, AD 27

**THIRD EVENT**: Jesus is resurrected (Matthew 28:1–10). Jesus appears to his disciples.
**TIME FRAME**: Eternity Present—Creation 4003, Jewish, the beginning of Sunday 18 Nisan 3787, Western Saturday April 10, AD 27 (There is a six hour difference in the beginning of a day between Jewish and Western time count.)

By viewing the following Scriptures, we can see God's plan for mankind's redemption at the time of the fall. Genesis 3:22–23:

> Then the LORD God said, "Behold, the man has become like one of us, knowing good and evil; and now, *lest he put forth his hand and take also of the tree of life, and eat, and live forever"*—(23) therefore the LORD God sent him forth from the garden of Eden, to till the ground from which he was taken. (24) He drove out the man; and at the east of the garden of Eden *he placed the cherubim, and a flaming sword which turned every way, to guard the way to the tree of life.* (italics added)

What is the fruit of the tree of life? It is *spiritual*, and it is *love*.

John 3:16–21:

> *For God so loved the world that he gave his only Son, that whoever believes in him should not perish but have eternal life.* (17) For God sent the Son into the world, not to condemn the world, but that the world might be saved through him. (18) He who believes in him is not condemned; he who does not believe is condemned already, because he has not believed in the name of the only Son of God. (19) And this is the judgment, that the light has come into the world, and men loved darkness rather than light, because their deeds were evil. (20) For everyone who does evil hates the light, and does not come to the light, lest his deeds should be exposed. (21) *But he who does what is true comes to the light, that it may be clearly seen that his deeds have been wrought in God.* (italics added)

What is the "flaming sword" which guards the way to the Tree of Life? It is the Word of God. Hebrews 4:12–13:

> *For the word of God is living an active, sharper than any two-edged sword*, piercing to the division of soul and spirit, of joints and marrow, and *discerning the thoughts and intentions of the heart*. (13) And before him no creature is hidden, but all are open and laid bare to the eyes of him with whom we have to do. (italics added)

So how does this work?

Ephesians 2:8–9:

> For by grace you have been saved through faith; and this is not your own doing, *it is the gift of God*—(9) *not because of works, lest any man should boast*. (italics added)

Grace is the sovereign and divine intervention into your life by the Holy Spirit to make you aware that you are a sinner in God's sight. Also, that you are lost in a world of darkness and chaos and need to be delivered from the conditions that are destroying your life. The Holy Spirit makes it very clear that Jesus is the person you are to commit your life too and follow. Through this process, true sorrow begins to take place in your heart with repentance, and you see the futility of life on earth without God. When you make the commitment to invite Jesus into your life, you are exercising faith in what God has revealed to you. When this is done, you have partaken of the Tree of Life and spiritual rebirth takes place. Now the Holy Spirit takes up residence in your body and makes the Word of God, Jesus, come alive to you. With this event, the spiritual kingdom of God has come into you, and you have entered into God's kingdom. Jesus becomes Lord over your life to give you guidance and fulfill the purpose of your life that God the Father designed for you upon this earth. Jesus is the High Priest before the Father, and the Holy Spirit is the counselor of your life in all knowledge, understanding, truth, and wisdom that come from God. Jesus is the love offering by God that paid the price for your sins, past, present, and future, so long as you repent and ask forgiveness when you sin. Eternal life with God is yours as a gift by God by his grace, through the exercise of your faith, and not by works! The works that you will do after your salvation on earth will be *the result of your relationship with God in obedience* and that will bring further reward into your life.

**EVENT: Resurrection of Jesus and the beginning of the spiritual rebirth for mankind**
**TIME FRAME: Eternity Present—Creation 4003, Jewish 18 Nisan 3787, Western April 10, AD 27**

## Let There Be Light

Spiritual rebirth took place in his disciples after Jesus was resurrected on Sunday.

John 20:19–23:19:

> On the evening of that day, the first day of the week [Sunday at 3:00 p.m. the day Jesus was resurrected, 18 Nisan 3787, which is April 10, AD 27], the doors being shut where the disciples were, for fear of the Jews, Jesus came and stood among them and said to them, "Peace be with you." (20) When he had said this, he showed them his hands and his side. Then the disciples were glad when they saw the Lord. (21) Jesus said to them again, "Peace be with you. As the Father has sent me, even so I send you." (22) And when he had said this, *he breathed on them, and said to them, "Receive the Holy Spirit.* [Spiritual rebirth takes place in the disciples with the Holy Spirit taking residence in them] (23) If you forgive the sins of any, they are forgiven; if you retain the sins of any, they are retained." (italics added)

During the forty days from his resurrection, he appears to his disciples at various times and places. Then on the day of his ascension into heaven he speaks to them. It is Wednesday May 19, AD 27, which is Jewish 26 Iyyar 3787. Acts 1:3–11:

> To them he presented himself alive after his passion by many proofs, appearing to them during forty days, and speaking of the kingdom of God. (4) And while staying with them he charged them not to depart from Jerusalem, *but to wait for the promise of the Father, which he said, "you heard from me, (5) for John baptized with water, but before many days you shall be baptized with the Holy Spirit."* (6) So when they had come together, they asked him, "Lord, will you at this time restore the kingdom of Israel?" (7) He said to them, "It is not for you to know times or seasons which the Father has fixed by his own authority. (8) *But*

*Let There Be Light*

> *you shall receive power when the Holy Spirit has come upon you; and you shall be my witnesses in Jerusalem and in all Judea and Samaria and to the end of the earth.*"[18] (9) And when he had said this, as they were looking on, he was lifted up, and a cloud took him out of their sight. (10) And while they were gazing into heaven as he went, behold, two men stood by them in white robes, (11) and said, "Men of Galilee, why do you stand looking into heaven? *This Jesus, who was taken up form you into heaven, will come in the same way as you saw him go into heaven.*" (italics added)

Jesus will return to earth on Thursday May 20, 2021 AD, when he puts his foot on the Mount of Olives 1,994 years later.

**EVENTS: The Feast of Pentecost**
**TIME FRAME: Eternity Present—Creation 4003,**
**Jewish 6 Sivan 3787, Western Friday May 28, AD 27**

Acts 2:1–21:

> When the day of Pentecost had come, they were all together in one place. (2) And suddenly a sound came from heaven like the rush of a mighty wind, and it filled all the house where they were sitting. (3) And there appeared to them tongues as of fire, distributed and resting on each one of them. (4) And they were all filled with the Holy Spirit and *began to speak in other tongues, as the Spirit gave them utterance*.
> (5) Now there were dwelling in Jerusalem Jews, devout men from every nation under heaven. (6) And at this sound the multitude came together, and they were bewildered, because each one heard them speaking in his own language. (7) And they were amazed and wondered, saying, "Are not all these who are speaking Galileans? (8) And who is it that we hear, each of us in his own native language? (9) Parthians and Medes and

## Let There Be Light

Elamites and residents of Mesopotamia, Judea and Cappadocia, Pontus and Asia, (10) Phrygia and Pamphylia, Egypt and the parts of Libya belonging to Cyrene, and visitors from Rome, both Jews and proselytes, (11) Cretans and Arabians, we hear them telling in our own tongues the mighty works of God." (12) And all were amazed and perplexed, saying to one another, "What does this mean?" (13) But others mocking said, "They are filled with new wine."

(14) But Peter, standing with the eleven, lifted up his voice and addressed them, "Men of Judea and all who dwell in Jerusalem, let this be known to you, and give ear to my words. (15) For these men are not drunk, as you suppose, since it is only the third hour of the day; (16) but this is what was spoken by the prophet Joel: (17) 'And in the last days it shall be, God declares that *I will pour out my Spirit upon all flesh, and your sons and your daughters shall prophesy, and your young men shall see visions, and your old men shall dream dreams;* (18) *yea, and on my menservants and my maidservants in those days I will pour out my Spirit; and they shall prophesy.* (19) And I will show wonders in the heaven above and signs on the earth beneath, blood, and fire, and vapor of smoke; (20) *the sun shall be turned into darkness and the moon into blood, before the day of the Lord comes, the great and manifest day.*[19] (21) And it shall be that whoever calls on the name of the Lord shall be saved.'"

Verse (20) will begin on May 14, AD 2014. This will be a terrifying event that the entire world is going to experience, and darkness will cover the earth for seven days! (If this event does not begin at 10:16 p.m. UTC, it will begin sometime during the next hour and forty-four minutes.)

Now, the Holy Spirit dwells within people to reveal the light of God to the heart and mind. And the Holy Spirit comes upon the life of people in power to minster the life of

God to others, in preaching the gospel, prophesying, healing the sick, performing miracles, casting out demons, and performing other wonderful deeds. Human flesh is wedged between the life of God's revelation and the power of the Holy Spirit moving each person to accomplish the work of God, *for those who believed in Jesus and have received both baptisms.* So the gospel of Jesus began to be preached to Jews and gentiles around the world. The Gentiles were grafted into the New Covenant of grace when they believed and received Jesus as their Lord and Savior. The very issue that separated humans from God, failure to trust in God through faith in God's Word, became the only gateway for our return. That is, faith in Jesus, the Son of God, the Word of God, the truth, and his atonement for our sins on the cross! *"And without faith it is impossible to please him"* (Hebrews 11:6; italics added).

At the time of the crucifixion, the unbelievers of the Jewish nation who wanted Jesus dead proclaimed to Pilot, "His blood be upon us and our children!" (Matthew 27:25). After the day of Pentecost, disciples of Jesus preached the gospel to the Jews for forty-three years. While many Jews were converted, the nation still rejected their Messiah, and they entered into a new judgment. In AD 70 the Jews were again thrown out of their God-given country when the Romans destroyed the city and the temple. At the same time, for the Jews and gentiles who accepted Jesus as their Messiah and who walked by faith in Christ, the blessings of Leviticus 26:1–13 were enacted upon their lives as one body of people in Christ around the world now known as the body of Christ, the church.

In the Book of Revelation 1:4–3:22, the Lord speaks to the seven churches in Asia Minor.[20] He gives praise, prophecy, and warnings of judgment due to sinful conduct, and he acknowledges the persecution and tribulation which comes upon believers and must be endured. In five of the churches, he deals with the issue of their works. To all of the churches, he makes the statement: "He who conquers…" It refers to receiving the reward for those who overcome the sinful nature and demonic attacks that we must deal with until his return. If we will be faithful to him, he will give us the victory!

The first churches were made up of groups of believers in fellowship with God and one another in different locations. They were not institutions. They were governed by God through the administration of the Holy Spirit in and through the people that God called and gifted for leadership.

Jesus was the focal point and the head of any given body of believers. Jesus states in John 4:6: "I am the way, and the truth, and the life; no one comes to the Father, but by me." In John 15:5–19 Jesus defines the working relationship of his body of believers:

> I am the vine, you are the branches. He who abides in me, and I in him, he it is that bears much fruit, *for apart from me you can do nothing.* (6) If a man does not abide in me, he is cast forth as a branch and withers; and the branches are gathered, thrown into the fire and burned. (7) If you abide in me, and my words abide in you, ask whatever you will, and it shall be done for you. (8) By this my Father is glorified, that you bear much fruit, and so prove to be my disciples. (9) As the Father has loved me, so have I loved you; abide in my love. (10) If you keep my commandments, you will abide in my love, just as I have kept my Father's commandments and abide in his love. (11) These things I have spoken to you, that my joy may be in you, *and that your joy may be full.*
>
> (12) This is my commandment, that you love one another as I have loved you. (13) Greater love has no man than this, that a man lay down his life for his friends. (14) You are my friends if you do what I command you. (15) No longer do I call you servants, for the servant does not know what his master is doing; but I have called you friends, for all that I have heard from my Father I have made known to you. (16) *You did not choose me, but I chose you and appointed you that you should go and bear fruit and that your fruit should abide*; so that whatever you ask the Father in my name, he may give it to you. (17) This I command you, to love one another.
>
> (18) If the world hates you, know that it has hated me before it hated you. (19) If you were of the world, the world would love its own; but because you are not of the world, but I chose you out of the world, *therefore the world hates you.* (Italics added)

In this working relationship with God, there are different gifts and callings as stated in Ephesians 4:11–16:

> And his gifts were *that some should be apostles, some prophets, some evangelists, some pastors and teachers, (12) to equip the saints for the work of ministry, for building up the body of Christ, (13) until we all attain the unity of the faith and of the knowledge of the Son of God, to mature manhood, to the measure of the stature of the fullness of Christ; (14) so that we may no longer be children, tossed to and fro and carried about with every wind of doctrine,* by the cunning of men, by their craftiness in deceitful wiles. (15) Rather, speaking the truth in love, we are to grow up in every way into him who is the head, into Christ, (16) from whom the whole body, joined and knit together by every joint with which it is supplied, *when each part is working properly, makes bodily growth and up builds itself in love.* (italics added)

In 1 Corinthians 12:4–11 there are additional gifts given to the body of Christ:

> Now there are varieties of gifts, but the same Spirit; (5) and there are varieties of service, but the same Lord; (6) and there are varieties of working, but it is the same God who inspires them all in every one. (7) To each is given the manifestation of the Spirit for the common good. (8) To one is given through the Spirit the utterance of wisdom, and to another the utterance of knowledge according to the same Spirit, (9) to another faith by the same Spirit, to another gifts of healing by the one Spirit, (10) to another working of miracles, to another various kinds of tongues, to another the interpretation of tongues. (11) *All these are inspired by one and the same Spirit, who apportions to each one individually as he wills.* (italics added)

In 1 Corinthians 12:27–31, Paul the Apostle sums it up:

> *Now you are the body of Christ and individually members of it.* (28) And God has appointed in the church first apostles, second

prophets, third teachers, then workers of miracles, then healers, helpers, administrators, speakers in various kinds of tongues. (29) Are all apostles? Are all prophets? Are all teachers? Do all work miracles? (30) Do all possess gifts of healing? Do all speak with tongues? Do all interpret? (31) *But earnestly desire the higher gifts.* (italics added)

With God in control of the lives of those who enter into a loving relationship with him through Jesus, the church from the day of Pentecost begins to grow.

Acts 2:44-47:

And all who believed were together and had all things in common; (45) and they sold their possessions and goods and distributed them to all, as any had need. (46) And day by day, attending the temple together and breaking bread in their homes, they partook of food with glad and generous hearts, (47) praising God and having favor with all the people. And the Lord added to their number day by day those who were being saved.

With signs and wonder taking place through the body of Christ, the religious hierarchy of Judaism began to persecute the Christians. In Acts chapter 7, Stephen, a man filled with the Holy Spirit, preaches the Word of God to the high priest and the religious order about the salvation of Jesus and the plan of God. They became so angry with Stephen that they stoned him to death. Stephen became the first of many martyrs for the spreading of the gospel of Christ. Forty three years after Jesus was crucified and many Jews had been saved, the nation of Israel still rejected their Messiah. As Jesus had predicted in Matthew 24:2, the Romans destroy Jerusalem and the temple. The Jewish nation is removed from their homeland as another judgment upon them. The Christians are dispersed to other countries to spread the gospel of Jesus around the world until the return of Jesus to rule the world for a thousand years.

By AD 300, the gospel of Jesus had permeated the Roman Empire. Constantine, the leader of the Roman Empire, proclaimed Christianity to be the leading religion of the Empire. Then, some three hundred years later, Muhammad establishes the religion of Islam, and the conflicts begin between Islam and Christianity. The territory of the Roman Empire eventually becomes divided by these two religious faiths. The western to northern section become predominately Christian and the eastern to southern section become Islamic. This event is pictured in the dream of King Nebuchadnezzar that is given to and interpreted by Daniel.

Daniel 2:31–35:

> You saw, O king, and behold a great image. This image, mighty and of exceeding brightness, stood before you, and its appearance was frightening. (32) The head of this image was of fine gold [the head represents the Babylonian Empire], its breast and arms of silver [represents the Media-Persian Empire], its belly and thighs of bronze [represents the Grecian Empire], (33) *its legs of iron, its feet partly of iron and partly of clay* [represents the Roman Empire]. (34) As you looked, a stone was cut out by no human hand, *and it smote the image on its feet of iron and*

*clay, and broke them in pieces* [the stone represents Jesus, the Christ, the Son of the living God, the foundation of the Christian church]; (35) then the iron, the clay, the bronze, the silver, and the gold, all together were broken in pieces, and became like the chaff of the summer threshing floors; and the wind carried them away, so that not a trace of them could be found [all of the heathen empires will be permanently destroyed by the return of Jesus at the end of this age for the Battle of Armageddon]. But the stone that struck the image became a great mountain and filled the whole earth [for one-thousand years Jesus will rule over the entire earth]. (italics added)

The two legs of the Roman Empire represent the western and eastern territorial division of the country which became Christian on the western side and Islamic on the eastern side. The feet with the ten toes represent *the last three and a half years of Daniel's "seventy weeks of years"* after the rapture of the Christian church. The toes represent ten Islamic nations that join together and will be led by the Antichrist. He will be their awaited Messiah. The time period from the rise of Nebuchadnezzar's Babylonian Empire to the Battle of Armageddon is about 2,626 years that King Nebuchadnezzar's dream represents.

During the entire church age period upon the earth from the time Jesus was crucified and resurrected, the true church of Jesus was made up of all the people who repented of their sins, made Jesus Lord of their life, and followed him through the enlightenment and power provided by the Holy Spirit.

However, through the works of people over centuries, the living church became an institutional church, governed by rules, regulations, laws, and by men, who quite often did not know or walk with Jesus. Form and ritual dominated the services, and while part of the Word of God was preached, the true personal life of God in the individual relationship got smothered. But God knows who belongs to him, and he knows those who are just playing religious games. So down through the centuries, God brings true revival to those who are trapped in dead religion but have a heart to walk with God. The sinful nature of people is always at work to control God's church in the flesh. Sadly, the atrocities that people commit in the name of Jesus will continue until Jesus returns.

**POINTS TO REMEMBER**

1. Jesus is the Word of God that was with God the Father when creation began in Eternity Past. All things were made through him and without him nothing was made. He is our life and light.

2. John the Baptist announced the coming of the Messiah, Jesus, and prepared the people to receive him.

3. Mary, the mother of Jesus, is a descendant of Aaron the first high priest of the Mosaic Covenant established by God which gives Jesus the right by law to be a high priest. Joseph, the legal father of Jesus, is a descendant of King David, giving Jesus the right to the throne. The real father of Jesus was God through the power of the Holy Spirit, making Jesus the high priest and king over the Jewish nation, and over all the people of every nation who believe in him and have been born again through their faith and commitment to follow Jesus.

4. Jesus brings to us a New Covenant in his shed blood (life) upon the cross. The Son of God laid his life down for us to atone for our sins as a love offering from the Tree of Life, God's divine system, to cover the evil we have done, and allow us to return into his spiritual Garden of Paradise. We enter into the kingdom of God, and the kingdom enters into us through the person and power of the Holy Spirit. We become children of God, heirs to all of his promises with eternal life in his presence being the most important promise.

5. With the fulfillment of the Feast of Pentecost after Jesus was resurrected, the power of the Holy Spirit came upon the believers with different supernatural gifts of the Spirit for the work of the ministry in serving God.

6. Christians are constantly attacked by demonic spirits in spiritual warfare. But we are given the victory in the Spirit if we remain faithful to Jesus in his power and authority.

7. Christians who wander away from the Lord are subject to disciplinary actions by God, just as parents discipline their children for their welfare.

8. God wants his children to be productive and fruit bearing. With the gifts given to us through the Holy Spirit and our walking in obedience, we can perform miracles under the anointing of the Holy Spirit.

9. When Jesus returns to the earth to rule the world for a thousand years, Lucifer and the rest of the fallen angelic realm will be locked up in the abyss. Then true peace will reign over the entire earth.

## CHAPTER 11

# INTRODUCTION TO THE GREAT TRIBULATION PERIOD

**INTRODUCTION NARRATIVE:** *At the close of the church age of God's educational program that our generation has entered into, a time period of great tribulation is clearly defined in the Book of Revelation. We are the generation that will see the second coming of Jesus for his saints.*

In calculating the total of the prophetic time periods presented in the tabernacle of Moses—being 1,500 years dispensation for the Covenant of Law, 2,000 years for the Covenant of Grace, plus 1,000 years for the reign of Jesus upon the earth—they total 4,500 years. By using this total,

Scripture locks together all of the specific time-oriented prophecies of events that are to take place in the future. However, in the process of checking to make sure all of the calculations were balanced, I discovered the 1,500 years dispensation of law was actually 1,505 years. Then, the 2,000 years for the Covenant of Grace was only 1,995 years. The first period was five years over, the second period was five years short, but the total remained the same. And everything else correlated and locked together.

The answer for this change is found in Matthew 24:22 which states: "*And if those days had not been shortened*, no human being would be saved; but for the sake of the elect *those days will be shortened*" (italics added). This statement was presented just before Jesus went to the cross. The statement uses the past tense and future tense. It was 1,505 years from the establishment date of the Jews securing the Promised Land and setting the tabernacle up in Shiloh to the date Jesus was crucified. Then, there was another 1,995 years to the entrance into the millennia rule of Jesus on earth. Five years had been deducted from the great tribulation period during the Covenant of Grace and added to the Covenant of Law before Jesus went to the cross. That change would remain as a permanent adjustment for the tribulation.

So the next question is: how long is the great tribulation period? By deduction, based upon all of the parallels of the Jewish exodus and their forty years of testing, the parallel would be forty years. The number forty in Scripture is consistently used for testing in either days or years. So they original time period was preset for forty years of testing to separate the sheep from the goats for the final tally of those who would go into God's Promised Land in the rapture. But due to the severity of conditions and God's mercy, it was reduced to thirty-five years. Because the Battle of Armageddon ends the great tribulation period on Sunday July 4, AD 2021, we can deduct thirty-five years to find the starting date. That gives us the beginning date of AD 1986. If the time period is to the exact day, the beginning would be July 5, AD 1986.

The first five seals of Revelation begin the great tribulation period and are all exercised in the natural order of events of the world system. It begins slowly and progressively gets worse as chaos and death compound. Before the opening of the sixth seal, we will have reached the pinnacle of the words of Jesus in Matthew 24:21: "For then there will be great tribulation, such as has not been from the beginning of the world until now, no, and never will be." I believe that this event will take place sometime around the year AD 2014, everything becomes a compounding of supernatural judgments with great destruction worldwide direct form the throne of God. The sixth seal opens seven days before the beginning of Daniel's Seventieth Week of prophecy. Daniel's Seventieth Week begins on May 21, AD 2014, when the sky is rolled back like a scroll and we will see into God's throne room. The last day of the Seventieth Week will be May 20, AD 2021, when Jesus returns to the Mount of Olives. The great tribulation will end forty-five days later at the Battle of Armageddon on July 4, AD 2021.

In Revelation 4:1, the Apostle John, who is recording the Word of the Lord, is called up into heaven to the throne of God with the words, "Come up hither, and I will show you what must take place after this." The statement, "take place after this," concerns five major events: (1) the closing of this age; (2) the millennial rule an reign of Jesus over the entire earth; (3) the destruction of this heaven and earth and the angelic heaven; (4) the great white throne judgment; (5) the creation of the new heaven and earth, with the new Jerusalem coming down from heaven to the new earth.

Revelation 4:2–6:

> At once I was in the Spirit, and lo, a throne stood in heaven, with one seated on the throne! (3) And he who sat there appeared like jasper and carnelian, and round the throne was a rainbow that looked like an emerald. (4) Round the throne were twenty-four thrones, and seated on the thrones were twenty-four elders, clad in white garments, with golden crowns upon their heads. (5) From the throne issue flashes of lightening, and voices and peals of thunder, and before the throne burn seven torches of fire, which are the seven spirits of God; (6) and before the throne there is as it were a sea of glass, like crystal

When John says that he immediately entered into the Spirit, it is a reference to the third person of the Trinity, the Holy Spirit of God. John's sprit entered into the Spirit of God where God is, and he is now able to spiritually see what God the Father wants to reveal to him on behalf of all of the saints. This experience might be compared to sitting in a movie theater watching a film taken in a foreign country. But being in the Spirit, you are totally oblivious to the environment of your physical body on earth, and all of your senses are experiencing what you are seeing. John sees a spiritual form of God the Father seated on his throne in an environment of glorious color and charged with supreme energy marked by lightning and thunder.

There are seven burning torches before the throne symbolizing the seven spirits of God. They are the seven spiritual facets of God governing all creation through the administration of the Holy Spirit. He is surrounded by twenty-four elders who hold positions of authority. They are covered in righteousness and purity (white garments) and have golden crowns upon their heads, symbolizing accomplishments of divine honor in serving God. Jesus tells us in Matthew 25:14–30, the parable of the master who entrusts to his servants a sum of money to invest and to those who were faithful over little, he entrusted much more upon his return. That is the picture of the elders who surround God. They have proved themselves worthy to hold positions of responsibility. They are not his counselors, for God needs no one to counsel him. The entire setting of this scene is upon a "sea of glass, like crystal." God lives in a pure spiritual state where he sees every detail of his creation in clarity.

Revelation 4:6–11:

> And round the throne, on each side of the throne, are four living creatures, full of eyes in front and behind: (7) the first living creature like a lion, the second living creature like an ox, the third living creature with the face of a man, and the fourth living creature like a flying eagle. (8) And the four living creatures, each of them with six wings, are full of eyes all round and within, and day and night they never cease to sing, "Holy, holy, holy, is the Lord God Almighty, who was and is and is to come!" (9) And whenever the living creatures give glory and honor and thanks to him who is seated on the throne, who lives for ever and ever, (10) the twenty-four elders fall down before him who is sated on the throne and worship him who lives for-

ever and ever; they cast their crowns before the throne, singing, (11) "Worthy art thou, our Lord and God, to receive glory and honor and power, for thou didst create all things, and by thy will they existed and were created."

Now we are presented with "four living creatures" around the throne. There is no name given to them other than "four beasts." They represent the ferocity of the lion, the strength of the ox, the intelligence of man, the soaring of the eagle. In Ezekiel 1:4–26, there is a more detailed description of these four living creatures. Ezekiel encounters them with the Lord at the river Chebar during the Babylonian captivity of the Jewish nation. These creatures serve God the Father and render praise and worship to his everlasting glory.

Revelation 5:1–5:

> And I saw in the right hand of him who was seated on the throne a scroll written within and on the back, sealed with seven seals; (2) and I saw a strong angel proclaiming with a loud voice, "Who is worthy to open the scroll and break its seals?" (3) And no one in heaven or on earth or under the earth was able to open the scroll or to look into it, (4) and I wept much that no one was found worthy to open the scroll or to look into it. (5) Then one of the elders said to me, 'weep not; lo, the Lion of the tribe of Judah, the root of David, has conquered, so that he can open the scroll and its seven seals."

Jesus is "Lord of lords and King of kings" (Revelation 17:14), and he is also our "High Priest" (Hebrews 4:14). The will of the Father contained in the seals and the scroll will be placed into the hand of the Son to reveal the contents to the church, and bring about their fulfillment. The seals and the scroll present the future plan of God at the end of the church age period: first, to separate those who are to be saved from those doomed for destruction; second, to gather the bride of Christ to himself in the rapture; third, to destroy the wicked upon the face of the earth; fourth, to exercise his sovereign control over the earth for one thousand years with his bride. All of this will be accomplished through the Son of God, the Word of God, Jesus, and the empowerment of the Holy Spirit.

Revelation 5:6–14:

> And between the throne and the four living creatures and among the elders, I saw a Lamb standing, as though it had been slain, with seven horns and with seven eyes, which are the seven spirits of God sent out into all the earth; (7) and he went and took the scroll from the right hand of him who was seated on the throne. (8) And when he had taken the scroll, the four living creatures and the twenty-four elders fell down before the Lamb, each holding a harp, and with golden bowls full of incense, which are the prayers of the saints; (9) and they sang a new song, saying "Worthy art thou to take the scroll and to open its seals, for thou wast slain and by thy blood didst ransom men for God from every tribe and tongue and people and nation, (10) *and hast made them a kingdom and priests to our God*, and they shall reign on earth." (11) Then I looked, and I heard around the throne and the living creatures and the elders the voice of many angels, numbering myriads of myriads and thousands of thousands, (12) saying with a loud voice, "Worthy is the Lamb who was slain, to receive power and wealth and wisdom and might and honor and glory and blessing!" (13) And I heard every crea-

ture in heaven and earth and under the earth and in the sea, and all therein, saying, "To him who sits upon the throne and to the Lamb be blessing and honor and glory and might for ever and ever!" (14) And the four living creatures said, "Amen!" and the elders fell down and worshiped. (italics added)

John sees the symbolic Lamb who was slain, who is Jesus. He is between the throne and the four living creatures. His position is next to the Father. No one will ever be closer in the position of authority to God the Father than Jesus and the Holy Spirit. The Lamb is shown with seven horns, which are seven powers, and the seven eyes are the seven spirits of God to comprehend, empower, create, and control all creation. The horns and the eyes of the Lamb are a symbolic picture of Jesus in his ability to see everything and possess all power in a state of purity. Jesus takes the scroll from his Father.

## POINTS TO REMEMBER

1. The great tribulation period was reduced in time from forty years to thirty-five years. It began in AD 1986 and will conclude July 4, AD 2021, with the Battle of Armageddon. It began slowly and is increasing in intensity.

2. The first five seals are exercised in the natural order of life on earth.

3. The sixth seal will open on May 14, AD 2014, and the earth will be covered with darkness for seven days.

4. Daniel's Seventieth Week of prophecy will begin May 21, AD 2014, when the sky rolls back like a scroll and the entire world will be able to see into the throne room of God. The last day of Daniel's Seventieth Week will be May 20, AD 2021, when Jesus returns to the earth and puts his foot on the Mount of Olives, and it splits north and south. On that day he will take over Jerusalem.

## CHAPTER 12

# THE FIRST SEAL—FIRST RIDER OF THE APOCALYPSE

EVENT: Opening of the first seal, the first rider of the Apocalypse, the beginning of the great tribulation period.

TIME FRAME: From Eternity Present—Creation 5962, Jewish 5746, Western AD 1986 to Eternity Present—Creation 5993, Jewish 1 Kislev 5778, Western November 19, AD 2017

INTRODUCTION NARRATIVE: *Revelation chapter 6 begins the great tribulation period. It sets forth the events and judgments that will take place in a sequential order but will be interrupted with overviews concerning the time periods.*

*Because a great deal of the writing is the symbolic language from the Old Testament, it must be interpreted. From chapter 6 on, God is dealing with the destruction of the wicked, the redemption of the saints, and setting up the rule and reign of Jesus for a thousand years over the entire earth.*

Revelation 6:1–2: "Now I saw when the Lamb opened one of the seven seals, and I heard one of the four living creatures say, as with a voice of thunder, 'Come!' (2) And I saw, and behold, a white horse, and its rider had a bow; and a crown was given to him, *and he went out conquering and to conquer*" (italics added). Jesus opens the first seal. One of the four living creatures says come. The word "come" also means "appear." So what takes place is a vision to John of the future events, which will not take place for almost two thousand years. He sees a white horse. White is a symbol of light and purity. The rider has a bow, which is a symbol of warfare and hunting. A crown is given to him. The crown is a symbol of royalty, honor, and victory for winning. It is given to him before he enters into battle, which means that he is guaranteed the victory. It is stated that he "went out conquering and to conquer." That means he will not only win the battles, but also win the war. What is the war? It is the battle for the minds and hearts of mankind. This rider on the white horse is Jesus. He is coming from the throne of God in heaven, not to battle the enemy of darkness, the Devil and his followers, but to deliver those who are chosen from the idolatry of the world system, God's elect, from those who reject the authority of God.

The Devil was beaten at the cross when Jesus shed his blood for the forgiveness of our sins with his death and resurrection. In Christ, we who have submitted our lives to his authority have the positional victory over sin and death unto eternal life with God. But while God has the power and ability to fulfill his every promise to us, he has not taken away our free will choice. We must make the decision daily to follow Jesus through the continuous revelation of the Holy Spirit. The issue of the entire end time scenario is to separate those who will become the last segment of saints on earth from the world system controlled by Satan. They will be caught up in the rapture to become a part of the bride of Christ. The process will also separate those who will enter the millennial reign of Christ in their natural bodies as born again believers after the rapture. Our separation into Christ is from the idolatry of the world system. Hebrews 12:25–29 states:

See that you do not refuse him who is speaking. For if they did not escape when they refused him who warned them on earth, must less shall we escape if we reject him who warns from heaven. (26) His voice then shook the earth [God speaking from Mount Sinai to the Jews]; but now he has promised, "Yet once more I will shake not only the earth but also the heaven." (27) This phrase, "Yet once more," indicates the remove of what is shaken, as of what has been made, in order that what cannot be shaken may remain [the truth]. (28) Therefore let us be grateful for receiving a kingdom that cannot be shaken, and thus let us offer to God acceptable worship, with reverence and awe; (29) for our God is a consuming fire.

Everything in our lives will be shaken that is not right with God. If money is our god above God, it will be purged from us. If worldly pleasures rank higher than our relationship with God, it will be put into proper perspective. Nothing in our lives that separates us from total dependency upon the living God and his relationship with us will remain. Every aspect of corruption, ignorance, pride, greed, lust, and the vanity of our pursuits, individually and collectively, will be exposed. Psalm 127:1 sums up the issue: "Unless the LORD builds the house, those who build it labor in vain. Unless the LORD watches over the city, the watchman stays awake in vain." *Exposure and judgment is God's purpose for the entire world from the work of the first ride of the Apocalypse to the Feast of Atonement, judgment day on earth, just before the entrance into the millennial reign of Jesus at the Feast of Tabernacles.* If you are not taken in the rapture and survive to the day of the Feast of Atonement without giving control of your life to Jesus, you will be put to death on that day. No person on earth will enter into the reign of Jesus over the world without submitting their life to his control. Only God can orchestrate the end time scenario to bring the world into perfect harmony of love, peace, joy, and righteousness. God has established his Word to us. His Word is God, and his name is Jesus and fulfillment comes through God's Word. *Jesus is the leader of the apocalyptic riders to bring forth those who are to be saved and destroy those who will not repent.*

How will this play out in the world? Let us look at the pattern in the Old Testament when God wanted to deliver his chosen people, the Jews, from their bondage in Egypt (the world system) and take them into the Promised Land. Their exodus from Egypt was filled with miraculous signs and plagues of judgment that fell upon the Egyptians but not the Jews. It was a time of great upheaval for both Jew and Egyptian. It was a time when God proved to his chosen people his ability to keep them safe while he dealt with those who stood against him. He took the Jews and believing Gentiles out of Egypt from worldly bondage into the wilderness, and there he established a Covenant of Law with them.

It took them forty years of testing before they were ready to enter the Promised Land.

We are sojourners on this earth. God's promises are fulfilled in our lives today while we live among unbelievers. Our Promised Land is eternal life with Jesus as his bride with new glorified bodies, ruling with him for a thousand years on this earth, and then in the new heaven and earth of Revelation 21:1–4.

In Matthew 24:9–14, in answer to the questions of his disciples concerning the destruction of Jerusalem, the sign of his coming, and the end of the age, Jesus states:

> Then they will deliver you up to tribulation, and put you to death; and you will be hated by all nations for my name's sake. (10) And then many will fall away, and betray one another, and hate one another. (11) And many false prophets will arise and lead many astray. (12) And because wickedness is multiplied, most men's love will grow cold. (13) *But he who endures to the end will be saved.* (14) And this gospel of the kingdom will be preached throughout the whole world, as a testimony to all nations; *and then the end will come.* (italics added)

In Matthew 24:15–28 Jesus tells us about the rise of the Antichrist and the great tribulation of those days, and we should not believe tales that Jesus has come, for his coming will be like lightning flashing from the east to the west. It will be a major, breathtaking even that everyone will be able to see. In Matthew 24:29–30, he tells us the sign of his coming will start with the opening of the sixth seal by quoting that "...the sun will be darkened, and the moon will not give its light, and the stars will fall from heaven, and powers of the heavens will be shaken; (30) *then will appear the sign of the Son of man in heaven...*" (italics added). After the sun is darkened, the sky will vanish, and we will be able to see into the throne room of God, and there will be the sign of the Son of man (most likely the cross right next to God the Father or a lamb with seven eyes an seven horns). After that, several years later, at the sound of the last trumpet (the seventh trumpet of the seventh seal) he will come on the clouds, like lighting comes from the east to the west, to gather his elect.

What is the end of the age? It will be the return of Jesus to the earth, the retaking of Jerusalem, and the total destruction of every wicked person on the face of the earth who will not submit to his authority. Then all of his saints will occupy the earth. Those people who received their new glorified bodies as his bride, and those with their natural bodies who became Christians after the rapture. Jesus will begin to rule the entire earth for one thousand years and the Devil will be locked up. These events will mark the end of the church age period that we are now in.

As God gave the victory to the Jews over a segment of land upon the earth under the Old Covenant, under the new Covenant Jesus is going to give us the entire world. While the Jews were not obedient in every aspect of their conquest, they did not receive all of the land that was promised, and the enemy became thorns in their sides and pricks in their eyes. God clearly stated to them in Numbers 33:55: "But if you do not drive out the inhabitants of the land from before you, then those of them whom you let remain shall be as pricks in your eyes and thorns in your sides, and they shall trouble you in the land where you dwell."

Under the New Covenant, God is personally convicting us of sin in our lives so he can replace it with his blessings. Jesus states in John 8:32: "...you will know the truth, and the truth will make you free." Our bondage is to sin and it destroys our life on earth. The freedom from sin comes through the Word of God, Jesus, by the power of the Holy Spirit. If we will follow Jesus, the promises of God will be fulfilled in our lives individually. The question is, "How much freedom do we want in our life here on earth?" The purpose of the great tribulation period is the deliverance from our bondage to all idolatry. It has been placed into the hand of Jesus to accomplish in accordance with the seven seals and the scroll. The futility of idolatry must be seen by everyone in every aspect, along with the destruction of those who refuse to repent.

During the days of Jeremiah the prophet, the Jews rebelled against God and entered into idolatry. God sent warnings to repent. He exercise disciplinary actions, and still no repentance. Finally, after four stages of disciplinary action without repentance, he exercised a stage five judgment, which is destruction. After that event, Jeremiah states in Lamentation 2:3–5:

> He has cut down in fierce anger all the might of Israel; he has withdrawn from them his right hand in the face of the enemy; he has burned like a flaming fire in Jacob, consuming all around. (4) *He has bent his bow like an enemy, with his right hand set like a foe; and he has slain all the pride of our eyes in the tent of the daughter of Zion*; he has poured out his fury like fire. (5) The Lord has become like an enemy, he has destroyed Israel; he has destroyed all its palaces, laid in ruins its strongholds; and he has multiplied in the daughter of Judah mourning and lamentation. (italics added)

The rider on the white horse in Revelation carried no arrows because the bow is only a symbol for the purpose of his mission. The term bow in Scripture carries different meanings in its figurative use. In the above passage of Lamentation 2:3–5, the translation of "bow" in the Hebrew is "bending a bow for shooting, figuratively, strength." God executed judgment on their idolatry, "pride of their eyes," and placed them into bondage under the Babylonian Empire. The term "bow" used for the first rider of the Apocalypse, in the Greek is literally or figuratively to: "bear, be born, bring forth, be delivered, be in travail." This figurative "bow" is being used not for destruction of his people, but for the bringing forth of those who are to be redeemed unto the Lord from those who are to be destroyed by the Lord. That has been, and always will be part of the purpose of Jesus on this earth.

For the nation of Israel, Leviticus chapter 26:1–2 establishes the focal point of God's requirement of his people. Through obedience, verses 3–13 guarantees the blessings that God will provide on their behalf. In verse 14–39, God proclaims the judgments that will take place for breaking their Covenant relationship, which we looked at in chapter 9.

Under the New Covenant, God's disciplinary actions continue with each of us individually as sons and daughters. He also exercises corporate discipline upon the individual bodies of believers that gather together all over the world called his church. In Revelation chapters 2 and 3, the Lord speaks to seven different churches with words of praise, correction, rebuke, disciplinary actions, and warnings. In five the churches, he deals with works, and in all seven churches he makes the statement: "He who has an ear to hear, let him hear what the Sprit says to the churches." He also uses the phrase, "He who conquers…," which is a reference to receiving the reward that God wants you to have. Revelation 3:14–22 is an example of where many of the churches are today:

> And to the angel of the church in La-odicea write: "The words of the Amen, the faithful and true witness, the beginning of God's creation"
> (15) I know your works: you are neither cold nor hot. Would that you were cold or hot! (16) So, because you are lukewarm, and neither cold nor hot, I will spew you out of my mouth. (17) For you say, I am rich, I have prospered, and I need nothing; not knowing that you are wretched, pitiable, poor, blind, and naked. (18) Therefore I counsel you to buy from me gold refined by fire, that you may be rich, and white garments to clothe you and to keep the shame of your nakedness from being seen, and salve to anoint your eyes, that you may see. (19) Those whom I love, I reprove and chasten; so be zealous and repent. (20) Behold, I stand at the door and knock; if any one hears my voice and opens the door, I will come in to him and eat with him, and he with me. (21) *He who conquers*, I will grant him to sit with me on my throne, as I myself conquered and sat down with my Father on his throne. (22) *He who has an ear, let him hear what the Spirit says to the churches.* (italics added)

There are three major groups of people that God is dealing with during the great tribulation. The first group is the church. 1 Peter 4:17–18 states: "For the time has come for judgment to begin with the household of God; and if it begins with us, what will be the end of those who do not obey the gospel of God? (18) And 'If the righteous man is scarcely saved, where will the impious and sinner appear?'" This judgment has been going on since the church was established after the resurrection of Jesus and will continue in accordance with Revelation chapters 2 and 3 until the rapture. A major judgment began in the United States with the collapse of Jim and Tammy Bakker's ministry in May of AD 1987 due to violations of law and immorality. For the next three years, other major ministries were exposed.

The second group God is dealing with are the nations and peoples of the world who have not committed their lives to Christ, the unsaved. The collapse of the Soviet Union in 1989 took place without any invading forces. It was a financial collapse. The oppressing control of the godless ideology of communism was broken. The countries that were in bondage to the system wanted to become independent democratic countries. The Cold War ended. But with the oppressive control of Communism diminished, new power plays began to take place and long repressed hatreds of peoples were ignited. Warlords arose, and the slaughtering of peoples began. It also opened the way for radical Islam to pursue their quest for world domination unto Allah. Pandora's Box was opened! At the same time, there was a tremendous evangelistic outreach that produced a great harvest of souls in those countries. All of this is the work of the Lord with his bow. Through all of the upheaval, God knows every individual that will come unto him for salvation, and he will bring it to completion. When the tribulation of the world exceeds our individual ability to control our life, we will call upon God for help.

The third group is the nation of Israel. They have been suffering for rejecting their Messiah, Jesus, ever since his first coming. There is a veil that covers their mind unless they turn to the Lord (2 Corinthians 3:14–16). That veil will remain until the rapture of the saints. Then the veil will be lifted and they will know, as a nation, that Jesus is their Messiah, but Jerusalem will again be taken over for forty-two months. Many Jews will escape and be divinely protected. This time the overthrow of Jerusalem will be the Antichrist leading ten Islamic nations. When Jesus returns to Jerusalem at the end of Daniels' Seventieth Week, he will take over Jerusalem. The Jews, as a nation, will then submit to his authority and be grafted into the new Covenant. Israel, with Jesus ruling from Jerusalem, will then become the capitol of the world.

What about the United States? The United States of American is an example of a nation that came into being by God-fearing men, who established a country upon their commitment to God, the Word of God, and the laws of God in the development of the Constitution as a Christian nation. By the power of God, working through the people, the United States became the greatest nation in the world. After the settlement of our country from World War I up until September 11, AD 2001, during all of the wars that we fought, our homeland was not invaded. That was a period of some eighty-seven years.

From the time of the 1960s with material prosperity, our moral values, based upon the Word of God, began to slide. Today our country sanctifies what God condemns and calls an abomination. On September 11, AD 2001, our hedge of protection by God was removed, and our enemy now lives in our backyard as a constant threat to our security. That is a stage-one judgment that God brought against the Jewish nation for their violation of his commandments. Now our economy has taken a major hit that is taking a toll on our productivity. Extreme greed and corruption are the cause. The result is a stage-two judgment that God exercised upon the Jewish nation, and we have not seen the worst of it. Our

*Let There Be Light*

President Obama does not even classify us as a Christian nation. Fear is now a predominant issue in the lives of the people of our country, and true repentance is nowhere in sight. The shaking of our country and God's judgments are taking place now. But through it all, God takes care of those who walk with him daily in obedience. Yet we are subject to persecution and martyrdom from the unsaved. When the rapture of the saints takes place, the entire world will experience a stage-five judgment. The Devil will then dominate the world for forty-two months until the return of Jesus.

**POINTS TO REMEMBER**

1. John the Apostle is taken into heaven and given a complete picture of five major future events that will take place. The first is the end of the age of the Covenant of Grace, also called the church age period. The second event is the entrance into the millennial reign of Jesus on the earth. The third event is the end of this creation. The fourth event is the great white throne judgment. The last event is the creation of a new heaven and earth with a new Jerusalem coming down to the new earth.

2. A scroll with seven seals is given to Jesus by God the Father. It contains all of the events that will take place for the closing of this age. The seals are numbered from one through seven plus the scroll. They are all established in sequential order form start to finish.

3. There are four living creatures and twenty-four elders that surround the throne of God.

4. Jesus is presented as the Lamb of God with seven horns and seven eyes. The Lamb is the symbol of the pure and innocent offering for our sins to make atonement. The seven horns represent seven powers. The seven eyes represent the clarity of vision in the seven spirits of God. The two added together reveal the totality of power and vision that only God possesses.

5. Jesus is the first rider of the apocalyptic riders. He is sent forth from God the Father "conquering and to conquer." That means he will not only win the battles, he will win the war.

6. The purpose of the first rider is to destroy idolatry and bring forth those who are to be saved from those who will be destroyed.

7. Our separation is from the idolatry of this world. We are to be transformed to the image of Christ and become his bride to rule over the world with him for a thousand years when he returns.

8. Everything that is not of God in this world is going to be shaken during the thirty-five years of tribulation from the time Jesus starts his ride to the Battle of Armageddon when he returns to the earth to set up his kingdom. The process begins slowly and grows in intensity over the years and will reach the point in the words of Jesus, "For then there will be great tribulation, such as has not been from the beginning of the world until now, no, and never will be" (Matthew 24:21).

9. Judgment begins in the house of the Lord. Not for its destruction, but for its cleansing from its adaption to the world system.

10. The second group that Jesus deals with is the unsaved population of the nations to bring them to salvation.

11. The third group of people that Jesus deals with is the nation of Israel. They will come to know their Messiah, Jesus, and occupy the capitol of the world, Jerusalem.

## CHAPTER 13

# THE SECOND SEAL—THE SECOND RIDER OF THE APOCALYPSE

**EVENT:** The second rider of the Apocalypse

**TIME FRAME:** From Eternity Present—Creation 5962, Jewish 5746, Western AD 1986 to Eternity Present—Creation 5993, Jewish 1 Kislev 5778, Western November 19, AD 2017.

**INTRODUCTION NARRATIVE:** *The sword of division comes forth to divide and separate those who will worship and serve the true living God in Christ from those who prefer the deception and idolatry of the Devil. The ultimate culmination of this process will be Christianity verses Islam.*

Revelation 6:3–4: "When he opened the second seal, I heard the second living creature say, 'Come!' (4) And out came another horse, bright red; its rider was permitted to take peace from the earth, so that men should slay one another; and he was given a great sword."

During the ministry of Jesus upon the earth, he states very clearly in Matthew 10:34–39:

> Do not think that I have come to bring peace on earth; I have not come to bring peace, *but a sword*. (35) For I have come to set a man against his father, and a daughter against her mother, and a daughter-in-law against her mother-in-law; (36) and a man's foes will be those of his own household. (37) He who loves father and mother more than me is not worthy of me; (38) and he who loves son or daughter more than me is not worthy of me; and he who does not take his cross and follow me is not worthy of me. (39) He who finds his life will lose it, and he who loses his life for my sake will find it. (italics added)

The word "sword" given to the second rider in the Greek is translated figuratively: "war, judicial punishment, controversy:—fighting, strive, striving."

To follow Jesus, Jesus must take first place in our life. When he is in first place, we are against the world system that is directed by the Devil. There are battles that must be fought. Our responsibility is to follow the Lord's personal direction for each of us. Quite often, his direction will be in conflict with those who are closest to us, our family. So what is the purpose of the second rider of the Apocalypse? It concerns the sword of the rider, which is also a symbol of the Word of God, and the rider is coming from God to divide the world into two groups. Those who believer and follow Jesus, and those who will be destroyed. Each individual that God calls into salvation is accountable to the Lord. To surrender our life to the world system of sin is death. To stand with Jesus in his power, authority, and truth is life.

Some three hundred years after the death and resurrection of Jesus in AD 27, the Word of God had gone forth through the Roman Empire, and Constantine, head of the Empire, declared Christianity to be the predominant religion of the nation. Then, in AD 626, God lets the Devil raise up Muhammad, a descendant from the illegitimate son of Abraham, Ishmael. The Koran is given to the so-called prophet Mohammad. He is given a mandate to conquer the world and turn it over to Allah, his god. Any person that will not commit his life to Allah, under the Koran, is to be put to death. So war began against Christianity and Judaism by Islam.

Jesus made a statement in Matthew 24:14 concerning his gospel: "And this gospel of the kingdom will be preached throughout the whole world, as a testimony to all nations;

and then the end will come." The gospel of Jesus is now available to the entire world at this point in time. It can be received through missionaries, television, and the internet. What were the territorial boundaries of the Roman Empire at its peak are now predominantly divided today by Christianity in the western to northern section and Islam in the eastern to southern section.

The nation of Israel is surrounded by Islamic nations who hate the Jews. The Jews are supported by the Christians because Judaism is the foundation of Christianity. Jesus states in Matthew 5:17–18: "Think not that I have come to abolish the law and the prophets; I have come not to abolish them but to fulfill them. (18) For truly, I say to you, till heaven and earth pass away, not an iota, not a dot, will pass from the law until all is accomplished." Jesus, the Jewish Messiah, came to fulfill the Old Covenant of law within us through the power of the Holy Spirit, and Jerusalem will become the Christian capitol city of the world with the Jewish nation grafted into the New Covenant, but not until the permanent return of Jesus to the earth.

The end of the church age period will be primarily a battle between Christianity and Islam, the two dominating religions of the world. With worldwide chaos increasing, the

Antichrist will rise up through Islam, proclaim himself to be God, their Messiah, with signs and wonders, "and seek to change the times and the law" (Daniel 7:25). Then will come the opening of the sixth seal with a clear perspective that Jesus is the Son of God and the true Messiah. It will mark the beginning of Daniel's Seventieth Week, and it will be a deathblow to the Antichrist. When the rapture of the saints takes place, then Islam will dominate the world for a period of "forty-two months" (Revelation 11:2; 13:5). The Antichrist will take over Jerusalem and do battle with other countries that will not submit to Islamic control.

The collapse of the USSR in 1989 was the result of the first rider of the Apocalypse bringing down idolatry. The sword of division is the work of the second rider of the Apocalypse. Peace was taken away, and the killing began. Since then, we have had more wars taking place than ever before in world history.

In Zachariah 1:7–17 we have a picture of the Lord and his angelic riders who have patrolled the earth throughout the ages before the four riders of the Apocalypse:

> In the twenty-fourth day of the eleventh month which is the month Shebat, in the second year of Darius, the word of the LORD came to Zechariah the son of Berechiah, son of Iddo, the prophet; and Zechariah said, (8) "I saw in the night, and behold, a man riding upon a red horse! He was standing among

## Let There Be Light

the myrtle trees in the glen; and behind him were red, sorrel, and white horses. (9) Then I said, 'What are these, my lord?' The angel who talked with me said to me, 'I will show you what they are.' (10) So the man who was standing among the myrtle trees answered, *'These are they whom the LORD has sent to patrol the earth.'* (11) And they answered the angel of the LORD who was standing among the myrtle trees. 'We have patrolled the earth, and behold, all the earth remains at rest.' (12) Then the angel of the LORD said, 'O LORD of hosts, how long wilt though have no mercy on Jerusalem and the cities of Judah, against which thou hast had indignation these seventy years?' (13) And the LORD answered gracious and comforting words to the angel who talked with me. (14) So the angel who talked with me said to me, 'Cry again, Thus says the LORD of hosts: I am exceedingly jealous for Jerusalem and for Zion. (15) And I am very angry with the nations that are at ease; for while I was angry but a little they furthered the disaster. (16) Therefore, thus says the LORD, I have returned to Jerusalem with compassion; my house shall be built in it, says the LORD of hosts, and the measuring line shall be stretched out over Jerusalem. (17) Cry again. Thus says the LORD of hosts: My cities shall again overflow with prosperity, and the LORD will again comfort Zion and again choose Jerusalem.'" (italics added)

This prophecy was given to Zechariah in 536 BC at the end of the seventy year judgment that was exercised upon the Jews for their rebellion. God used the Babylonian Empire to take them into captivity. Then he used the Media-Persian Empire to overthrow the Babylonian Empire at the end of the seventy years as a judgment against Babylon. Through Darius King of the Media-Persian Empire, some of the Jews are returned to Jerusalem to rebuild the temple and the walls.

God has always been in control over this creation. The unseen angelic realm, both holy and fallen angels, is actively engaged in the affairs of mankind. While God has the power to bring a halt to any activity at any point in time, we are allowed to make the free will decisions that govern our life. God is constantly bringing light to us, and the Devil brings darkness. God has predetermined the end time events that will usher in the return of Jesus to this earth. Those events are already in process. It is part of the great tribulation period that Jesus told us about. What he did not tell us was the length of its duration. My observation and by inductive deduction is that it starts slowly and builds in size and momentum and has a total duration of thirty-five years, reduced from an original period of forty years. It will end at the Battle of Armageddon on July 4, AD 2021.

**POINTS TO REMEMBER**

1. The second rider of the Apocalypse brings the sword of division

2. The division concerns those who want to worship the true living God from those who want to hold onto their false

gods. Allah of Islam will be the predominant false god of the world that people will follow before Armageddon take place.

3. God has never lost control of his creation.

4. God continually brings us light, and Lucifer continually brings us darkness.

5. The holy angels and fallen angels are actively involved in the affairs of mankind. Each person must make a decision to live in the light of God or the darkness of Lucifer. The division between the two will become very clear before the rapture of the church takes place.

## CHAPTER 14

# THE THIRD SEAL—THE THIRD RIDER OF THE APOCALYPSE

**EVENT:** The third rider of the Apocalypse

**TIME FRAME:** From Eternity Present—Creation 5962, Jewish 5746, Western AD 1986 to Eternity Present—Creation 5993, Jewish 1 Kislev 5778, Western November 19, AD 2017

**INTRODUCTION NARRATIVE:** *Those who have received the light through God's grace but have rejected it are marked for destruction. Those who are sitting on the fence are being distressed.*

Revelation 6:5–6: "When he opened the third seal, I heard the third living creature say, 'Come!' And I saw, and behold, a black horse, and its rider had a balance in his hand; (6) and I heard what seemed to be a voice in the midst of the four living creatures saying, 'A quart of wheat for a denarius, and three quarts of barely for a denarius; but do not harm oil and wine!'"

The black horse is a symbol of darkness moving through the world. The rider has a balance in his hand. A quart of wheat or three quarts of barley for a denarius is a symbol of a day's wage for a small amount of food, which is a sever condition to live in. He is told not to harm oil and wine. The term "harm" in the Greek is also translated "to hurt," which means: "to be unjust, do wrong (morally, socially or physically)." The oil is a symbol of the anointing of the Holy Spirit, and the wine is a symbol of our participation in the shed blood of Jesus (his life) that cleanses us from our sins. Those who belong to the Lord are under his protection unless they are living in sin and rebellion.

There is a dividing point here for those who labor to feed their bellies and those who labor unto the Lord. For those who labor to feed their own appetites and have rejected the Lord, there will be a high price to pay. Their daily labor will only produce a starved existence with no hope for the future. Progress and productivity will be distressed. *The scale concerns how you weigh in, in the sight of the Lord and what will be measured out to you.* Are you sold out to the Lord? Are you standing in the middle of the road? Or are you living totally apart from Jesus?

In Luke 21:25-28, Jesus gives us a picture of the time period we have entered:

> And there will be signs in sun and moon and stars, [21] and upon the earth distress of nations in perplexity at the roaring of the sea and the waves, (26) men fainting with fear and with foreboding of what is coming on the world; for the powers of the heavens will be shaken. (27) *And then they will see the Son of man coming in a cloud with power and great glory.*[22] (28) Now when these things begin to take place, look up and raise your heads, because your redemption is drawing near. (italics added)

The first five seals are the prelude to the opening of the sixth seal, and all five of them are played out in the natural order of life on earth. From the opening of the sixth seal, all of the judgments are supernatural, direct from God's throne, undeniable and indisputable.

Luke 21:29-36:

> And he told them a parable: "Look at the fig tree [the symbol of Israel returning as a nation May 14, AD 1948], and all the trees; (30) as soon as they come out in leaf, you see for yourselves and know that the summer is already near. (31) So also, when you see these things taking place, you know that the kingdom of God is near. (32) Truly, I say to you, this generation will not

pass away till all has taken place. (33) Heaven and earth will pass away, but my words will not pass away.

(34) But take heed to yourselves lest your hearts be weighted down with dissipation and drunkenness and cares of this life, *and that day come upon you suddenly like a snare*; (35) for it will come upon all who dwell upon the face of the whole earth. (36) *But watch at all times, praying that you may have strength to escape all these things that will take place, and to stand before the Son of man.*" (italics added)

The statement, "will come upon all who dwell upon the face of the whole earth," refers to those who remain or reside in the fallen worldly condition. For the Christian, our dwelling place is in the kingdom of God even though we are living on the earth. If you are a worldly Christian, you will be taken by surprise!

In Daniel 5:26–28 we have an example of being weighed in God's balance. God rendered a miraculous sign with the handwriting on the wall to King Belshazzar. He was a descendant of King Nebuchadnezzar. He made a great feast for a thousand of his lords and used the holy vessels from the Jewish temple in Jerusalem to serve his guests. It was sacrilegious unto God. So God wrote his reply on the wall where they were eating and drinking. No one could interpret the message except the servant of God, Daniel. He gave the interpretation of the handwriting. "This is the interpretation of the matter: *menemene*, God has numbered the days of your kingdom and brought it to an end; (27) *tekeltekel*, you have *been weighed in the balances and found wanting*; (28) *peresperes*, your kingdom is divided and given to the Medes and Persians" (italics added). That very night the Babylonian kingdom was overthrown. Christians who walk with God and know their Bible will be able to know and understand what is taking place, as the signs appear for the end times we are in.

Many Christians today believe that the rapture of the saints will take place before the events of Revelation occur. Contrary to that theology when they do take place, terror and chaos will grip their lives. For those who have their eyes truly focused on living for the Lord and who are prepared for the events, they will readily adjust to the conditions, knowing that their redemption from this world is close at hand. At the same time, while God has saved us from the destruction of the unsaved, we are not without his disciplinary action upon our lives to correct our conduct from destructive behavior. Also, God puts us to the test through difficult times to reveal what is in us in order to draw us into a closer relationship with him. He is our life and protector, and we must come to the full realization of that issue.

## POINTS TO REMEMBER

1. The third rider of the Apocalypse is segregating those who are not walking with God from those who are walking with him. Those who are not, are marked for death. Those who are, will be protected. Those who are on the fence will be distressed.

2. Now is the time to take a good look at what is taking place worldwide and where you stand with Jesus, the Christ, the Son of the living God!

## CHAPTER 15

# THE FOURTH SEAL—THE FOURTH RIDER OF THE APOCALYPSE

**EVENT:** The fourth rider of the Apocalypse

**TIME FRAME:** From Eternity Present—Creation 5962, Jewish 5746, Western AD 1986 to Eternity Present—Creation 5993, Jewish 1 Kislev 5778, Western November 19, AD 2017

**INTRODUCTION NARRATIVE:** *During the time period of the four riders of the Apocalypse, one-fourth of the world's landmass will be the target for war, famine, pestilence, and wild beasts to destroy those who have been marked for death and eternal damnation. It is taking place now.*

Revelation 6:7–8: "When he opened the fourth seal, I heard the voice of the fourth living creature say, 'Come!' (8) And I saw, and behold, a pale horse, and its rider's name was Death, and Hades followed him; and they were given power over a fourth of the earth, to kill with sword and with famine and with pestilence and by wild beasts of the earth."

The fourth rider's name is Death. There are two forms of death. The first is spiritual, and the second physical. This rider is sent to kill those who are spiritual dead in their sins and will not repent. They are destined for eternal damnation. Hades follows this rider. One-fourth of the earth's landmass is his territorial jurisdiction. The sword represents war. Famine represents the depletion of the food supply through war or crop failure, floods, drought, and even pestilence that disables farmers to plant and harvest their crops. Pestilence is the spread of disease such as AIDS, which has killed millions of people. Wild beasts are animals in a wide variety that take the lives of people. The landmass areas are not identified in Scripture. But looking at the continent of Africa, many of its countries have been hard hit with all of the above killing methods.

John 8:31-38:

> Jesus then said to the Jews who had believed in him, "If you continue in my word, you are truly my disciples, (32) and you will know the truth, and the truth will make you free." (33) They answered him, "We are descendants of Abraham, and have never been in bondage to anyone. How is it that you say, 'You will be made free'?"
> (34) Jesus answered them, "Truly, truly, I say to you, everyone who commits sin is a slave to sin. (35) The slave does not continue in the house for ever; the son continues for ever. (36) So if the Son makes you free, you will be free indeed. (37) I know that you are descendants of Abraham; yet you seek to kill me, because my word finds no place in you. (38) I speak of what I have seen with my Father, and you do what you have heard from your father [the Devil].

The purpose of Jesus is to establish the truth concerning the world drowning in deception because we believe that we can live our lives without God. When God brought the Jews out from Egyptian bondage, the first commandment in Exodus 20:3 was: "You shall have no other gods before me." Ever since the fall in the Garden of Eden, the battle between truth and deception has been the central issue of life on earth. When Adam and Eve were driven out of the garden, two cherubim and a flaming sword were placed at the entrance to guard the way to the Tree of Life (the symbol of the system of life in the paradise of God). The sword and bow are symbols of warfare both spiritual and literal. The translation of the sword of the two cherubim is spiritual. It is translated in Hebrew as "draught" and also as "a cutting instrument (from its destructive effect), as a knife, sword or other sharp implement." It means: "to parch (though drought), that is, (by analogy) to desolate, destroy, and kill:—decay." Those who do not have the Word of God in their life and live by it are left desolate. Drought, decay, and death become their heritage. The Word of God, Jesus, came to establish the truth in our lives and reunite us with God the Father. Jesus states in John 10:10: "The thief comes only to steal and kill and destroy; I came that they may have life, and have it abundantly." So the purpose of the first rider of the Apocalypse is to break down every form of idolatry where mankind places his dependency and bring forth those who will see the truth and be saved. This is the work of Jesus. The second rider brings about a major division between those who want to live in the light and those who want to live in darkness. Peace is taken away and killing begins among the people. The third rider makes it very clear for those who try to develop lifestyles apart from God that it is an exercise in futility, and they will pay a very high price for their folly. The fourth rider kills with war, pestilence, famine, and wild beasts, those who refuse to repent, and Hades awaits their arrival. While the first three riders cover the earth, the fourth rider is limited by God to one-fourth of the earth's landmass that is spread around the world. The exact areas are not defined in Scripture. The four riders are executing a team effort in sequence worldwide in a progressive compounding movement that is now overwhelming the world's ability to handle the problems. The numbers of refugees and deaths are astronomical.

## POINTS TO REMEMBER

1. One-fourth of the world's landmass is targeted for war, famine, pestilence, and wild bests to kill those who have been marked by the third rider of the Apocalypse during the tribulation period.

2. Jesus wants to set us free from the fallen world system drowning in deception.

3. Without a personal relationship with Jesus, life on planet earth is an exercise in futility that will result in eternal separation from God.

## CHAPTER 16

# THE FIFTH SEAL—THE MARTYRDOM OF THE SAINTS

**EVENT:** The fifth seal, the martyrdom of the saints

**TIME FRAME:** From Eternity Present—Creation 5962, Jewish 5746, Western AD 1986 to Eternity Present—Creation 5997, Jewish 9 Sivan 5781, Western May 20, AD 2021, the return of Jesus to the earth

**INTRODUCTION NARRATIVE:** *Christians are now being persecuted and martyred all over the world for sharing their faith in Christ. Most of the killing is being done by Islam. In addition to this, there are four major events that must take place before the opening of the sixth seal.*

Revelation 6:9–11:

> When he opened the fifth seal, I saw under the altar the souls of those who had been slain for the word of God and the witness they had borne; (10) they cried out with a loud voice, "O Sovereign Lord, holy and true, how long before thou wild judge and avenge our blood on those who dwell upon the earth?" (11) Then they were each given a white robe and told to rest a little longer, until the number of their fellow servants and their brethren should be complete, who were to be killed as they themselves had been.

From the beginning of the New Covenant with the sacrificial offering of Jesus on the cross, many Christians have been killed because of their spreading of the gospel. While every saint who dies is rewarded with eternal life with God in Paradise, for those who were murdered for their faith, there is an additional reward. The "white robe" is translated in the Greek as a "stole" or long fitting gown (as a mark of dignity). They are given a mark of distinction.

Our salvation is clearly stated in Ephesians 2:8–10: "For by grace you have been saved though faith; and this is not your own doing, it is the gift of God—not because of works, lest any man should boast. For we are his workmanship, created in Christ Jesus *for good works*, which God prepared beforehand, that we should walk in them" (italics added). Our salvation is a gift, but when we accept it, we are called to accomplish good works on earth directed by the Holy Spirit.

In doing so, there are additional rewards in our life on earth and also when we go home to be with the Lord. The issue of works and rewards is stated in 1 Corinthians 3:10–15:

> According to the grace of God given to me, like a skilled master builder I laid a foundation, and another man is building upon it. Let each man take care how he builds upon it. (11) For no other foundation can any one lay than that which is laid, which is Jesus Christ. (12) Now if any one builds on the foundation with gold, silver, precious stones, wood, hay, stubble—(13) each man's work will become manifest; for the Day will disclose it, because it will be revealed with fire, and the fire will test what sort of work each one has done. (14) If the work which any man has built on the foundation survives, he will receive a reward. (15) *If any man's work is burned up, he will suffer loss, though he himself will be saved, but only as through fire.* (italics added)

The gold is a symbol of the divine nature of God, which is love. The "silver" represents God's plan for our life after we are saved, not our own plans. The precious stones are a symbol of the individual gifting that God gives to us to accomplish his work as he directs. The wood, hay, and stubble are symbols of productive activity not directed by the Lord through the Holy Spirit. Your efforts to serve God, outside of his direction and timing for your life, will be consumed with fire and you lose your reward but not your life with God. Serving God with compassion and love in whatever field of work God has planned for you to accomplish is far more valuable to God than our building monumental empires to our own egos and pleasures. To share your life and the Word of God for the salvation and welfare of others, at the cost of your life, if required is a precious gift to the Lord in his honor and for his glory that will not go unrewarded! Just as Jesus laid his life down for us, he wants us to lay our life down for others but not without his direction and power.

There is an extreme hatred between Satan and Christians, darkness and light. The end time plan of God is to take complete control over this earth and remove the darkness that has destroyed our lives. It is a fierce battle in the separation of those who want to live in the light and those who want to live in darkness. God is going to win the battle. He has never given up his supreme power and authority over all creation. What he has done is subject this creation to the rebellion of Lucifer and its futility upon the development of mankind, so that we will come to a free will decision concerning who and what we want to control our lives. Will it be light or darkness, truth or deception, love or hatred, harmony or chaos, God or Satan, eternal glory or eternal damnation?

Right now the entire world is being split into these two groups: those who walk with God in the light of Christ and those who want to follow the Devil in darkness and deception. It is a decision that every person must make, and the battle is growing in magnitude worldwide. Christians, from the time of the stoning of Steven in the Book of Acts to the beginning of the four riders of the Apocalypse, have been giving their lives in the ultimate sacrifice of service to Jesus. But now, with the opening of the fifth seal, the martyrdom of Christians is a major issue around the world. When September 11, AD 2001, took place there was a video clip on the news with radical Muslims chanting, "Kill Christians kill Jews! Kill Christians, kill Jews!" Christianity is at war with Islam, and our missionaries, churches, and people are being attacked and murdered all over the world, and the news media has remained extremely quiet concerning the intensity of the problem. *For those who can see, we are in the end times of the Book of Revelation!*

At this hour a large segment of the church "sleeps in the durst of the earth [the flesh]." (Daniel 12:2–3) They have been lulled to rest with doctrines of blessings and the assurance that the saints will be raptured before the great tribulation ever takes place. A pastor of one large church today will not ever talk about sin. The issue of the believer being crucified with Christ is no longer a topic for teaching (Galatians 2:20). Sin and ignorance run rampant in the church and all in the name of Jesus. The church has become more "seeker sensitive" than Jesus sensitive! The church will never save anyone without the Lord personally being involved and directing the program individually and collectively.

Tribulation has always been a part of the growth of the church. It is the purging process that forces and teaches the Christian to become totally dependent upon Christ for his or her salvation and to seek the Lord daily for guidance upon this earth. Tribulation, discipline, and punishment are used for the destruction of the flesh so we can live in the Spirit under God's control. The only difference between tribulation and the great tribulation is the magnitude in which it is presented. The final "shaking" is designed to clean up the saints and bring in those who have not been harvested. To think for one moment that the saints will not be shaken while they violate the Word of God is an exercise in delusion and blindness. It is for our benefit, not for our destruction, unless we rebel against God. It is the wrath of God that is sent for the destruction of the wicked, not the saints. Tribulation and wrath are two different things.

God's punishment and discipline have always been part of the educational system of his saints (Hebrews 12:3–11). We are God's children. God's wrath has been shown to us in the flood of Noah. It was tribulation for Noah and destruction for the wicked. Likewise, it was tribulation for Lot but destruction for Sodom and Gomorrah. It was great tribulation for the Israelites when God took them out of Egypt to move them into the Promised Land. But it was God's wrath that fell upon the Egyptians in the form of plagues, the killing of their firstborn sons, and the destruction of their army. The Jews were spared from God's wrath! So will it be in this end time scenario. Christian will die as martyrs for their faith and receive a crown of glory, but they will not die from God's wrath. Christians can die early as a result of disobedience due to immorality and contracting AIDS, just like Lot's wife died of her disobedience, but they do not lose their salvation. They do lose reward! Wrath is a wipe out for wicked conduct in rebellion against God. Punishment is a disciplinary action as a corrective measure against sinful conduct. The consequences of sin may cost you your life on planet earth, but not your loss of salvation. Christians lose their lives on the battlefields of war along with the heathen, fighting for good and evil. The Christian is taken to be with the Lord because of his faith while the heathen goes to eternal damnation for their rejection of faith in God. War is a battle between good and evil on the earth and under the control of God. God's supernatural wrath is poured out from heaven when man exceeds the limit God has allowed for unrighteousness to exist. The wrath of God, as seen in the Book of Revelation, is supernatural destruction from the throne room, poured upon the unrighteous that refuse to repent. It is not poured upon his saints. His saints are divinely protected (Revelation 9:3–4).

**EVENTS: (1) Matthew 24:21—great tribulation, (2) the forming of ten Islamic nations, (3) the beginning of the reconstruction of Babylon, (4) the rise of the Antichrist TIME FRAME: From Eternity Present—Creation 5987, Jewish 5771, Western AD 2011 to Eternity Present—Creation 5990, Jewish 14 Iyyar 5774, Western May 14, AD 2014**

There are four events that must take place before the opening of the sixth seal on May 14, AD 2014. There are no specific dates. However, there is a specification in Matthew 24:21: "For then there will be *great tribulation*, such as has not been from the beginning of the world until now, no, and never will be" (italics added). While the tribulation period is already taking place, we have not reached the pinnacle of this verse, and Scripture does not reveal what will cause the event. But based upon the events that are taking place now from the opening of the first five seals (war, pestilence, famine, and martyrdom of the saints) and the short period of time left before the opening of the sixth seal, it appears that it will be the result of upheaval and financial collapse of nations worldwide during the years of AD 2011 and 2012 (which is the work of the first rider of the Apocalypse, Jesus). This upheaval may be the catalyst for the ten Islamic nations to join together. That is my opinion, not Scripture. It is Scripture that dictates the reconstruction of the old city of Babylon, which is in the territory of Iraq.

It is my opinion that construction will begin before the rise of the Antichrist and the opening of the sixth seal. It is Scripture that dictates the worldwide chaos and that the ten nations are joined together and functioning before the Antichrist comes on the scene. It is also clear that the great tribulation is already in process when he appears. Then he will present a solution for the problems confronting the world that will cause the unsaved population to follow him as their messiah, and he will be the long awaited messiah of Islam.

In Matthew 24:15–31, Jesus deals with the rise of the Antichrist:

> So when you see[23] the desolating sacrilege spoken of by the prophet Daniel,[24] standing in the holy place (let the reader understand),[25] (16) then let those who are in the Judea flee to the mountains;[26] (17) let him who is on the housetop not go down to take what is in his house; (18) and let him who is in the field not turn back to take his mantle. (19) And alas for those who are with child and for those who give suck in those days! (20) Pray that your flight may not be in winter or on a Sabbath. (21) For then there will be great tribulation, such as has not been from the beginning of the world until now, no, and never will be. (22) And if those days had not been shortened, no human being would be saved; for the sake of the elect those days will be shortened. (23) Then if any one says to you, "Lo, here is the Christ!" or "There he is!" do not believe it. (24) For false Christs and false prophets will arise and show great signs and wonders so as to lead astray, if possible, even the elect. (25) Lo, I have told you beforehand. (26) So, if they say to you, "Lo, he is in the wilderness," do not go out; if they say, "Lo, he is in the inner rooms," do not believe it. (27) For as the lightning comes from the east and shines as far as the west, so will be the coming of the Son of man.[27] (28) Wherever the body is, there the eagles will be gathered together.[28]
>
> (29) Immediately after the tribulation of those days[29] the sun will be darkened, and the moon will not give its light, and the stars will fall from heaven, and powers of the heavens will be shaken;[30] (30) then will appear the sign of the Son of man in heaven, and then all the tribes of the earth will mourn,[31] and they will see the Son of man coming on the clouds of heaven with power and great glory;[32] (31) and he will send out his angels with a loud trumpet call, and they will gather his elect from the four winds, from one end of heaven to the other.[33]

The forming of ten Islamic nations must happen before the rise of the Antichrist. It is defined in Daniel 7:1–8:

In the first year of Belshazzar king of Babylon, Daniel had a dream and vision of his head as he lay in his bed. Then he wrote down the dream, and told the sum of the matter. (2) Daniel said, "I saw in my vision by night, and behold, the four winds of heaven were stirring up the great sea. (3) And four great beasts came up out of the sea, different from one another. (4) The first was like a lion and had eagles' wings.[34] Then as I looked its wings were plucked off, and it was lifted up from the ground and made to stand upon two feet like a man; and the mind of a man was given to it. (5) And behold, another beast, a second one, like a bear.[35] It was raised up on one side; it has three ribs in its mouth between its teeth; and it was told, 'Arise, devour much flesh.' (6) After this I looked, and lo, another, like a leopard, with four wings of a bird on its back; and the beast had four heads; and dominion was given to it.[36] (7) After this I saw in the night visions, and behold, a fourth beast, terrible and dreadful and exceedingly strong; and it had great iron teeth;[37] it devoured and broke in pieces, and stamped the residue with its feet. It was different from all the beasts that were before it; and it had ten horns.[38] (8) I considered the horns, and behold, there came up among them another horn, a little one, before which three of the first horns were plucked up by the roots; and behold, in this horn were eyes like the eyes of a man, and a mouth speaking great things."[39]

## SUMMARY

The following is a list of the events that must take place before the opening of the sixth seal. They are listed in the order that I believe they will take place. It is my calculated opinion. Scripture dictates that *the events will take place before the opening of the sixth seal.*

1. There will be compounding financial breakdown during the years of AD 2011 and AD 2012. It will cause nations of the world to go bankrupt. This is already taking place. With the continued activity of the opening of the first five seals and the financial collapse of nations, this will bring us to the fulfillment of the words of Jesus in Matthew 24:21: "For then there will be great tribulation, such as has not been from the beginning of the world until now, no, and never will be."

2. During this same time period, Iraq will begin reconstruction of the old city of Babylon.

3. There will also be an upheaval in the Islamic nations that will cause ten nations to join together during this time period.

4. Sometime after the uniting of ten Islamic nations, the Antichrist will come on the scene. He will be the long awaited messiah of Islam. He will proclaim himself to be God. He will take over three of the ten Islamic nations.

5. When the Antichrist proclaims to be God, God will reveal to the Christians in Judea who he really is and that they are to flee from the country.

6. On May 14, AD 2014, the sixth seal will be opened. Darkness will cover the earth for seven days, and on the eighth day, May 21, the sky will vanish like a scroll (Revelation 6:14), "then will appear the sign of the Son of man in heaven..." (Matthew 24:30). May 21, AD 2014, will mark the beginning of the final seven year countdown of Daniel's Seventieth Week.

## POINTS TO REMEMBER

1. Christians who are killed because of their sharing the gospel of Jesus in his service are given a mark of distinction in heaven.

2. Our salvation is a free gift given to us through God's grace and the exercise of our faith in repentance and committing our life to Jesus. While the gift is free, there is a responsibility that comes with our acceptance. We are called to

undertake good works directed by his Holy Spirit that now dwells within us.

3. God gives us spiritual gifts to accomplish the work he calls us to do.

4. We have already entered into the end times of the Book of Revelation. God is separating those who are to be saved from those who refuse to repent. The world is being prepared for the return of Jesus.

5. Four major events must take place before the opening of the sixth seal: (1) the pinnacle of the great tribulation will take place; (2) the beginning of the reconstruction of Babylon will start; (3) ten Islamic nations will join together; and (4) the Antichrist will present himself.

6. The sixth seal will open on May 14, AD 2014.

## CHAPTER 17

# THE SIXTH SEAL

**EVENT**: The opening of the sixth seal
**TIME FRAME**: Eternity Present—Creation 5990, Jewish 14 Iyyar 5774, Western May 14, AD 2014

**INTRODUCTION NARRATIVE**: *The opening of the sixth seal on May 14, AD 2014, is the prelude for the beginning of Daniel's Seventieth Week of prophecy to be fulfilled. Darkness will engulf the world for seven days as a symbol of the spiritual darkness that has enveloped the seven days that God created our heaven and earth in a state of holiness and light. On the eighth day, May 21, AD 2014, the sky will roll back like a scroll and the entire world will be able to see into the throne room of God! This day will mark the begin-*

*ning of Daniel's final seven year countdown of God's supernatural judgments from heaven that will take place before the Battle of Armageddon. The judgments are against evil. During this time, God will confirm the New Covenant established in the death and resurrection of Jesus to all mankind. There will be no questions about who Jesus is and the salvation that he offers for any man or woman who will repent and make Jesus Lord of their life. It will be a mortal wound to the Antichrist until the rapture of the saints. Then Islam, led by the Antichrist, will dominate the world for forty-two months.*

Revelation 6:12–17:

> When he opened the sixth seal, I looked, and behold, there was a great earthquake; and the sun became black as sackcloth, the full moon became like blood, (13) and the stars of the sky fell to the earth as the fig tree sheds its winter fruit when shaken by a gale; (14) the sky vanished like a scroll that is rolled up, and every mountain and island was removed from its place. (15) Then the kings of the earth and the great men and the generals and the rich and the strong, and every one, slave and free, hid in the caves and among the rocks of the mountains, (16) calling to the mountains and rocks, "Fall on us and hide us from the face of him who is seated on the throne, and from the wrath of the Lamb; (17) for the great day of their wrath has come, and who can stand before it?"

The opening of the seal begins with an earthquake to get everyone's attention worldwide. For those who are in daylight, the sun will be darkened. For those who are on the darkened side of the earth, the moon will turn the color of blood. Then there will be stars falling from the sky to the earth in the natural order (they will not hit the earth or it would all be over at this point). There is also a figurative reality represented in this statement. It deals with the saints and those ministering spirits in the body of Christ who have violated the Word of God and who have sanctified doctrines of filth in the sight of God to his people. They will be the first to be shaken from their positions by the glory of the Lord that is revealed.

Revelation 2:20–23:

> But I have this against you, that you tolerate the woman Jezebel, who calls herself a prophetess and is teaching and beguiling my servants to practice immorality and to eat food sacrificed to idols. (21) I gave her time to repent, but she refuses to repent of her immorality. (22) Behold, *I will throw her on a sickbed, and those who commit adultery with her I will throw into great tribulation*, unless they repent of her doings; (23) and I will strike her children dead. And all the churches shall know that I am he who searched mind and heart, and I will give to each of you as your works deserve. (italics added)

In Revelation 6:14 where it states, "…and every mountain and island was removed from its place," is a figurative statement. Mountains in Scripture are a symbol of the governments of large nations. Islands are a symbol of smaller bodies of people bound together under a government format. "Removed from its place," means that it is no longer business as usual. The geological location will remain the same. Everyone will now have to deal with what has been revealed to mankind by God. So terrifying is the event that everyone flees to hide from God the Father "and the wrath of the Lamb." The message is clear! It is a rude awakening! But even with the visual reality of God seated upon his throne and knowing of the "wrath of the Lamb" that is to come God and his Son will be rejected. The issue is clearly stated in John 3:19–20: "And this is the judgment, that the light has come into the world, and men loved darkness rather than light, because their deeds were evil. (20) For everyone who does evil hates the light, and does not come to the light, lest his deeds should be exposed."

May 14, AD 2014, is not any ordinary day! It happens to be the sixty-sixth year anniversary of Israel becoming a nation in AD 1948. The number of the seal is six. Added to the anniversary date of Israel, and *we have the number of the beast* in Revelation, 666, and darkness covers the entire world. It is a sign as a prelude to the final seven year countdown of Daniel's Seventieth Week of prophecy. On the, eighth say, May 21, AD 2014, is the beginning of the

Seventieth Week of Daniel. The sky will vanish like a scroll that is rolled up, and we will be able to see right into the throne room of God.

In Genesis 1:2 there is the chaos and darkness of Lucifer's rebellion. "The earth was without form and void, and *darkness* [it is spiritual chaos and darkness] was upon the face of the deep." This literal darkness upon the earth in Revelation is a sign of the spiritual darkness of the working of the Antichrist who is present at this point in time! The number of the name of the beast is 666 (Revelation 13:18). It is broken down into three symbolic components: 600, 60, and 6. Six hundred is a symbol of destruction. In the six-hundredth year of the life of Noah, the flood that destroyed the world took place, and the righteous were delivered (Genesis 7:6). Sixty is a symbol of idolatry. During the reign of King Nebuchadnezzar he constructed an image of gold that was sixty cubits high with a breadth of six cubits. Everyone was required to bow down before the image and worship (Daniel 3:1–7). The future Antichrist will have an image in his likeness constructed after he takes over Iraq and rules from the reconstructed city of Babylon (Revelation 13:11–18). This image will not be constructed until after the rapture. Six is the symbol of man because he was crated on the sixth day of creation (Genesis 1:27).

So what is the name of the beast? First, we need to look at the Greek translation of the term "name": "a name (literally or figuratively), (authority, character)." Because of the use of the numbers, it is the figurative description that must be used, not the literal. Also, it is not the name of the Antichrist that is to be defined. It is the number of the symbolic *beast*. Revelation 13:18: "This calls for wisdom: let him who has understanding reckon the number of the beast, for it is a human number, its number is six hundred and sixty-six." In Revelation 12:3 the Devil is labeled as "the great red dragon," which is a beast. The meaning of the three numbers tied together is, "*destruction* through *idolatry* by *man*." The authority and character of the beast is "darkness upon the face of the deep" representing the fall and rebellion of Lucifer, which is figuratively defined in Genesis 1:2. The Antichrist is a servant of Satan and is called "the beast." He will carry out Satan's evil plan upon the earth. God's response to Lucifer's rebellion in Genesis 1:3 was: "Let there be light!" In 2 Corinthians 4:6 it states: "For it is the God who said, '*Let light shine out of darkness,*' who has shone in our hearts to give the light of the knowledge of the glory of God in the face of Christ" (italics added). With the rise of the Antichrist backed by the Devil, God is going to bring the glory of Christ to the entire world when the sky is rolled back like a scroll after seven days of darkness, and the world will be able to see into the throne room of God.

Daniel 9:27 (KJV):

> And he [Jesus] shall confirm the covenant [the New Covenant] with many for one week: and in the midst of the week he [Jesus] shall cause the sacrifice and the oblation to cease,[40] and for the overspreading abominations [idolatry and filth] he [Jesus] shall make it desolate [ruined with the wrath of God from heaven], even until the consummation, and that determined shall be poured upon the desolate [destruction of the unrepentant living in sin at Armageddon and at the Feast of Atonement].

Matthew 24:29–31:

> Immediately after the tribulation of those days the sun will be darkened, and the moon will not give its light, and stars will fall from heaven, and the powers of the heavens will be shaken; then will appear the sing of the Son of man in heaven, and then all the tribes of the earth will mourn, and they will see the son of man coming on the clouds of heaven with power and great glory; and he will send out his angels with a loud trumpet call, and they will gather his elect from the four winds, from one end of heaven to the other.

Jesus quotes the opening of the sixth seal! He gives reference to the tribulation that comes before it. He tells us that there will be a "sign of the son of man" that will appear. This is a direct answer to the question of his disciples on the Mount of Olives in Matthew 24:3: "...*what will be the sign of your coming* and of the close of the age?" (italics added). After the sign will come the gathering up of the saints, which is the rapture! He clearly establishes the fact that the rapture will not take place until after the opening of the sixth seal. This also reveals that the tribulation period begins long before the final seven year countdown of Daniel's prophecy with the opening of the first five seals. The eighth day in Scripture was the day for the circumcision of a new child. Eight is also a symbol of restoration and new beginnings. This final week of Daniel is going to bring a circumcision to the hearts of the Jews and convert their nation to Christ. It will be a new beginning for them. It will also lead to the total destruction of Satan and all of his followers.

**EVENTS: The beginning of Daniel's Seventieth Week**
**TIME FRAME: Eternity Present—Creation 5990, Jewish 21 Iyyar 5774, Western May 21, AD 2014**

There are two dates in Revelation 6:12–17. There is a seven day period of darkness around the world from the beginning of "the sun became black as sackcloth, the full moon became like blood" and then in verse 14 when "the sky vanished like a scroll that is rolled up, and every mountain and island was removed from its place." At this point we have the beginning of the final week of Daniel's prophecy in compliance with Daniel 9:27 as stated above in the previous section. The first seven days of darkness is a prelude to the final seven year countdown, when Jesus confirms the New Covenant with the entire world for seven years through supernatural signs and judgments upon the wicked that refuse to repent. Because the sky is rolled back, we will see God the Father seated upon his throne and the sign of Jesus which will most likely be in the form of a cross or a lamb with seven horns and seven eyes.

Then in the last half of the verse in Daniel 9:30–31, there is another time separation just short of three and a half years, in which Jesus defines the rapture of the saints: "... and they will see the Son of man coming on the clouds of heaven with power and great glory; (31) and he will send out his angels with a loud trumpet call, and they will gather his elect from the four winds, from one end of heaven to the other" (Matthew 24:30–31). This is not an event that will be done in secret. It will be a public display for the entire world because Jesus is confirming the New Covenant in his blood with everyone. While we will not know "the day or the hour," the season has been formulated for those who have eyes to see and ears to hear what the Spirit says to his saints in Scripture. The actual "day" refers to a twenty-four hour period with the exact hour of that day when the rapture takes place. It will not be known until it happens. But it will happen shortly before the middle of Daniel's Seventieth Week at the sound of the seventh trumpet of the seventh seal. That is the season!

**POINTS TO REMEMBER**

1. The opening of the sixth seal beings with seven days of darkness around the entire world. God is going to bring the full force of his judgments (seven trumpet judgments, seven thunders, and seven bowls of wrath, and then finalize the issue with the Battle of Armageddon) upon the earth and will destroy the wicked who will not repent.

2. On the eighth day of the opening of the sixth seal, the sky will roll back like a scroll, and we will be able to see into the throne room of God. We will see the sign of the Son of God signifying that Jesus is the Messiah. This day will mark the beginning of Daniel's Seventieth Week.

3. The mark of the beast in the number 666 translates into: "*Destruction* through *idolatry* by *man.*" It is the same issue of the rebellion of Lucifer in Genesis 1:2, symbolized by "darkness was upon the face of the deep" when God acted upon that rebellion in Eternity Past. Now, God is acting upon the rebellion of mankind in our day, Eternity Present! God is going to destroy the destroyers of the earth! God will deliver all who belong to him.

4. The rapture will take place shortly before the halfway point of Daniel's Seventieth Week. We will not know the day or the hour.

# CHAPTER 18

# THE SEVENTH SEAL — THE FIRST HALF OF THE SEVENTIETH WEEK

EVENTS: The opening of the seventh seal with its seven trumpet judgments[41]

TIME FRAME: From Eternity Present—Creation 5990, Jewish 21 Iyyar 5774, Western May 21, AD 2014 to Eternity Present—Creation 5993, 1 Kislev 5778, Western November 19, AD 2017

INTRODUCTION NARRATIVE: *With the sky rolling back after the opening of the sixth seal and God confirming the New Covenant of life in Christ by his shed blood, it will be a mortal wound to the Antichrist who proclaims himself to be God. All of the judgments that are to follow will be supernatural from the throne of God. It will be very clear to the entire world!*

Revelation 7:1–8:

> After this I saw four angels standing at the four corners of the earth, holding back the four winds of the earth, that no wind might blow on earth or sea or against any tree. (2) Then I saw another angel ascend from the rising of the sun, with the seal of the living God, and he called with a loud voice to the four angels who had been given power to harm earth and sea, (3) saying, "Do not harm the earth or the sea or the trees, till we have sealed the servants of our God upon their foreheads." (4) And I heard the number of the sealed, a hundred and forty-four thousand sealed, out of every tribe of the sons of Israel, (5) twelve thousand sealed out of the tribe of Judah, twelve thousand of the tribe of Reuben, twelve thousand of the tribe of Gad, (6) twelve thousand of the tribe of Asher, twelve thousand of the tribe of Naphtali, twelve thousand out of the tribe of Manasseh, (7) twelve thousand of the tribe of Simeon, twelve thousand of the tribe of Levi, twelve thousand of the tribe of Issachar, (8) twelve thousand of the tribe of Zebulun, twelve thousand of the tribe of Joseph, twelve thousand sealed out of the tribe of Benjamin.

Before the seventh seal is opened and enacted upon the earth, we see the results of the sky having been rolled back and mankind being able to see into the throne room of God. This terrifying event will produced some amazing results. First, 144,000 thousand Jews will be converted to salvation in Christ. This will mark the beginning of the redemption of the Jewish nation from a Covenant of Law into the Covenant of Grace. But the eyes of the rest of the nation will still be blind to their Messiah.

The second thing that takes place is seen in Revelation 7:9–14:

> After this I looked, and behold, a great multitude which no man could number, from every nation, from all tribes and peoples and tongues, standing before the throne and before the Lamb, clothed in white robes, with palm branches in their hands, (10) and crying out with a loud voice, "Salvation belongs to our God who sits upon the throne, and to the Lamb!" (11) And all the angels stood round the throne and round the elders and the four living creatures, and they fell on their faces before the throne and worshiped God, (12) saying, "Amen! Blessing and glory and wisdom and thanksgiving and honor and power and might be to our God for ever and ever! Amen."
> (13) Then one of the elders addressed me, saying, "Who are these, clothed in white robes, and whence have they come?" (14) I said to him, "Sir, you know." And he said to me, "These are they who have come out of the great tribulation; *they have washed their robes and made them white in the blood of the Lamb.*" (italics added)

This multitude that John sees are not new Christians, they already had robes. They are Christians who were living a life in the fleshly system of the world and had spotted the white robe that each one received when they committed their life to Christ. The white robe is an invisible spiritual covering of righteousness that allows you to have communion with God. With the terrifying experience of the sixth seal, they repented of their sins and made peace with God. They are holding palm branches in their hands, which is a symbol of peace.

In Revelation 7:15–17 it states:

> Therefore are they before the throne of God, and serve him day and night within his temple; and he who sits upon the throne will shelter them with his presence. (16) They shall hunger no more, neither thirst anymore; the sun shall not strike them, nor any scorching heat. (17) For the Lamb in the midst of the throne will be their shepherd, and he will guide them to springs of living water; and God will wipe away every tear from their eyes.

These saints have come out of the great tribulation and entered into the divine protection of God from the judgments that are coming upon the unrepentant. They are still upon the earth awaiting the rapture! If you are a Christian living in sin, you will be in tribulation. The only difference between tribulation and great tribulation is the magnitude in which it comes. All Christians will have tribulation in their life upon the earth. How you deal with it depends upon your relationship with Jesus. It can be dealt with through fear, kicking, yelling, screaming, anger, bitterness, denial, cursing, crying, and fighting, or you can have the peace of the Lord in his wisdom, insight, understanding, guidance, power, and calmness, and protection.

Revelation 8:1–6:

> When the Lamb opened the seventh seal, there was silence in heaven for about half an hour. (2) Then I saw the seven angels who stand before God, and seven trumpets were given to them. (3) And another angel came and stood at the altar with a golden censer; and he was given much incense to mingle with the prayers of all the saints upon the golden altar before the throne; (4) and the smoke of the incense rose with the prayers of the saints from the hand of the angel before God. (5) Then the angel took the censer and filled it with fire from the altar and threw it on the earth; and there were peals of thunder, voices, flashes of lightning, and an earthquake.
>
> (6) Now the seven angels who had the seven trumpets made ready to blow them.

There is silence in heaven. It is a solemn time because God is going to clean up the entire worldly system during the next seven years. He will save those who will submit their life to Jesus, and he will kill those who refuse and cast them into the abyss. And when he is finished, *the entire world will live in peace and righteousness.* It is a very serious time!

Revelation 8:7: "The first angel blew his trumpet, and there followed hail and fire, mixed with blood, which fell on the earth; and a third of the earth was burnt up, and a third of the trees were burnt up, and all green grass was burnt up." The first trumpet sounds. Hail and fire mixed with blood falls upon the earth from heaven, creating tremendous ecological damage. One-third of the earth's land will be hit around the world. This is a literal event. One-third of the trees and all of the green grass in every area will be burned up. It will have a major impact on mankind and the animal population. The prophet Joel sums up the issue in Joel 1:19–20: "Unto thee, O LORD, I cry. For fire has devoured the pastures of the wilderness, and the flame has burned all the trees of the field. (20) Even the wild beasts cry to thee because the water brooks are dried up, and fire has devoured the pastures of the wilderness."

When we look at the three elements poured out upon the earth, they hold spiritual significance. The hail is a symbol of the cold, hard indifference of man toward God. The fire is a symbol of God's purifying process to counteract the cold indifference. And the blood is the symbol of the life of the New Covenant in Christ, the focal point of God's revelation. The blood of Christ (his life) has the power to heal or destroy mankind. In Exodus 9:23–24, God sent hail and fire upon the Egyptians before he delivered the Jews from bondage. This time the judgments will be greater as God delivers the world from bondage to evil and wickedness.

Revelation 8:8–9: "The second angel blew his trumpet, and something like a great mountain, burning with fire, was thrown into the sea; (9) and a third of the sea became blood, a third of the living creatures in the sea died, and a third of the ships were destroyed." With this event, the world will suffer another major loss of food, along with suffering a major impact to commerce due to the loss of ships. This will hinder the world's ability to carry on.

Revelation 8:10–11: "The third angel blew his trumpet, and a great star fell from heaven, blazing like a torch, and it fell on a third of the rivers and on the fountains of water. (11) The name of the star is Wormwood. A third of the waters became wormwood, and many men died of the water, because it was made bitter." The great star that falls from heaven is an angel who fell during the rebellion of Lucifer. The name "Wormwood" means "rottenness, accursed, and bitterness." The angel comes to earth to poison one-third of the natural rivers and fountains of water. The judgment in the natural order parallels the spiritual. Mankind needs water to drink for survival of the body and spirit. The water of the spirit comes in the form of knowledge, understanding, and wisdom coupled with truth from God. They are the building blocks of the soul and spirit. The poison comes in the form of lies and deceit. The Devil told Eve in the garden, "You will not die. For God knows that when you eat of it your eyes will be opened, and you will be like God, knowing good and evil" (Genesis 3:4–5). Adam and Eve exchanged the truth for a lie, and every one of us has suffered spiritual death since that time. Our ability to reason has been disabled because of deception. Rottenness and bitterness have become our heritage.

In John 4:13–14, Jesus speaks to the woman at the well and tells her about "living water." That water is the knowledge, understanding, and wisdom all encased in truth in the Word of God imparted to us by grace through the Holy Spirit. Jesus states, "You will know the truth, and truth will make you free" (John 8:32). The natural poisoning of the water is a fitting judgment for all those who want to live lives of deception. The security of the Christian for this judgment lies in the promise of God in Mark 16:18: "... and if they drink any deadly thing, it will not hurt them." The saints are under divine protection.

Revelation 8:12: "The fourth angel blew his trumpet, and a third of the sun was struck, and a third of the moon, and a third of the stars, so that a third of their light was darkened; a third of the day was kept from shining, and likewise a third of the night." This is a literal event that will take place by the supernatural power of God. We are not told how long this event will last. If the condition were to be long-term, it would destroy life on planet earth and that is not the purpose. The intention is to bring mankind to their knees in the reality that we do not have control over our creation. Only God is sovereign in that department. As for the issue of "one-third," it deals with the demonic order and the fall of Lucifer (Revelation 12:3–4). When he rebelled, he took *one-third* of the angels with him. The consistent use of that number in the trumpet judgments is the focus of God toward those who embrace the world system, which is controlled by the fallen angelic realm through the lives of people not submitted to Jesus.

Revelation 8:13: "Then I looked, and I heard an eagle crying with a loud voice, as it flew in midheaven, 'woe, woe, woe to those who dwell on the earth, at the blasts of the other trumpets which the three angels are about to blow!'" While the first four trumpet judgments fall upon the natural earth and affect the people, the last three judgments fall upon the unrepentant, not the saints. The term "dwell" in the Greek means to "house permanently." The term concerns those who embrace this life on earth. The Christians are only temporary residents. Their permanent dwelling place is with, and in Christ. The "woe, woe, woe" doesn't apply to Christians!

Revelation 9:1–6:

And the fifth angel blew his trumpet, and I saw a star fallen from heaven to earth, and he was given the key of the shaft of the bottomless pit; (2) he opened the shaft of the bottomless pit, and from the shaft rose smoke like the smoke of a great furnace, and the sun and the air were darkened with the smoke from the shaft. (3) Then from the smoke came locusts on the earth, and they were given power like the power of scorpions of the earth; (4) *they were told not to harm the grass of the earth or any green growth or any tree but only those of mankind who have not the seal of God upon their foreheads*; (5) they were allowed to torture them for five months, but not to kill them, and their torture was like the torture of a scorpion, when it stings a man. (6) And in those days men will seek death and will not find it; they will long to die, and death will fly from them. (italics added)

There is a description of these demonic creatures in Revelation 9:7–11. The fallen angelic realm has absolutely no love for mankind. In reference to the Devil and his followers, Jesus makes the statement in John 10:10: "The thief comes only to steal and kill and destroy; I came that they may have life, and have it abundantly." So God uses these fallen creatures that have been confined to "pits of nether gloom" (2 Peter 2:4) to harm those humans who hate God and refuse to repent. For those who reject God, the source of the lifestyle they have chosen becomes the means for their extensive pain, suffering, and destruction. In 1 Kings 22:1–23 the King of Israel and the King of Judah wanted the Word of God concerning doing battle with Syria, but only if it was consistent with their desires. They rejected the truth from the Prophet Micah. So God sent them a "lying spirit," which they believed, and they lost the battle. It is called divine justice! Galatians 6:7 "Do not be deceived; God is not mocked, for whatever a man sows, that he will also reap."

Revelation 9:13-19:

> Then the sixth angel blew his trumpet, and I heard a voice from the four horns of the golden altar before God, (14) saying to the sixth angel who had the trumpet, "Release the four angels who are bound at the great river Euphrates." (15) So the four angels were released, who had been held ready for the hour, the day, and month, the year, to kill a third of mankind. (16) The number of the troops of cavalry was twice ten thousand times ten thousand; I heard their number. (17) And this was how I saw the horses in my vision: the riders wore breastplates the color of fire and of sapphire and of sulphur, and the heads of the horses were like lions' heads, and fire and smoke and sulphur issued from their mouths. (18) By these three plagues *a third of mankind was killed*, by the fire and smoke and sulphur issuing from their mouths. (19) For the power of the horses is in their mouths and in their tails; their tails are like serpents, with heads, and by means of them they wound. (italics added)

The army used for this destruction is angelic, neither human nor demonic. They are holy. There are four angels in charge of two hundred million troops. Each will cover one-fourth of the earth, killing a total of one-third of the world's unrepentant population. They will not touch anyone belonging to Christ. This event parallels the release of the Jews from Egyptian bondage on the night of the Passover when an angel of God killed the firstborn son of every family that had not the sign of the blood on the doorposts and lintel of the house where they lived. This time, it is the seal of the Holy Spirit upon the life of the believer that spares the person from destruction. Joel 2:1–11 gives a picture of this event:

> Blow the trumpet in Zion sound the alarm on my holy mountain! Let all the inhabitants of the land tremble, for the day of the LORD is coming, it is near, (2) a day of darkness and gloom, a day of clouds and thick darkness! Like blackness there is spread upon the mountains a great and powerful people; their like has never been from of old, nor will be again after them through the years of all generations. (3) Fire devours before them, and behind them a flame burns. The land is like the garden of Eden before them, but after them a desolate wilderness, and nothing escapes them. (4) Their appearance is like the appearance of horses, and like war horses they run. (5) As with the rumbling of chariots, they leap on the tops of the mountain, like the crackling of a flame of fire devouring the stubble, like a powerful army drawn up for battle. (6) Before them peoples are in anguish, all faces grow pale. (7) Like warriors they charge, like soldiers they scale the wall. They march each on his way, they do not swerve from their paths. (8) They do not jostle one another, each marches in his path; they burst through the weapons and are not halted. (9) They leap upon the city, they run upon the walls; they climb up into the houses, they enter through the windows like a thief. (10) The earth quakes before them, the heavens tremble. The sun and the moon are darkened, and the stars withdraw their shining. (11) The LORD utters his voice before his army, for his host is exceedingly great; he that executes his word is powerful. For the day of the LORD is great and very terrible; who can endure it?

This is the second woe to mankind, and there is one more woe yet to follow.

Between the sixth and seventh trumpet sounding, there are seven more judgments that are to take place under the label of seven thunders.

Revelation 10:1–4:

> Then I saw another mighty angel coming down from heaven, wrapped in a cloud, with a rainbow over his head, and his face was like the sun, and his legs like pillars of fire. (2) He had a little scroll open in his hand. And he set his right foot on the sea, and his left foot on the land, (3) and called out with a loud voice, like a lion roaring; when he called out, the seven thunders sounded. (4) And when the seven thunders had sounded, I was about to write, but I heard a voice from heaven saying, "Seal up what the seven thunders have said, and do not write it down."

We are not told what form the judgments will take. But they will take place just before the rapture.

Revelation 10:5–7:

> And the angel whom I saw standing on sea and land lifted up his right hand to heaven (6) and swore by him who lives for ever and ever, who created heaven and what is in it, the earth and what is in it, and the sea and what is in it, that there should be no more delay, (7) *but that in the days of the trumpet call to be sounded by the seventh angel, the mystery of God*, as he announced to his servants the prophets, *should be fulfilled.*" (italics added)

What is the "mystery?" It is the completion of our redemption when God's people are caught up in the air to meet Jesus and receive new glorified bodies, leaving behind the sinful nature that was inherited through the fall of Adam with the continual plague of death, both spiritually and physically. It is the reward for those, who through faith in Christ have overcome the fallen world system of Lucifer in the power and glory of the Lord. For us, our redemption is complete, but God's redemption for the rest of the world still remains as part of his educational program for all creation. Revelation 10:8–11 states:

> Then the voice which I had heard from heaven spoke to me again, saying, "Go, take the scroll which is open in the hand of the angel who is standing on the sea and on the land." (9) So I went to the angel and told him to give me the little scroll; and he said to me, "Take it and eat; it will be bitter to your stomach, but sweet as honey in your mouth." (10) And I took the little scroll from the hand of the angel and ate it; it was sweet as honey in my mouth, but when I had eaten it my stomach was made bitter. (11) And I was told, "You must again prophecy about many peoples and nations and tongues and kings."

Before the seventh trumpet sounds, which is the rapture of the saints, we are given a view of what will take place during the last half of the Seventieth Week. The scroll contains the wrath of God that will be poured out upon the people who refuse to repent and be saved along with the events that God has pre-ordained. The final destruction of the wicked is sweet to taste but sorrowful to digest because of the loss of human life.

Revelation 11:1–3:

> Then I was given a measuring rod like a staff, and I was told: "Rise and measure the temple of God and the altar and those who worship there, (2) but do not measure the court outside the temple; leave that out, for it is given over to the nations, and they will trample over the holy city for forty-two months. (3) And I will grant my two witnesses power to prophesy for one thousand two hundred and sixty days, clothed in sackcloth."

To understand these verses, one must understand the issue of the temple. In the Garden of Eden, God walked with man in perfect harmony. There was no material temple. The Spirit of God dwelt in the heart of man from the breath of life that was breathed into man when he was created. When man sinned, he lost the Spirit of God. Man and God were separated, and man was required to sacrifice to gain God's favor, but close personal, intimate union was no longer possible. For the first 2,500 years, there was no temple established by God. Then, when God established the Mosaic Covenant with his people, the descendants of Abraham, he established a portable tabernacle.

The tabernacle was broken down into three parts. The first part was an open courtyard surrounded by a fence with a single gateway entrance. In the courtyard were a brazen altar and a brazen laver for sacrifices to be offered unto God. It was the place for ministry to be conducted between God and his people. There was also a tent of meeting that was set up in the courtyard. It consisted of two compartments: a holy place and the Holy of Holies. The designated priests ministered in the Holy place before God. The presence of God dwelt in the Holy of Holies upon the ark of the covenant, which was a box designed in a symbolic form that defined the person of God's forthcoming Son, Jesus. There was a veil separating the two compartments. The veil would remain for a period of 1,500 years when animal sacrifice would end with the offering of God's Son upon the cross. Then the Spirit of God would return to live in the hearts of men who would believe in Jesus and trust God with the control of their life through the work of the Holy Spirit.

The temple of Solomon was a replica of the tabernacle, only on a grander scale. The temple at the time of Herod's reign over Jerusalem, during the control of the Roman Empire when Jesus was born, was the last material temple that would ever be established by God. With the death and resurrection of Jesus, the heart of man was again the temple where God would dwell forever in those who would believe and trust in Jesus. Herod's temple was destroyed in AD 70. The temple that was revealed to Ezekiel the prophet (Ezekiel chapters 40–48) for the millennial reign of Jesus on earth is written in the Old Testament symbolic form and ritual language. It must be translated into the New Testament life. The tabernacle of Moses, in form and ritual, represented the ministry of Jesus during the time period between his first and second coming. The temple form given to Ezekiel presents the ministry of Jesus during his reign on earth for the final thousand years of this creation. The presentation of Ezekiel's temple is a symbolic picture of God's relationship with mankind. It is not in a material temple. Within the courtyards there is a portrayal of the different forms of ministries and functions that will exist during that thousand year period governing the people worldwide. The entire design reveals a picture of the kingdom of God ruling over the lives of men and women around the world. It is not a material structure to be built!

As for the courtyard of the temple in Revelation 11:1–4, being given over to the nations for forty-two months, it identifies the ministry outreach of the believers in Christ who are "a kingdom of priests" (Revelation 1:6), ministering the life of God to the people of this world under the New Covenant. Daniel 9:27: "... and for half of the week [forty-two months] he shall cause sacrifice and offering to cease." Jesus tells his disciples in Mark 16:15–16: "Go into all the world and preach the gospel to the whole creation. (16) He who believes and is baptized will be saved; but he who does not believe will be condemned." With the rapture of the saints, sacrifice and offering in the work of the ministry throughout the world will cease. Christians offer and sacrifice their lives to serve the Lord, and when they leave the earth, no one will be left to fulfill that obligation. The rapture takes place at the sound of the seventh trumpet of the seventh seal. Yet God will continue to confirm the New Covenant for the last forty-two months with supernatural signs and events to those who will believe after the fact of the rapture. But ministry outreach as we know it today will not be in effect because the world will be given over to the Antichrist for forty-two months, the last half of Daniel's Seventieth Week.

When John is told to, "Rise and measure the temple of God and the altar and those who worship there" (Revelation 11:1), the reference is to the saints and the hearts of the people in their service to God. When the saints are raptured, each person will stand before the judgment seat of Christ and be rewarded for their service to Jesus according to what he called them to do while on earth. Many will lose reward because they did not build upon the foundation of Christ through the leading of the Holy Spirit but simply built in the flesh without the direction of God (1 Corinthians 3:10–15). But, their salvation is intact.

The seventh trumpet sounds; it is the third woe to mankind.

Revelation 11:15–19:

> Then the seventh angel blew his trumpet, and there were loud voices in heaven, saying, "The kingdom of the world has become the kingdom of our Lord and of his Christ, and he shall reign for ever and ever." (16) And the twenty-four elders who sit on the thrones before God fell on their faces and worshiped God, (17) saying, "We give thanks to thee, Lord God Almighty, who art and who wast, that thou hast taken thy great power and begun to reign. (18) The nations raged, but thy wrath came, and the time for the dead to be judged, for rewarding thy servants, the prophets and saints, and those who fear thy name, both small and great, *and for destroying the destroyers of the earth*." (19) Then God's temple in heaven was opened, and the ark of his covenant was seen within his temple; and there were flashes of lightning, voices, peals of thunder, and earthquake, and heavy hail. (italics added)

All who believed God and walked with him, from the time of Adam to the sounding of the seventh trumpet, are now completely redeemed in body, soul, and spirit to God, forever and ever. Paul summed up the event in 1 Corinthians 15:51–53: "Lo! *I tell you a mystery.* We shall not all sleep, but we shall all be changed, (52) in a moment, in the twinkling of an eye, at the last trumpet. For the trumpet will sound, and the dead will be raised imperishable, and we shall be changed. (53) For this perishable nature must put on the imperishable, and this mortal nature must put on immortality." (italics added)

With the third "woe," every tribe of people around the world will lose loved ones that are family or friends that they depended upon as part of their social structure. Total confusion and anguish will be worldwide for those who are left behind. The "woe" is a blessing to God's saints, and wrath to unbelievers. Jesus tells us in Matthew 24:30: "... and they will see the Son of man coming on the clouds of heaven with power and great glory." For the unbeliever, Jesus will come like a thief, unexpected. For the believer, his coming will be expected. The event will not be a secret. It will be a visual event for the entire world to see as God continues to confirm the New Covenant in the blood of Christ to everyone.

In Revelation 11:18, it is made clear that the wrath of God will be upon the unbelievers of the world system. The unrepentant, spiritually dead are to be judged. With the rapture, the servants, prophets, and saints are to be rewarded. The last half of Daniel's Seventieth Week is the time for the destruction of those who are destroying the earth in evil conduct and redeeming those who now believe because of the rapture.

Immediately after the rapture of the saints, another view of God's dwelling in heaven takes place. This time, the ark of God's Mosaic Covenant will be seen in heaven (Revelation 11:19). It is the symbol of the Jew's Messiah that identifies Jesus as their Holy One, their redeemer. In Isaiah 66:7–9 the prophet explains the conversion of the nation of Israel in their acceptance of Jesus when God takes away the veil that has kept them from knowing their Messiah.

> Before she was in labor she gave birth; before her pain came upon her she was delivered of a son. (8) Who has heard such a thing? Who has seen such things? Shall a land be born in one day? Shall a nation be brought forth in one moment? For as soon as Zion was in labor she brought forth her sons. (9) Shall I bring to the birth and not cause to bring forth? says the LORD; shall I, who cause to bring forth, shut the womb? says your God.

When Jesus was born, the Jews were at peace under Roman domination, and they did not recognize Jesus as their Messiah. Some two thousand years later during the great tribulation (identified as birth pangs for the Jewish nation), 144,000 Jews will be saved at the beginning of Daniel's Seventieth Week, and then with the vision of their ark of the covenant at the rapture of the saints, spiritual awakening and salvation will take place for the rest of the nation of Israel. But for those saved after the rapture, they will have to flee for their lives and will be divinely protected for the forty-two months when Jerusalem will be taken over by the Antichrist (Revelation 11:2). With the rapture of the saints, the United States will no longer be a backup power for the support of Israel due to the loss of the Christian population. Isaiah 66:7–9 also refers to Israel being birthed as a nation on May 14, AD 1948. The spiritual rebirth takes place almost seventy years later.

**EVENT: The season for the rapture of the saints**
**TIME FRAME: Eternity Present—Creation 5993, Jewish 1 Kislev 5778, Western November 19, AD 2017**

Concerning the rapture of the saints, Jesus stated in Matthew 24:36, "But of that day and hour no one knows, not even the angels of heaven, nor the Son, but the Father only." While the day and hour will not be known until the event takes place, I believe we can predict the year and the season now that we know the date that Israel returned to their land as a nation, being May 14, AD 1948. There is a prophecy in Isaiah 23:14–18 that states:

> Wail, you ships of Tarshish; your fortress is destroyed! (15) At that time Tyre will be forgotten for seventy years, the span of a king's life. But at the end of these seventy years, it will happen to Tyre as in the song of the prostitute: (16) "Take up a harp, walk through the city, O prostitute forgotten; play the harp well,

sing many a song, so that you will be remembered." (17) At the end of seventy years, the LORD will deal with Tyre. She will return to her hire as a prostitute and will ply her trade with all the kingdoms on the face of the earth. Yet her profit and her earnings will be set apart for the LORD; they will not be stored up or hoarded. (18) Her profits will go to those who live before the LORD, for abundant food and fine clothes.

In Ezekiel 28:1–10, God addresses the Prince (ruler) of Tyre. Then in verses 28:11–19, he addresses the King of Tyre, who is Lucifer, and the issue is his original fall, which was pride. Tyre was in the service of the Devil.

There are two separate time periods of seventy years incorporated into Isaiah's prophecy. On the first reading, it would appear they were one of the same. But when God repeats himself concerning the same issue, within a few verses, there is a reason for it, and we must take a close look at why it was done. An example of this is in Genesis 2:8 and 2:15. God placed Adam in the Garden of Eden twice because there were two gardens, a material garden and a spiritual garden. To see and understand the difference in Isaiah's prophecy, it is important to know the history and relevance that Tyre has to Israel.

Tyre was a thriving, wealthy Phoenician seaport before the Jews ever came into the Promised Land. It is located just above the northwest corner of the territory given to the Jews by God. It was known for its famous Temple of Melkart.

# Let There Be Light

Today it is the fourth largest city in Lebanon. During the reign of David and Solomon, the King of Tyre (Hiram) was on friendly terms with them and supplied materials for the building of David's house and for Solomon's Temple (1 Kings 5:1 and 9:11). The time period was around 1015 BC. Some 427 years later in 588 BC, the Lord had the Babylonian Empire overthrow Jerusalem due to the Jew's idolatry (prostitution) and rebellion. At that time Tyre was an enemy to the Jews.

Ezekiel 26:2–4:

> Mortal, because Tyre said concerning Jerusalem, "Aha, broken is the gateway of the peoples; it has swung open to me; I shall be replenished, now that it is wasted." (3) Therefore, thus says the Lord GOD: "See, I am against you, O Tyre! I will hurl many nations against you, as the sea hurls its waves. (4) They shall destroy the walls of Tyre and break down its towers. I will scrape its soil from it and make it a bare rock."

Tyre went into Jerusalem after the Babylonian Empire sacked the city in AD 588. Tyre took what was left. Then God pronounced judgment upon them. In 573 BC, Tyre was overthrown by the Babylonian Empire. While the judgment of seventy years ended in 503 BC, Tyre became a "prostitute" to other nations. After the conquest of the Babylonian Empire by the Media-Persian Empire, they took over Tyre. In 332 BC, Alexander the Great conquered the city. After that, it became part of the Roman Empire, then the Byzantine Empire. Later, Christian crusaders occupied it. The Muslims captured it in AD 1291 and have held it to this day.

The first seventy year prophesy of Isaiah was fulfilled. Due to the domination of foreign countries over Tyre and Israel, along with the dispersion of the Jews in AD 70, the second seventy-year prophecy could not be fulfilled. Tyre was overthrown because of her vile treatment toward the Jews during the reign of the Babylonian empire. When the Jews returned again to Jerusalem on May 14, AD 1948, as a nation, hatred was ignited by the Muslims who occupied Tyre due to the Palestinians displacement. This date begins *the second seventy years prophesy* of Isaiah concerning Tyre. These seventy years are a countdown of hatred and ill treatment toward the Jews, and before the end of the prophecy, Tyre will take part with the nations that will overthrow Jerusalem. Tyre is again being controlled by Lucifer. At the end of the period of the prophecy, while playing the "prostitute" (worship of a false god; this time it's Allah instead of Melkart), they will again go and sack Jerusalem. But this cannot happen until after the rapture of the church. Tyre will be part of the Antichrist's kingdoms. Tyre will profit once again from the overthrow the Jews. It is right after this event that the Lord will deal with Tyre. God's judgment, the seven bowls of wrath, will come upon her and the other nations along with their destruction at Armageddon.

Concerning Tyre, "... her profit and her earnings will be set apart for the LORD; they will not be stored up or hoarded. Her profits will go to those who live before the LORD, for abundant food and fine clothes" (Isaiah 23:18). Jerusalem is going to receive the wealth of the nations that are slaughtered at Armageddon. This is the only time that this prophecy could be fulfilled in the lives of the people of Tyre. From the end of the first seventy years, concerning Isaiah's prophecy, to the beginning of the second seventy years (AD 1948), there are 2,450 years. Because of the governing conditions controlling Tyre and Jerusalem, the second seventy year prophecy could not begin until the return of the Jews in AD 1948. It will end on the seventieth Jewish anniversary on May 14, AD 2018, with Jerusalem under the control of Islam. Before the overthrow of Jerusalem beings, the rapture of the saints will take place. Because of the rapture, total control will be given to the Antichrist over all ten Islamic nations on November 8, AD 2017. Then God will allow the overthrow of Jerusalem to begin for the last time on November 19, AD 2017. This date, noon on November 19, AD 2017, marks the beginning of the last half of Daniel's Seventieth Week. It is only after the Battle of Armageddon on July 4, AD 2021, that the Jews will have the spoils of war and the servitude of the nations as they "live before the Lord." This gives us clarity for the season for the rapture, but not the day or the hour.

## SUMMARY

If I have correctly divided the Word of God by the Spirit of God, here is a simple list of the sequence of events concerning Daniel's Seventieth Week. First, the sixth seal opens on May 14, AD 2014, at 10:16 UTC. The sun will turn black as sackcloth, and the moon will turn the color of blood. Darkness will envelope the entire earth for seven days. On the eighth day, which will be May 21, AD 2014, the sky will vanish like a scroll that is rolled up. This day in Revelation 6:14 marks the beginning of Daniel's Seventieth Week when the sky rolls back and the entire world will look into the throne room of God. It is the beginning of God confirming the New Covenant with supernatural signs and judgments upon the unrepentant population of the entire world for seven years through the glory of his son, Jesus!

Second, the seventh seal will open shortly after the sixth seal. There are seven trumpet judgments that attend the seventh seal and will take place during the first three and a half years of Daniel's Seventieth Week. The first four trumpet judgments will damage the earth and its productivity. The last three trumpet judgments will harm and destroy unrepentant people that will not commit their lives to Jesus. The seventh trumpet of the seventh seal is the rapture of the saints. On November 8, AD 2017, the Antichrist will be given total authority over ten Islamic nations. While the Bible spells out the exact number of days to the crowning of the Antichrist, it does not tell us if the rapture occurs before or after that event. My personal conclusion is that the rapture takes place within days or weeks before the Antichrist is crowned. The reason he is given total control is due to the chaos that is created worldwide because of the rapture.

Third, noon on November 19, AD 2017, marks the exact middle of Daniel's Seventieth Week. Revelation 11:2 clearly states that the courtyard outside of the temple "is given over to the nations, and they will trample over the holy city for forty-two months." It should be noted here that the reference to the temple is not the physical building. It is the Christian population that has become the temple of the living God since the death and resurrection of Jesus. The heart of man is where God wants to dwell. It is the holy place. The courtyard is a symbol of where the ministry of the priests to the people was carried out under the Mosaic Covenant. Today, Christians are the priests on earth under the New covenant (Revelation 5:9–10). We were commanded to spread the gospel of Christ as his witnesses, beginning with Jerusalem, Judea, Samaria, and to the ends of the earth (Acts 1:8). The trampling over the holy city of Israel will begin on that day and will continue in the hands of Islam until Jesus returns on May 20, AD 2021, and retakes Jerusalem. That is the last day of Daniel's Seventieth Week. November 19, AD 2017, marks the beginning of the overthrow. It is sixty-nine years, six months, and seven days to that day when Tyre is part of the nations that overthrow Jerusalem. That places it at the end of seventy years in exact accord with the Isaiah 23:17 prophecy concerning Tyre. This prophecy locks together all of the other specific time-oriented prophecies into a clear, cohesive, timeline picture concerning God's plan for Israel and our creation.

## POINTS TO REMEMBER

1. With the terrifying event of the opening of the sixth seal, and clarity that Jesus is the Messiah, 144,000. Jews get saved. Millions of Christians around the world repent of their sins and put Jesus first in their life instead of second, third, or fourth.

2. It is clearly defined that these Jews and Christians have come out of the great tribulation that is in process. They have not been raptured; they are still on the earth. Finding peace and security in Christ, they have been delivered from the chaos of the world system. They have come out of the great tribulation.

3. The opening of the seventh seal is the first event that takes place after the beginning of Daniel's Seventieth Week. There is silence in heaven for a half-hour before the beginning of the seven trumpet judgments.

4. Seven trumpets are given to seven angels. At the sound of each trumpet, a supernatural judgment of God will come upon the earth against the unrepentant population, not against

the Christians. We are protected. It is a very serious time period in separating the sheep from the goats, those who will go in the rapture.

5. The first four trumpet judgments will damage the earth, creating a major impact on the supply of food, and the flow of commerce worldwide. There will be a poisoning of the water supply and a reduction of light in the sun, moon, and stars.

6. The last three trumpet judgments will fall upon the people. First, there will be physical affliction. Second, there will be the death of one-third of the world's population. Third, there will be the removal of the Christian population in the rapture.

7. In between the sixth and seventh trumpet judgments, there will come seven thunders which are events that will take place. But we are not enlightened with the details. That makes fourteen major events that will take place during the first half of Daniel's Seventieth Week.

8. The Scroll that was covered with seven seals is now given to John the Apostle to eat. That means he will read and digest the contents, and then tell us the events that will take place during the last half of Daniel's Seventieth Week.

# CHAPTER 19

# THE LAST HALF OF THE SEVENTIETH WEEK AND ARMAGEDDON

**EVENT:** An overview of events during the last half of Daniel's Seventieth Week and the Battle of Armageddon forty-five days later

**TIME FRAME:** From Eternity Present—Creation 5993, Jewish 1 Kislev 5778, Western November 19, AD 2017 to Eternity Present—Creation 5997, Jewish 24 Tammuz 5781, Western July 4, AD 2021

**INTRODUCTION NARRATIVE:** *Because of the rapture and the sign given to the Jews, confirming that Jesus is their Messiah, the nation will convert to Christianity. Part of the*

*population will flee the country and be divinely protected during the last forty-two months of Daniel's Seventieth Week. At that time, the Devil and his angels will all be thrown down from heaven and confined to the earth. At the beginning of the last forty-two months, Moses (?) and Elijah will return to Jerusalem to bear witness to Jesus and exercise power and authority over those who would kill them. Jerusalem will be overthrown by Islam on November 19, AD 2017. Shortly thereafter, a False Prophet will arise in Babylon, the capitol city of the Islamic ten nations, performing great signs in support of the Antichrist. Islam will dominate the world for forty-two months but will suffer the judgments of God during that time with seven bowls of wrath poured upon them. During this forty-two month period, God will harvest more souls for his kingdom.*

From the beginning of Revelation 12:1 through 15:1–4, we are presented with the overviews of events taking place that enlighten us with the issues of Daniel's Seventieth Week. The symbolic language of the Old Testament is used and must be interpreted to understand the events. The brackets define the terms and issues that need to be translated.

## Revelation 12:1–12:

And a great portent appeared in heaven, a woman [Israel] clothed with the sun [the light of God], with the moon under her feet [the governing body of light reflected from the Son to bring light into darkness during the night around the world], and on her head a crown of twelve stars [the twelve tribes of Israel]; (2) she was with child [Jesus] and she cried out in her pangs of birth [great tribulation], in anguish for delivery [from the tribulation]. (3) And another portent appeared in heaven; behold, a great red dragon [the Devil], with seven heads [seven empires] and ten horns [ten powers],[42] and seven diadems [crowns of authority] upon his heads. (4) His tail swept down a third of the stars of heaven [angels], and cast them to the earth [the rebellion of Lucifer]. And the dragon [the Devil] stood before the woman [Israel] who was about to bear a child [give birth as a nation to faith in Jesus], that he might devour her child [destroy faith in Jesus] when she brought it [faith] forth; (5) she brought forth a male child [Jesus], one who is to rule all the nations with a rod of iron, but her child was caught up to God and to his throne [after his death, resurrection, and ascension some 1,991 years prior], (6) the woman [Israel] fled into the wilderness [before the last captivity of Jerusalem], where she has a place prepared by God, in which to be nourished for one thousand two hundred and sixty days [the last half of Daniel's Seventieth Week].

(7) Now war arose in heaven, *Michael and his angels fighting against the dragon; and the dragon and his angels fought,* (8) *but they were defeated and there was no long any place for them in heaven.* (9) And the great dragon was thrown down, that ancient serpent, who is called the Devil and Satan, *the deceiver of the whole world*—he was thrown down to the earth, and his angels were thrown down with him. (10) And I heard a loud voice in heaven, saying, "Now the salvation and the power and the kingdom of our God and the authority of his Christ have come, for the accuser of our brethren has been thrown down, who accuses them day and night before our God. (11) And they have conquered him by the blood of the Lamb [the life of Jesus] and by the word of their testimony, for they loved not their lives even unto death. (12) Rejoice then, O heaven and you that dwell therein [all of the saints caught up

in the rapture]! But woe to you, O earth and sea, for the Devil has come down to you in great wrath, because he knows that his time is short!" (italics added)

Since the creation of this heaven and earth, the Devil has had the freedom to roam through the heavens and the earth. Now, after the rapture, he is confined to the surface of the earth. God is in complete control and is using the Devil as the trash collector of this world to gather those who refuse to believe the truth for the day of God's wrath.

Revelation 12:13–13:18:

> And when the dragon [the Devil] saw that he had been thrown down to the earth, he pursued the woman [Israel] who had borne the male child [accepted Jesus as their Messiah]. (14) But the woman was given the two wings of the great eagle [an airlift] that she might fly from the serpent into the wilderness, to the place where she is to be nourished for a time, and times, and half a time [three and a half years, the last half of the Seventieth Week]. (15) The serpent [the Devil] poured water like a river out of his mouth after the woman, to sweep her away with the flood [a campaign of anti-Semitism along with troops to destroy her]. (16) But the earth came to the help of the woman, and the earth opened its mouth and swallowed the river which the dragon had poured from his mouth [as the red Sea destroyed the troops that pursued Israel when God delivered them from Egypt, now the earth will swallow up the troops of the Antichrist]. (17) Then the dragon was angry with the woman [Israel], and went off to make war on the rest of her offspring, on those who keep the commandments of God and bear testimony to Jesus. And he [the Devil] stood on the sand of the sea [the borderline of the sea of humanity and its movement toward worldwide domination of the earth].
> 
> (13:1) And I saw a beast rising out of the sea, with ten horns and seven heads, with ten diadems upon its horns [the final form of the idolatress people under the control of the

Devil in the religious system of Islam under a confederacy of ten Islamic nations] and a blasphemous name upon its heads [idolatry]. (2) And the beast that I saw was like a leopard [a functioning body paralleling that of Alexander the Great in the conquests of the Grecian Empire], its feet were like a bear's [it takes the territorial stance of the Media-Persian Empire from which the ten Islamic nations come from], and its mouth was like a lion's mouth [the capitol city of the empire will be the reconstructed city of Babylon in Iraq]. And to it the dragon [the Devil] gave his power and his throne and great authority. (3) One of its heads [the seventh head] seemed to have a mortal wound [from the Word of God, the sword, by the rapture of the church clearly establishing Jesus as the Son of God, the Messiah], but its mortal wound was healed [through lies and deception to all who rejected the light of God and were not taken in the rapture and now refuse to repent of their sins], and the whole earth followed the beast [the Devil working through the Antichrist in a false religion known as Islam] with wonder. (4) Men worshiped the dragon [the Devil], for he had given his authority to the beast [the Antichrist leading Islam], and they worshiped the beast, saying, "Who is like the beast, and who can fight against it?"

(5) And the beast was given a mouth uttering haughty and blasphemous words, and it was allowed to exercise authority for forty-two months [the last half of Daniel's Seventieth Week]; (6) it opened its mouth to utter blasphemies against God, blaspheming his name and his dwelling, that is, those who dwell in heaven [who were redeemed by God in the rapture]. (7) Also it was allowed to make war on the saints and to conquer them [those who came to faith in Christ after the rapture will not have any kind of a unified body to set up an opposition force, and many will die as martyrs for their faith]. And authority was given it over every tribe and people and tongue and nation, (8) and all who dwell on earth will worship it, everyone whose name has not been written before the foundation of the world in the book of life of the Lamb that was slain.[43] (9) If anyone has an ear, let him hear: (10) If anyone is to be taken captive, to captivity he goes; if anyone slays with the sword, with the sword must he be slain. Here is a call for the endurance and faith of the saints.

## Let There Be Light

(11) Then I saw another beast which rose out of the earth; it had two horns like a lamb and it spoke like a dragon (12) It exercises all the authority of the first beast [the Antichrist] in its presence, and makes the earth and its inhabitants worship the first beast, whose mortal wound was healed [through deception]. (13) It works great signs, even making fire come down from heaven to earth in the sight of men; (14) and by the signs which it is allowed to work in the presence of the beast, it deceives those who dwell on earth, bidding them make an image for the beast which was wounded by the sword [the Word of God revealing the true God at the rapture and causing many to convert to faith in Christ] and yet lived [continue in evil domination under Islamic rule]; (15) and it was allowed to give breath to the image of the beast so that the image of the beast should even speak, and to cause those who would not worship the image of the beast to be slain. (16) Also it causes all, both small and great, both rich and poor, both free and slave, to be marked on the right hand or the forehead, (17) so that no one can buy or sell unless he has the mark, that is, the name of the beast [the name of the beast will be Madhi, meaning "the guided one"] or the number of its name. (18) This calls for wisdom: let him who has understanding reckon the number of the beast, for it is a human number, its number is six hundred and sixty six [*destruction* through *idolatry* by *man*].

While the covering name of the Antichrist, Madhi, can be established, and what his purpose is, destruction through idolatry by man, his real birth name is not given to us. We will have to discern that when he makes his appearance from the facts that we know. The beast that rises from the earth is another individual who carries with him two powers (horns). The two powers consist of a prophet and priest. The lamb depicts the kind of relationship Christ has with God the Father. Only this individual comes from the earth, not heaven. His position will be to support the Antichrist as "God" and carry out his will. This prophet and priest will speak the words of the dragon (the Devil). As Jesus glorified his Father and did mighty works through the Holy Spirit, the earth will experience a counterfeit system. This False Prophet and priest will glorify the Antichrist as God. The Devil will do the miraculous behind the scenes, even making fire come down from heaven to earth. We can label this the unholy trinity. Deception is the foundation of this structure. Those who reject the truth will embrace the Devil through his signs and wonders.

The image of the beast will be a computerized system designed to carry out the will of the Antichrist in governing all the people that support his authority. The mark of the beast, on the hand or forehead is a sign of commitment to the Antichrist and his government. It will most likely be a computer chip inserted into the hand or forehead. The technologies for the system already exist and are being used. While we use this advanced technology today, it does not constitute committing your life to the worship of the Antichrist. But when the Antichrist takes control, after the rapture, those who use it in compliance to him will be in bondage to the Devil and marked for the judgment of God. Computerized control of commerce, including satellite tracking of every individual, will enable the Antichrist to keep the people under his control. Without the mark of the beast, no one can buy or sell. It should be noted here that from the seven trumpet judgments, the world population will have been reduced to about two billion people.

At the beginning of Revelation 14, we are taken to heaven after the rapture and see the issue of the 144,000 Jews that were saved and taken with the saints in the rapture.

Revelation 14:1–5:

> Then I looked, and lo, on Mount Zion [the government of God in heaven] stood the Lamb, and with him a hundred and forty-four thousand who had his name and his Father's name written on their foreheads. (2) And I heard a voice from the heaven like the sound of many waters and like the sound of loud thunder; the voice I heard was like the sound of harpers playing on their harps, (3) and they sing a new song before the throne and before the four living creatures and before the elders. No one could learn that song [a special calling upon their lives] except the hundred and forty-four thousand who had been redeemed from the earth [taken in the rapture and given their new glorified bodies without a sinful nature]. (4) It is these who have not defiled themselves with women, for they are chaste [the defiling of Adam was placing his wife's desires in sin above the Word of the Lord ]; it is these who follow the Lamb wherever he goes; *these have been redeemed from mankind* as first fruits for God and the Lamb [in the plan of redemption for the nation of Jews], (5) and in their mouth no lie was found, for they are spotless [totally cleansed by the blood of Christ]." (italics added)

In Revelation 14:6–13, we are presented with three angels flying through the air around the earth (midheaven). The first angel is proclaiming the gospel to those on earth to repent and fear God because it is judgment time for the unrepentant. The second angel proclaims the fall of Babylon the Great in a feminine context in verse eight: "Another angel, a second, followed, saying, 'Fallen, fallen is Babylon the Great, *she who made all nations drink* [partake of] *the wine* [life] *of her impure passion* [just like Eve]'" (italics added). The forthcoming Babylon will be a city in Iraq that is doomed for destruction. It is also a symbol of a false religion and idolatry worldwide that is doomed for destruction. The city will be in the same area where Nimrod built a city called Babel in Genesis 11. It was a new rebellion against God after the flood. The construction of the Tower of Babel was the first form of religion after the flood in the plains of Shinar. That is where Iraq is today and where the old city of Babylon was built, and then decayed after the conquest of the Media-Persian Empire. The territory of Iraq has been a center for false religion and idolatry down through the ages. A third angel follows with the warning of eternal damnation for anyone who worships the beast and takes his mark. With the church gone, God is still confirming his covenant to the entire world and giving warnings about his wrath that is coming upon the world.

In Revelation 14:14–16 we are given another overview of the last half of Daniel's Seventieth Week:

> Then I looked, and lo, a white cloud, and seated on the cloud one like a son of man, with a golden crown on his head, and a sharp sickle in his hand. (15) And another angel came out of the temple, calling with a loud voice to him who sat upon the cloud, "Put in your sickle, and reap, for the hour to reap has come, for the harvest of the earth is fully ripe." (16) So he who sat upon the cloud swung his sickle on the earth, and the earth was reaped.

This is the harvest of souls for eternal life due to God's manifestation of supernatural powers and proclamations of warning straight from heaven. This same overview continues.

Revelation 14:17–20:

> And another angel came out of the temple in heaven, and he too had a sharp sickle. (18) Then another angel came out from the altar, the angel who has power over fire, and he called with a loud voice to him who had the sharp sickle, "Put in your sickle, and gather the clusters of the vine of the earth, for its grapes are ripe." (19) So the angel swung his sickle on the earth and gathered the vintage of the earth, and threw it into the great wine press of the wrath of God; (20) and the wine press was trodden outside the city, and blood flowed from the wine press, as high as a horse's bridle, for one thousand six-hundred stadia [about two hundred miles]."

This is the Battle of Armageddon. They are harvested for eternal damnation.

In Revelation 15:1-4, we are presented with another overview:

> Then I saw another portent in heaven, great and wonderful, seven angels with seven plagues, which are the last, for with them the wrath of God is ended. (2) And I saw what appeared to be a sea of glass mingled with fire, and those who had conquered the beast and its image and the number of its name, standing beside the sea of glass with harps of God in their hands. (3) And they sing the song of Moses, the servant of God, and the song of the Lamb, saying, "Great and wonderful are thy deeds, O Lord God the Almighty! Just and true are thy ways, O King of the ages! (4) Who shall not fear and glorify they name, O Lord? For thou alone art holy. All nations shall come and worship thee, for thy judgments have been revealed."

The seven plagues established the time period of the event, being the last half to the Seventieth Week. Then the picture presents those who have accepted Christ and were martyred for rejecting the Antichrist as God and refusing the mark of the beast and the destructive lifestyle of idolatry. They are in heaven singing a victory song for being delivered out of bondage. They have received their new glorified bodies and will return to the earth with all of the saints taken in the rapture who return with Jesus as his bride to rule and reign with him for a thousand years (Revelation 20:4).

## POINTS TO REMEMBER

1. The last half of Daniel's Seventieth Week begins on November 19, AD 2017, with the Antichrist coming against Israel to overthrow Jerusalem.

2. The Devil and his angels are thrown out of heaven and are confined to the earth.

3. At the time of the rapture, the Jews as a nation will be given the revelation that Jesus is their Messiah, and they will commit their lives to Christ. But it is too late to go in the rapture.

4. Part of the Jewish nation will flee from their country and be divinely protected in the wilderness by God until the return of Jesus.

5. A False Prophet will arise in support of the Antichrist and will perform miraculous signs by the Devil. He will set up an image of the Antichrist that can speak. Everyone who submits to the Antichrist will be marked on the hand or the

forehead. No one can buy or sell without the mark of the beast.

6. God will send three angels to fly around the world and proclaim the gospel of salvation; warn of the forthcoming destruction of Babylon and eternal damnation for those who do not repent.

7. There will be another harvest of souls unto salvation after the rapture. The rest of the people who refuse to repent will become a harvest unto eternal damnation.

# CHAPTER 20

# THE SEVEN BOWLS OF WRATH

**EVENT:** The seven bowls of God's wrath that will be poured upon the earth[44]

**TIME FRAME:** From Eternity Present—Creation 5993, Jewish 1 Kislev 5778, Western November 19, AD 2017 to Creation 5997, Jewish 19 Iyyar 5778, Western May 1, AD 2021

**INTRODUCTION NARRATIVE:** *There are seven bowls of wrath to be poured out upon the Antichrist's government over the world. This will take place during the last forty-two months of Daniel's Seventieth Week. The last bowl will be poured out on May 1, AD 2021. The purpose is to bring* repentance to those who are to be saved and destruction for those who will not repent. During this period, Christians will be protected from God's wrath, but many will be martyred for their faith. Elijah and Moses (?) will be on the earth in Jerusalem to give witness for the Lord and render judgments as they desire. The last bowl of wrath will destroy the capitol city of the Antichrist's kingdom, Babylon, and other cities around the world. Three foul spirits will go abroad and prepare the way for the Battle of Armageddon.

In Revelation 15:5–8, we go from the overview to the beginning of a sequential order of the bowls of wrath judgment that will take place:

> After this I looked, and the temple of the tent of witness in heaven was opened, (6) and out of the temple came the seven angels with the seven plagues, robed in pure bright linen, and their breasts girded with golden girdles. (7) And one of the four living creatures gave the seven angels seven golden bowls full of the wrath of God who lives for ever and ever; (8) and the temple was filled with smoke from the glory of God and from his power, and no one could enter the temple until the seven plagues of the seven angels were ended.

With the first bowl of wrath, pain and suffering are poured upon the rebellious in Revelation 16:2: "So the first angel went and poured his bowl on the earth, and foul and evil sores came upon the men who bore the mark of the beast and worshiped its image." Once again, God's wrath will not come upon the repentant believer in Christ during this time period.

The second bowl of wrath brings about an ecological disaster in Revelation 16:3: "The second angel poured his bowl into the sea, and it became like the blood of a dead man, and every living thing died that was in the sea." The food supply from the sea comes to an end.

With the third bowl of wrath, another ecological disaster takes place in Revelation 16:4–7:

> The third angel poured his bowl into the rivers and the fountains of water, and they became blood. (5) And I heard the angel of water say, "Just art thou in these thy judgments, thou who art and wast, O Holy One. (6) For men have shed the blood of saints and prophets, and thou hast given them blood to drink. It is their due!" (7) And I heard the altar cry, "Yea, Lord God the Almighty, true and just are thy judgments!"

While food and water will become a major problem, God will see to it that his people are taken care of just as God did with the Jews in their transition into the Promised Land.

The fourth bowl of wrath brings intensified heat as revealed in Revelation 16:8–9: "The fourth angel poured his bowl on the sun, and it was allowed to scorch men with fire; (9) men were scorched by the fierce heat, and they cursed the name of God who had power over these plagues, and they did not repent and give him glory." While the ungodly suffer, they are very much aware of who is causing the problems for them, yet there is no repentance. The godly are protected according to Revelation 7:16–17: "They shall hunger no more, neither thirst any more; the sun shall not strike them, nor any scorching heat. (17) For the Lamb in the midst of the throne will be their shepherd, and he will guide them to springs of living water; and God will wipe away every tear from their eyes."

The fifth bowl of wrath turns the evil kingdom into darkness in Revelation 16:10–11: "The fifth angel poured his bowl on the throne of the beast, and its kingdom was in darkness; men gnawed their tongues in anguish (11) and cursed the God of heaven for their pain and sores, and did not repent of their deeds." Turning the kingdom into darkness also took place during the Egyptian exodus by the Jews. But the Jews remained in the light.

With the sixth bowl of wrath, a main water supply to Syria and Iraq (Babylon) is cut off in Revelation 16:12–16:

> The sixth angel poured his bowl on the great river Euphrates, and its water was dried up, to prepare the way for the kings from the east. (13) And I saw, issuing from the mouth of the dragon [the Devil] and from the mouth of the beast [the Antichrist] and from the mouth of the false prophet, three foul spirits like frogs' (14) for they are demonic spirits, performing signs, who go abroad to the kings of the whole world, to assemble them

for battle on the great day of God the Almighty. (15) ("Lo, I am coming like a thief! Blessed is he who is awake, keeping his garments [coverings of righteousness by God] that he may not go naked and be seen exposed!") (16) And they assembled them at the place which is called in Hebrew Armageddon [the actual assembling takes place after Jesus returns].

All who participate in the Battle of Armageddon will die.

**EVENT: The seventh bowl of wrath is poured upon the earth from heaven**

**TIME FRAME: Eternity Present—Creation 5997, Jewish 19 Iyyar 5778, Western Saturday May 1, AD 2021**

The seventh bowl of wrath brings great destruction to cities and lives around the world in Revelation 16:17–20:

> The seventh angel poured his bowl into the air, and a loud voice came out of the temple, from the throne, saying, "It is done!" (18) And there were flashes of lightning, voices, peals of thunder, and a great earthquake such as had never been since men were on the earth, so great was that earthquake. (19) The great city [Jerusalem] was split into three parts, and the cities of the nations fell, and God remembered great Babylon, to make her drain the cup of the fury of his wrath. (20) And every island fled away and no mountains were to be found; and great hailstones, heavy as a hundredweight, dropped on men from heaven, till men cursed God for the plague of the hail, so fearful was that plague [the "islands" and "mountains" refer to governments].

In all of the seven bowls of wrath poured out upon the unrepentant population of the world, four of them are replications of the plagues that fell upon the Egyptians when God delivered the Jews from Egypt. The plagues were turning water to blood, boils upon men, hail and fire, and darkness as listed in Exodus chapters 7–9. The plagues were short in duration of time but caused long-term effects. In Revelation, all seven bowls of wrath come within a forty-two month period beginning when Jerusalem is overthrown after the rapture of the church. That will average one plague every six months. There is a clear-cut understanding of the people on earth that the plagues are supernatural judgments coming from God. Still, there is a hardness of heart maintained in those who have committed their lives to the Devil and his program. With the seventh bowl of wrath, Jerusalem is split into three parts and the city of Babylon is destroyed, and other cities around the world collapse. With the deceiving spirits going forth to the kings of the nation from the time of the sixth bowl of wrath, the stage is now set for the return of Christ and the gathering of the nations for the Battle of Armageddon to take place.

In Revelation 17:1–18, the sequence of events stops and we are given another overview of the issues of this time period of the last half of Daniel's Seventieth Week. The future city of Babylon in Iraq will be the ultimate "great harlot" of the corrupt evil life style.

Revelation 17:1–6:

> Then one of the seven angels who had the seven bowls came and said to me, "Come, I will show you the judgment of the great harlot who is seated upon many waters, (2) with whom the kings of the earth have committed fornication, and with the wine [life] of whose fornication the dwellers on earth have become drunk." (3) And he carried me away in the Spirit into a wilderness, and I saw a woman sitting on a scarlet beast which was full of blasphemous names, and it had seven heads and ten horns. (4) The woman was arrayed in purple and scarlet, and bedecked with gold and jewels and pearls, holding in her hand a golden cup full of abominations and the impurities of her fornication; (5) and on her forehead was written a name of mystery: "Babylon the great, mother of harlots and of earth's abominations." (6) And I saw the woman, drunk with the blood of the saints and the blood of the martyrs of Jesus.

The harlot is seated on many waters (peoples, nations, and tongues). The kings of the earth have embraced this system (spiritual fornication) to obtain what they want in violation of God's standards. The wine is a symbol of the life of the system. People become intoxicated with lust of every kind. The wilderness is not a fruit bearing environment. It is a wasteland of vanity. The woman (harlot) is seated (being carried) on a scarlet (glaring sin) beast (the Antichrist and his system). The blasphemous names relate to the open rebellion against God in the different forms of idolatry. The color purple is a symbol of royalty. The gold, jewels, and pearls symbolize wealth. The golden cup portrays a glorious lifestyle in sin. When all the symbols are together, it presents a picture of a highly esteemed, wealthy, sinful estate riding upon an evil system that is against God. It is the ultimate conduct in spiritual harlotry. So vile is this lifestyle that the mind is intoxicated by openly killing those who stand with God. The seven heads (Egypt, Assyria, Babylon, Media-Persian, Greece, Roman, and Islam) of the beast have all embraced this harlot. The definition of the harlotry is "giving one's talents and abilities to an unworthy cause." It is akin to idolatry, the worshiping of false gods. The two are united. The future city of Babylon in Iraq will be the ultimate "great harlot," also to be called "the great city."

In Revelation 17:7–14 there is a clear picture presented in symbolic form that reveals the details of the system that will be established:

> When I saw her I marveled greatly. (7) But the angel said to me, "Why marvel? I will tell you the mystery of the woman, and of the beast with seven heads and ten horns that the carries her. (8) The beast that you saw was, and is not, and is to ascend form the bottomless pit and go to perdition; and the dwellers on earth whose names have not been written in the book of life from the foundation of the world, will marvel to behold the beast, because it was and is not and is to come. (9) This calls for a mind with wisdom: the seven heads are seven mountains on which the woman is seated; (10) they are also seven kings,

five of whom have fallen, one is, the other has not yet come, and when he comes he must remain only a little while. (11) As for the beast that was and is not, it is an eighth but it belongs to the seven and it goes to perdition. (12) And the ten horns that you saw are ten kings who have not yet received royal power, but they are to receive authority as kings for one hour, together with the beast. (13) These are of one mind and give over their power and authority to the beast; (14) they will make war on the Lamb, and the Lamb will conquer them, for he is Lord of lords and King of kings, and those with him are called and chosen and faithful."

When John received the Book of Revelation from God, the Roman Empire was the ruling authority over the Jewish nation, God's people. The five heads or kings or mountains (governments) that were in power before the Roman Empire were the Egyptian, Assyrian, Babylonian, Grecian, and Media-Persian Empires. Rome was the sixth. The seventh will be a revised state of these empires. It will take the form of ten Islamic nations drawn into a confederacy from the territorial boundaries of the Media-Persian Empire during its reign. It will only be in existence for a short time under its first leadership. With the rise of the Antichrist, he will take over three of the ten nations (possibly in the form of a governing capacity without the use of force). While it is not stated in Scripture, I believe the three nations will be Iraq, Syria, and Lebanon. The capitol city for the confederacy will be Babylon. When the rapture takes place, all ten nations will vest their authority in the Antichrist, and he will be in full control. This becomes the eighth, but it belongs to the seven. When Jerusalem is overthrown after the rapture of the church, it will be a return of the Babylonian ruling power, which "was, and is not, and is to ascend from the bottomless pit and go to perdition." All seven have been ruled by the Devil, and this final ruling empire will go to perdition with the judgments of God and the return of Jesus. Islam is already at war with Christians and Jews. Radical Islam is the major cause of the wars and conflicts around the world today.

Revelation 17:15–18:

> And he said to me, "The waters that you saw, where the harlot is seated, are peoples and multitudes and nations and tongues. (16) And the ten horns that you saw, they and the beast will hate the harlot; they will make her desolate and naked, and devour her flesh and burn her up with fire, (17) for God has put it into their hearts to carry out his purpose by being one of mind and giving over their royal power to the beast [Antichrist], until the words of God shall be fulfilled. (18) And the woman that you saw is the great city [Babylon] which has dominion over the kings of the earth."

The United States has fought to establish a democracy in Iraq. Democracy allows great freedom for the people, but it requires strong moral values to maintain the system. When the moral values decline, repression, decay, and bondage become wide spread. The United States was formed from the Christian values of the Word of God by the Spirit of God. It is the foundation that has made our country the greatest nation in the world. But the democracy that will be formed in Iraq will not have the same value system, and the new city of Babylon as pictured in Revelation is an extremely decadent society in great wealth. Every foul spirit will dwell there. Even slave trading will be part of the system. When the Antichrist is given power after the rapture by the ten nations, strict Islamic rule under the Koran will be instituted. They will hate the harlotry and purge the system and place everyone into bondage of a unified religious order to control the people and the commerce.

The Devil wants complete control over the worldly system. While the holy people of God have departed, there will still be other nations and societies entrenched in false religious orders such as Hinduism and Buddhism that Islam will have to fight to gain control. His forty-two months of power will not be war free. Tribulation will be everywhere. But with the loss of about two-thirds of the world population from God's judgments and the rapture, plus worldwide chaos, the ten united Muslim nations will have a strong advantage over other nations as prophesied in Daniel 7:19, and they

"... stamped the residue with its feet" in reference to the "ten toes." This is the final thrust of what was called the Roman Empire. When Jesus returns to the earth, he will destroy the "ten toes" at the Battle of Armageddon along with the armies of the other nations that joined the Antichrist's kingdom.

In Revelation chapter 18, we have an overview of the reconstruction of the old city of Babylon that will become the capitol city for the ten Islamic nations for the last forty-two months of Daniel's Seventieth Week. We do not have a starting date for the reconstruction of Babylon. Saddam Hussein started the project, but it has a lot more work to be done to fulfill what is pictured in Revelation 18. However, we do have the destruction date. It will come with the seventh bowl of wrath that is poured upon the earth by God on May 1, AD 2021.

Revelation 18:1–3:

> After this I saw another angel coming down from heaven, having great authority; and the earth was made bright with his splendor. (2) And he called out with a mighty voice, "Fallen, fallen is Babylon the great! It has become a dwelling place of demons, a haunt of every foul spirit, a haunt of every foul and hateful bird; (3) for all nations have drunk the wine of her impure passion, and the kings of the earth have committed fornication with her, and the merchants of the earth have grown rich with the wealth of her wantonness."

Babylon embraces idolatry and harlotry. Idolatry is worshipping false gods, such as money, power, control, materialism, or any other item or person we place above God in substitution for a life controlled and nurtured by God. Harlotry is giving yourself over to an unworthy cause, such as the pleasures of the flesh in life without moral restraint in sex, food, material possessions, drugs, and alcohol. Idolatry and harlotry are intertwined and bring about very destructive behavior in human conduct. God has revealed it to us through almost six thousand years of our history!

Revelation 18:4–8:

> Then I heard another voice from heaven saying, *"Come out of her, my people, lest you take part in her sins, lest you share in her plagues*; (5) for her sins are heaped high as heaven, and God has remembered her iniquities. (6) Render to her as she herself has rendered, and repay her double for her deeds; mix a double draught for her in the cup she mixed. (7) As she glorified herself and played the wanton, so give her a like measure of torment and mourning. Since in her heart she says, 'A queen I sit, I am no widow, mourning I shall never see,' (8) so shall her plagues come in a single day, pestilence and mourning and famine, and she shall be burned with fire; for mighty is the Lord God who judges her." (italics added)

The angel that comes down from heaven calls out to the people in Babylon who have committed their lives to Christ after the rapture. They are to flee from the entire system of deception and wickedness. They are also informed of the judgment that is to come in a single day, which is the seventh bowl of wrath.

Revelation 18:9–20:

> And the kings of the earth, who committed fornication and were wanton with her, will weep and wail over her when they see the smoke of her burning; (10) they will stand far off, in fear of her torment, and say, "Alas! alas! thou great city, thou mighty city, Babylon! In one hour has thy judgment come." (11) And the merchants of the earth weep and mourn for her, since no one buys their cargo any more, (12) cargo of gold, silver, jewels and pearls, fine linen, purple, silk and scarlet, all kinds of scented wood, all articles of ivory, all articles of costly wood, bronze, iron, and marble, (13) cinnamon, spice incense, myrrh, frankincense, wine, oil, fine flour and wheat, cattle and sheep, horses and chariots, and slaves, that is, human souls. (14) "The fruit for which thy soul longed has gone from thee, and all thy dainties and thy splendor are lost to thee, never to be found again!" (15) The merchants of these wares, who gained wealth from her, will stand far off, in fear of her torment, weeping and mourning aloud, (16) "Alas, alas, for the great city that was clothed in fine line, in purple and scarlet, bedecked with gold, with jewels, and with pearls! (17) *In one hour all this wealth has been laid waste.*" And all shipmasters and seafaring men, sailors and all whose trade is on the sea, stood far off (18) and cried out as they saw the smoke of her burning, "What city was like the great city?" (19) And they threw dust on their heads, as they wept and mourned, crying out, "Alas, alas, for the great city where all who had ships at sea grew rich by her wealth! In one hour she has been laid waste. (20) Rejoice over her, O heaven, O saints and apostles and prophets, for God has given judgment for you against her!" (italics added)

The angel proclaims the destruction that will take place, and the effect upon the merchants of the earth that are supported by the trade that flows through the great city. It will cause the collapse of commerce worldwide!

Reverence 18:21–24:

> Then a mighty angel took up a stone like a great millstone and threw it into the sea, saying, "So shall Babylon the great city be thrown down with violence, and shall be found no more; (22) and the sound of harpers and minstrels, of flute players and trumpeters, shall be heard in thee no more; and a craftsman of any craft shall be found in thee no more; and the sound of the millstone shall be heard in thee no more; (23) and the light of a lamp shall shine in thee no more; and the voice of bridegroom and bride shall be heard in thee no more; for thy merchants were the great men of the earth, and all nations were deceived by thy sorcery. (24) And in her was found the blood of prophets and of saints, and of all who have been slain on earth."

With the destruction of the city of Babylon, commerce is destroyed. Babylon is a symbol of the work of the Devil throughout the world and for the martyrdom of all of the saints. At Armageddon, it will be finished.

Revelation 19:1–8 the Scripture picks up with another overview in a sequential order after the seventh bowl of wrath has been poured out:

> After this I heard what seemed to be the loud voice of a great multitude in heaven, crying, "Hallelujah! Salvation and glory and power belong to our God, (2) for his judgments are true and just; he has judged the great harlot who corrupted the earth with her fornication, and he has avenged on her the blood of his servants." (3) Once more they cried, "Hallelujah! The smoke from her goes up forever and ever." (4) And the twenty-four elders and the four living creatures fell down and worshiped God who is seated on the throne, saying, "Amen. Hallelujah!"

(5) And from the throne came a voice crying, "Praise our God, all you his servants, you who fear him, small and great." (6) Then I heard what seemed to be the voice of a great multitude, like the sound of many waters and like the sound of mighty thunderpeals, crying, "Hallelujah! For the Lord our God the Almighty reigns. (7) Let us rejoice and exult and give him the glory, *for the marriage of the Lamb has come, and his Bride has made herself ready;* (8) *it was granted her to be clothed with fine linen, bright and pure"—for the fine linen is the righteous deeds of the saints.* (italics added)

There is great rejoicing in heaven with the destruction of the evil system. The marriage of all of the saints that were resurrected and given new glorified bodies will now take place in heaven before Jesus returns to earth with his bride, to rule over the earth for a thousand years. Everyone taking their place in the bride of Christ will have a part to perform in the kingdom of God on planet earth. The details are attended too in heaven between the rapture and the second coming of Jesus. In heaven, the bride is bonded to the Lord forever. There is no divorce. The complete fullness of life, sought after on earth, now becomes a reality. This event is the fulfillment of Ephesians 5:27. Christ presents "*... the Church to himself in splendor, without spot or wrinkle, or any such thing, that she might be holy and without blemish*" (italics added).

Revelation 19:9–10:

And the angel said to me, "Write this: Blessed are those who are invited to the marriage supper of the Lamb." And he said to me, "These are true words of God." (10) Then I fell down at his feet to worship him, but he said to me, "You must not do that! I am a fellow servant with you and your brethren who hold the testimony of Jesus. Worship God. For the testimony of Jesus is the spirit of prophecy."

While the marriage takes place in heaven, the marriage supper takes place on earth. Those invited as guests are the people who have committed their lives to Christ after the fact of the rapture and are still alive after the Battle of Armageddon takes place. Those martyred during the period between the rapture and the return of Christ for their faith in Christ will be members of the bride (Revelation 20:4). They will rule with Christ on earth for one thousand years. The marriage supper is the great Feast of Tabernacles that will usher in the millennial rule of Jesus.

The two witnesses (believed to be Moses and Elijah) that God sends to Jerusalem at the beginning of the last half of Daniel's Seventieth Week for a period of 1,260 days are allowed to be killed by the Antichrist at the end of that time period (Revelation 11:3). Their bodies are left in the street for three and a half days while people celebrate their deaths. Then God speaks from heaven saying: "Come up hither!" They are resurrected in the sight of everyone, and they ascend into heaven. In that hour, a great earthquake hits Jerusalem and a tenth of the city falls. Seven thousand people die, and the rest of the people give glory to the God of heaven. I believe this is the same earthquake of the seventh bowl of wrath poured upon the earth which causes Jerusalem to be split into three parts (Revelation 11:4–13 and 16:17–19). By adding 1,260 days to the beginning of the last forty-two months of Daniel's Seventieth Week, being November 19, AD 2017, we have the date of May 1, AD 2021. From this date there are nineteen days left to the return of Jesus to the earth on May 20, AD 2021, which is the last day of Daniel's Seventieth Week. Lucifer and his angels know that they have very little time left on earth before God locks them up in hell. With the destruction of Babylon, they know the end is at hand and prepare for the Battle of Armageddon. Islam believes that Armageddon will give them the final victory.

## POINTS TO REMEMBER

1. There are seven supernatural bowls of wrath poured out from heaven upon the earth that destroy the ecology and the population. The purpose is to bring repentance into the lives of the people and destruction to the unrepentant.

2. During this time, Christians will be protected from God's wrath, but many will be martyred by the people who hate God.

3. The Christians who are martyred for their faith in God during the last forty-two months of Daniel's Seventieth Week will be joined with those who were taken in the rapture and become part of the bride of Christ.

4. The seventh bowl of wrath destroys cities and people all over the world. The "great city" of Babylon, the capitol of the Antichrist's system is totally destroyed.

5. At the beginning of the last half of Daniel's Seventieth Week, Moses (?) and Elijah are sent to Jerusalem to give witness to the true living God and exercise judgments upon the people for a period of 1,260 days. They will be divinely protected until three and a half days before the end, and then they will be killed. On the last day, they will be resurrected, and everyone will see them. Then they will ascend into heaven!

6. With the destruction of the Antichrist's system, preparation is made for the final battle at Armageddon. The Devil knows that the end of his rule has come, and this will be his last opportunity to exert his authority and power of deception on earth, in full force, against God.

## CHAPTER 21

# THE RETURN OF JESUS TO THE EARTH

**EVENT:** The return of Jesus to the earth

**TIME FRAME:** From Eternity Present—Creation 5997, Jewish 9 Sivan 5781, Western Thursday May 20, AD 2021 to Eternity Present—Creation 5998, Jewish 1 Tishri 5783, Western Monday September 26, AD 2022. The entrance into the millennial reign of Jesus beginning with the Feast of Trumpets

**INTRODUCTION NARRATIVE:** *Jesus will return to Jerusalem on the last day of Daniel's Seventieth Week and will take over Jerusalem. The Battle of Armageddon will take place forty-five days later on July 4, AD 2021. The*

enemy will be destroyed when Jesus speaks the Word! The Antichrist and the False Prophet will be thrown into the lake of fire. The Devil and all of the fallen angels will be locked up in the abyss for a thousand years. This day will mark the end of the great tribulation period.

Revelation 19:11–16:

> Then I saw heaven opened, and behold, a white horse! He who sat upon it is called Faithful and True, and in righteousness he judges and makes war. (12) His eyes are like a flame of fire, and on his head are many diadems; and he has a name inscribed which no one knows but himself. (13) He is clad in a robe dipped in blood, and the name by which he is called is The Word of God. (14) *And the armies of heaven, arrayed in fine linen, white, and pure, followed him on white horses.* (15) From his mouth issues a sharp sword with which to smite the nations, and he will rule them with a rod of iron; he will tread the wine press of the fury of the wrath of God the Almighty. (16) On his robe and on his thigh he has a name inscribed, King of kings and Lord of lords. (italics added)

Jesus is the rider on the white horse again. His robe was dipped in blood as the leader of the apocalyptic riders. "He judges and makes war." The sword (the Word of God) that issues from his mouth shall smite the nations. Now comes the treading of the wine press (Armageddon) for the grapes of wrath. Then Jesus will rule the nations with a rod of iron.

The standard accepted theology concerning the return of Jesus to the earth is that his bride comes with him for the Battle Armageddon. I personally believed this until some of the meticulous details caught my attention, which did not support what I believed. After researching the issue, I came up with some interesting facts that changed my position. It is not any great issue that will change the end result or outcome. It will only help to understand our position as the bride of Christ.

First, let us look at who is the bride of Christ. She is every human person, male and female, that committed their life to following the true living God through faith in accordance with the light given to them by God during the different educational time periods of God's enlightenment program, from Adam to the rapture. They did not fall away but remained faithful until their death or the rapture.

Second, let us look at our position with Christ. In accordance with Revelation 20:6 it states: "Blessed and holy is he who shares in the first resurrection! Over such the second death has no power, *but they shall be priests of God and of Christ, and they shall reign with him a thousand years*" (italics added). We will all be priests ministering to the people on earth in different capacities. Jesus took on human flesh and suffered and died. He personally experienced what we experience. Therein lies our bond and our salvation. Holy angels have watched what we have experienced. With our experience, we have great insight and understanding concerning the sinful nature of people. Due to this issue, we will be able to minister the life of God to all humans that go through the millennium reign with their sinful nature still in place, but they will not have the constant demonic attacks and control upon their lives.

Third, let us look at what we will be like. In accordance with Matthew 22:23-30, Jesus was confronted with a question from the Sadducees concerning a woman who was married seven times. The question was asked, "In the resurrection, therefore, to which of the seven will she be wife?" Jesus answered: "For in the resurrection they neither marry nor are given in marriage, *but are like angels in heaven*" (italics added). Holy angels are classified as messengers. In Hebrews 1:14 it states concerning angels: "Are they not all ministering spirits sent forth to serve, for the sake of those who are to obtain salvation?" The angels were created by God, not procreated as humans, and are not given in marriage. Throughout Scripture they have appeared to humans, like Daniel, and delivered messages. They can appear and disappear like Jesus did after his resurrection from death. They can travel through the three different dimensions of the heavens. In Revelation 12:7–8 there is physical combat that takes place between the holy angels and the fallen angels: "Now war arose in heaven, Michael and his angels fighting against the dragon; and the dragon and his angels fought, (8) but they were defeated and there was no longer any place for them in heaven." While we will be like angels in our resurrected bodies, we will not be angels! Jesus was never an angel. Jesus was, and is, the Word of God, and the Son of God who took on human flesh. When Jesus was resurrected from the grave he appeared to his apostles. In Luke 24:39, he states: "See my hand and my feet, that it is I myself; handle me, and see; *for a spirit has not flesh and bones as you see that I have*" (italics added). The Scripture does not tell us about the physical material makeup of angels. But when the two angels came to remove Lot from Sodom before God destroyed the city, the men of the city wanted to have sex with them.

We know from Scripture that the fallen angelic realm is labeled as: evil spirits, unclean spirits, and demons. Lucifer and all of those who followed him in rebellion against God experience spiritual death. That is separation from the divine life flow of God into their lives. Without that divine eternal, spiritual presence of God, the spirits of angels or humans will enter into moral decay. That moral decay will cause the physical body to malfunction. The compounding of the malfunction produces the death of the body. Because the soul of an angel or human is spirit, it is eternal in substance and will exist forever apart from the body. Thus, the fallen angels are all bodiless, unclean spirits that can enter into humans, or animals, as seen in Luke 8:26–32 when Jesus cast the demons out of a man and gave them permission to enter into a herd of swine. Lucifer entered the body of a serpent when he spoke to Eve in the Garden of Eden. He also entered into Judas to conduct the betrayal of Jesus in John 12:26–27. A holy angel has a body and cannot enter into humans or animals. Since Jesus ascended into heaven, he has given us the power through the baptism of the Holy Spirit to take authority over demonic spirits and command them to depart, and the demons must obey. It is done verbally through faith. But we cannot lock these spirits up in the abyss. God's holy army of angels will do this at the time of the Battle of Armageddon.

In summation of the bride of Christ, I do not believe that the bride returns with Jesus for the Battle of Armageddon because God has a holy army that has been trained in dealing with the fallen angels in accordance with God's will from the beginning of our creation. The bride of Christ is to function as priests, not warriors, in ministering life to humans during the millennial reign of Jesus on earth. We will not be battling demons during this time period; they will be locked in the abyss. At the entrance into the millennial reign, a year and three months after Armageddon, the bride will be presented at the marriage supper on earth. We are not needed at Armageddon; we would only be in the way of the trained angelic troops. Because we are like angels, we can return to earth at any time the Lord tells us.

Zechariah 14:4–5 depicts the Lord's return when he comes to the Mount of Olives.

> On that day his feet shall stand on the Mount of Olives which lies before Jerusalem on the east; and the Mount of Olives shall be split in two from east to west by a very wide valley; so that one half to the Mount shall withdraw northward, and the other half southward. (5) And the valley of my mountains shall be stopped up, for the valley of the mountains shall touch the side of it; and you shall flee as you fled from the earthquake in the days of Uzziah king of Judah. *Then* the LORD your God will come, and all the holy ones with him ["Then" introduces another time period]." (italics added)

With the return of Jesus and the changing of the landscape to the east of Jerusalem, people are going to flee in terror. The anointing of the Lord will fall upon the clans of

Judah that remained in the city, and they will rise up and destroy their enemies that controlled Jerusalem (Zechariah 12:4–8). May 20, AD 2021, marks the last day of Daniel's Seventieth Week when Jesus takes over Jerusalem. It will be another forty-five days before Armageddon takes place.

As for the splitting of the Mount of Olives, it will become a new valley that will be a new Garden of Eden about eight and one-eighth miles in width from Geba to Rimmon in a north to south direction. It will be part of the holy district of the Jewish nation, which will also go from the Jordan River to the Mediterranean Sea, in the east to west direction. This is where the new river will spring forth both in the spirit and the natural order. This is also where Ezekiel's temple (Ezekiel chapter 40–47) is to be placed, not on the Dome of the Rock where the last temple was constructed but southeast of that location. However the vision of the temple is not a material structure. The tabernacle of Moses was a portable material structure, and it was a symbolic form that pointed to the relationship that people would have with God in Christ after his death and resurrection for two thousand years. Ezekiel's temple is a symbolic picture of mankind's relationship with God in the Spirit worldwide for one thousand years. No material temple will ever be constructed again by God. Ever since the completed work on the cross by Jesus the dwelling place of God has been in every man, woman, and child that has accepted Jesus as Lord and Savior, and was born again by the Holy Spirit of God. There was no material temple in the Garden of Eden before the fall of humans, and since the destruction of the temple in Jerusalem in AD 70, God has not constructed another one. In the Book of Revelation at the end of the millennial reign of Christ, God destroys this heaven and earth with fire (2 Peter 3:8–10). Then we will have a new heaven and earth, and the new city of Jerusalem will come down to the new earth. Revelation 21:3: "... Behold, the dwelling of God is with men. He will dwell with them, and they shall be his people, and God himself will be with them." Revelation 21:22: *"And I saw no temple in the city, for its temple is the Lord God the Almighty and the Lamb"* (italics added).

With the new heaven and earth everyone will be growing in God as it was in Genesis 1:1 before the rebellion. God dwells in us now, and through our submission, we dwell in him. When God destroys this heaven and earth after the educational program is finished, we will have a new heaven and a new earth. We will dwell with God and in God, and there will be no distractions due to sin. We will all be united in perfect harmony, spiritually, forever! There is no material temple in the new creation. During the millennial reign of Christ on this earth, the Holy Spirit of God will dwell in each believer and speak very clearly the will of the Lord to each born-again individual. There will be gathering places, but each person will be the temple of the living God worldwide. No false religions will exist. At the end of our creation, the Devil will be locked up throughout Eternity Future in the lake of fire. The entire new creation will be controlled by a theocracy: Father, Son, and Holy Spirit.

**EVENT: The Battle of Armageddon**

**TIME FRAME: Eternity Present—Creation 5997, Jewish 24 Tammuz 5781, Western Sunday July 4, AD 2021**

The return of the Lord to Jerusalem will be known to the nations immediately. The final forty-five days will allow the Antichrist to gather the armies of the nations. He will bring them to the Valley of Jehoshaphat and the Plain of Megiddo outside Jerusalem. Preparation for the mustering of these troops will come through the work of the three foul spirits after the Euphrates dies up. Multitudes from the nations will be gathered to fight against the Lord.

Revelation 19:17–19 presents the prelude to the battle:

> Then I saw an angel standing in the sun, and with a loud voice he called to all the birds that fly in midheaven, "Come, gather for the great supper of God, (18) to eat the flesh of kings, the flesh of captains, the flesh of mighty men, the flesh of horses and their riders, and the flesh of all men, both free and slave, both small and great." (19) And I saw the beast and the kings of the earth with their armies gathered to make war against him who sits upon the horse and *against his army.* (italics added)

Now, Jesus will complete the final conquest for planet earth at Armageddon. On the actually day of battle, Zechariah 14:12–15 gives us a description about what will take place:

> And this shall be the plague with which the LORD will smite all the peoples that wage war against Jerusalem: their flesh shall rot while they are still on their feet, their eyes shall rot in their sockets, and their tongues shall rot in their mouths. (13) And on that day [the term "day" refers to the time period, not a twenty-four hour day] a great panic from the LORD shall fall on them, so that each will lay hold on the hand of his fellow, (14) and the hand of the one will be raised against the hand of the other; even Judah will fight against Jerusalem. And the wealth of all the nations round about shall be collected, gold, silver, and garments in great abundance. (15) And a plague like this plague shall fall on the horses, the mules, the camels, the asses, and whatever beasts may be in those camps.

During the battle which is a one day event, the Antichrist and False Prophet are captured. Revelation 19:20–21:

> And the beast was captured, and with it the false prophet who in its presence had worked the signs by which he deceived those who had received the mark of the beast and those who wor-

shiped its image. These two were thrown alive in the lake of fire that burns with sulphur. (21) And the rest were slain by the sword of him who sits upon the horse, the sword that issues from his mouth; and all the birds were gorged with their flesh.

With the return of Jesus to the earth and the Battle of Armageddon fought, a cleanup campaign begins.

Zechariah 14:6–11:

> On that day there shall be neither cold nor frost. (7) And there shall be continuous day (it is known to the LORD), not day and not night, for at evening time there shall be light. (8) On that day living waters shall flow out from Jerusalem, half of them to the eastern sea and half of them to the western sea; it shall continue in summer as in winter. (9) *And the LORD will become king over all the earth*; on that day the LORD will be one and his name one. (10) The whole land shall be turned into a plain from Geba to Rimmon south of Jerusalem. But Jerusalem shall remain aloft upon its site from the Gate of Benjamin to the place of the former gate, to the Corner Gate, and from the Tower of Hananel to the king's wine presses. (11) And it shall be inhabited, *for there shall be no more curse; Jerusalem shall dwell in security.* (italics added)

The cold, the frost, and the continuous day concern the light of God and the warmth of his love to a dark, cold world. It does not refer to a change in the seasons or the day and night process in the natural order. Now there will be a constant enlightenment worldwide. The living waters are truth, knowledge, understanding, and the wisdom of God that will flow around the world. Isaiah 11:9 relates to this issue when the prophet says: "for the earth shall be full of the knowledge of the LORD as the waters cover the sea." Jerusalem will be magnified and elevated above every other city, and it shall dwell in security and peace. It will be blessed of the Lord.

After the return of the Lord and the Battle of Armageddon, various tribes and peoples of the world will have no knowledge of the event that took place around Jerusalem. Before the marriage supper of the Lamb takes place, messengers will be sent forth to inform those who have not heard. In Daniel 7:12 after the destruction of the beast (Antichrist and the system), Daniel makes reference to the other kingdoms that were part of the system down through the ages. "As for the rest of the beasts, their dominion was taken away, but their lives were prolonged for a season and a time." The power and authority of these countries are taken away, but they will remain for a year and three months. If the people are not committed to Christ, they will die. Only those who belong to Jesus will be allowed into the banquet of the marriage super that begins with the Feast of Tabernacles on October 10, AD 2022. It is the inauguration of the millennium reign of Christ.

Beside the spiritual waters that will flow from Jerusalem around the world, bringing enlightenment, there will be a literal river flowing from God's throne (God's Garden of Eden).

Ezekiel 47:1-2, 8-9:

> Then he brought me back to the door of the temple; and behold, water was issuing from below the threshold of the temple toward the east (for the temple faced east); and the water was flowing down from below the south end of the threshold of the temple, south of the altar. (2) Then he brought me out by way of the north gate, and led me round on the outside to the outer gate, that faces toward the east; and the water was coming out on the south side. (8) And he said to me, "This water flows toward the eastern region and goes down into the Arabah; and when it enters the stagnant waters of the sea, the water will become fresh. (9) And wherever the river goes every living creature which swarms will live, and there will be very many fish; for this water goes there, that the waters of the sea may become fresh; so everything will live where the river goes."

With this water that flows from God's throne (the new Garden of Eden where the natural order and spiritual order are in perfect harmony), the rivers and seas will be replenished with life after the devastation of being turned to blood and poisoned. During the millennial reign of Jesus on earth, new life and new conditions will prevail. The longevity of life will increase and the animals will no longer be carnivorous. Plagues will no longer be a threat to mankind.

## POINTS TO REMEMBER

1. Jesus returns to Jerusalem with his army and will take the city on the last day of Daniel's Seventieth Week, May 20, AD 2021.

2. The Battle of Armageddon will take place forty-five days later when the Antichrist leads the nations that have followed him, into the Valley of Megiddo. The day of the battle will be Sunday July 4, AD 2021. Considering United States history, it could not fall on a more beautiful day!

3. There are two enemies of God that must be dealt with on the day of Armageddon. The first will be the armies of mankind that worshiped and follow the Antichrist as their god. For this battle, Jesus will simply speak the Word, and the armies will be destroyed. The second phase of this battle is to gather all of the fallen angelic spirits with the Devil, that were confined to the face of this earth at the beginning of the last forty-two months of Daniel's Seventieth Week. Then they will be thrown into the abyss for a thousand years. This is the purpose for the holy angelic army of God that came with Jesus. It is not the bride of Christ. The bride will be

presented at the Feast of Tabernacles which is the marriage supper and the official beginning of the thousand year period of the reign of Jesus with his bride.

4. The Antichrist (called the beast) and the False Prophet are thrown directly into the lake of fire. The souls of their followers are thrown into the abyss to wait for judgment day at the end of Eternity Present.

5. The rest of the people that followed the Antichrist that are still alive on earth will be put to death in one year and three moments later at the Feast of Atonement, judgment day on earth, October 5, AD 2022.

6. There will be a new Garden of Eden in the valley where the Mount of Olives was split north to south when Jesus returns to the earth.

## SUMMERY OF THE FOURTH PHASE OF GOD'S EDUCATIONAL PROGRAM

With the birth of Jesus the Son of God, his ministry, his death and resurrection, the foundation was laid for the return of mankind to have a close, personal relationship with God before the fall of Adam and Eve through our faith in Jesus. It was the breaking of faith in God that caused spiritual and physical death and the horrible conditions on earth through the activity of Lucifer and his fallen angels. The link between God and mankind is faith in what God reveals to us through his grace and our acceptance and obedience to it. With our commitment to Jesus and our obedience to what God reveals, spiritual rebirth takes place, and we have eternal life with God. Individually, we become part of the body of Christ, and collectively we are the church. When we commit our life to Jesus, the Holy Spirit takes up residence in us and reveals the will of God to us. When we ask Jesus to baptize us with his Holy Spirit that was given to the believers on the day of Pentecost, the Holy Spirit comes upon us, and we are given power and gifts to accomplish the will and work of God that the Holy Spirit reveals within us. Our fallen human flesh with its sinful nature is sandwiched in between the Spirit in us and the Spirit upon us, and we are enabled by God to overcome the demands of our sinful nature. All of us who are Christians are the temple of the living God to minister his life to others. The Spirit coming into us and the Spirit coming upon us are two separate events and manifestation of the work of the Holy Spirit that are part of our salvation. They can happen simultaneously with our committing our life to Jesus, or they can be two separate events separated by days, weeks, months, or years. My experience was a twelve year separation between the two. I was saved when I accepted Jesus into my life, but I did not have the power to serve him until I was baptized with the Holy Spirit and experienced the manifestation of his gifts.

While our sinful nature remains with us until God gives us a new glorified body, it is only through our growth and maturity in our relationship with God that we can overcome the condition. If we do not grow and mature and get victory over sin, sin will continue to dominate our life, even though we have eternal life with God through our faith in Jesus. Our quality of life improves with maturity. This is an everyday working relationship with God by placing his will for our life above everything else. The closer we walk with God, the greater the freedom we have from the evil corruption of this world. It is not a form and ritual activity. It comes through talking with God in prayer at any time, day or night, concerning any condition we are confronted with where we want or need his help. To the degree that we seek the life of Jesus in our life is the degree that the light of God will flow into us and through us for ministry to others. The way of life in Jesus is open to us. At the same time, God will not take away our free will choice, and God will not be mocked. Galatians 6:7–10 sums up his educational program for the church age period from the first coming of Jesus to his second coming:

> Do not be deceived; God is not mocked, for whatever a man sows, that he will also reap. (8) For he who sows to his own flesh will from the flesh reap corruption; but he who sows to the Spirit will from the Spirit reap eternal life. (9) *And let us not grow weary in well-doing, for in due season we shall reap, if we do not lose heart.* (10) So then, as we have opportunity, *let us do good to all men, and especially to those who are of the household of faith.*" (italics added)

## CHAPTER 22

# THE FIFTH PHASE OF GOD'S EDUCATIONAL PROGRAM: THE MILLENNIAL REIGN OF CHRIST

**EVENT:** The fulfillment of the last three feasts to enter the millennial reign of Jesus over the entire world
**TIME FRAME:** From Eternity Present—Creation 5998, Jewish 1 Tishri 5783, Western Monday September 26, AD 2022 to Eternity Present—Creation 5998, Jewish 15 Tishri 5783, Western Thursday October 10, AD 2022

**INTRODUCTION NARRATIVE:** *The last three feasts of the ceremonial law, explain the entrance into the millen-*

*nial reign of Jesus. They will take place one year and three months after the Battle of Armageddon.*

After the return of the Lord, the Battle of Armageddon, and notification to the people of the world about these events, the last three feasts in the ceremonial law of the Mosaic Covenant are to be fulfilled in Christ. They come in the seventh month of the Jewish religious calendar. It falls during our months of September and October. These three feasts will bring us into the millennial reign of Christ. The Feast of Trumpets comes first. Leviticus 23:23–25: "And the LORD said to Moses, (24) 'Say to the people of Israel, "In the seventh month, on the first day of the month, you shall observe a day of solemn rest, a memorial proclaimed with blast of trumpets, a holy convocation. (25) You shall do no laborious work; and you shall present an offering by fire to the LORD."'" The first day of the seventh month is symbolic of the seventh day of creation where God sanctifies it as a day of rest. It is a holy gathering. It is a day when there shall be no laboring (independent acts contrary to God's will). The offering by fire translates in the Spirit as a pure commitment of obedience to Jesus. It is God's spiritual feeding. His feast to the people is rest from the fallen worldly system.

This feast day also marks the beginning of the new civil calendar year for the Jews, which identifies the new time period in Christ. On the tenth day of this same month comes the Feast of Atonement. God separates the people. He segregates those who will follow Jesus from those who remain in rebellion. It is the cleansing of the people of God.

Leviticus 23:26–32:

> And the LORD said to Moses, (27) "On the tenth day of this seventh month is the day of atonement; it shall be for you a time of holy convocation, and you shall afflict yourselves and present an offering by fire to the LORD. (28) And you shall do no work on this same day; for it is a day of atonement, to make atonement for you before the LORD your God. (29) For whoever is not afflicted on this same day *shall be cut off from his people*. (30) And whoever does any work on this same day, that person *I will destroy from among his people*. (31) You shall do no work: it is a statute for ever throughout your generations in all your dwellings. (32) It shall be to you a Sabbath of solemn rest, and you shall afflict yourselves; on the ninth day of the month beginning at evening, form evening to evening shall you keep your Sabbath." (italics added)

Ten is symbolic of the law. On this day the law of God will be fulfilled in the lives of the people around the world. It is a day of gathering before the Lord in true repentance. It is the day of forgiveness, cleansing, and healing between God and all who will live upon the earth. Whoever is not afflicted (with sorrow and repentance), shall be cut off (separated and put to death). Anyone who tries to add to or take away from what God requires shall be cut off.

In Matthew 25:31–45, Jesus presents the spiritual reality of this Old Testament ceremonial law:

> When the Son of man comes in his glory, and all the angels with him, then he will sit on his glorious throne. (32) Before him will be gathered all the nations, and he will separate them one from another as a shepherd separates the sheep from the goats, (33) and he will place the sheep at his right hand, but the goats at the left. (34) Then the King will say to those at his right hand, "Come, O blessed of my Father, inherit the kingdom prepared for you from the foundation of the world; (35) for I was hungry and you gave me food, I was thirsty and you gave me drink, I was a stranger and you welcomed me, (36) I was naked and you clothed me, I was sick and you visited me, I was in prison and you came to me." (37) Then the righteous will answer him, "Lord, when did we see thee hungry and feed thee, or thirsty and give thee drink? (38) And when did we see thee a stranger and welcome thee, or naked and clothe thee? (39) And when did we see thee sick or in prison and visit thee?" (40) And the King will answer them, "Truly, I say to you, as you did it to one of the least of these my brethren, you did it to me." (41) Then he will say to those at his left hand, *Depart from me, you cursed, into the eternal fire prepared for the Devil and his angels*; (42) for I was hungry and you gave me no food, I was thirsty and you gave me no drink, (43) I was a stranger and you did not welcome me, naked and you did not clothe me, sick and in prison and you did not visit me." (44) Then they also will answer, "Lord, when did we see thee hungry or thirsty or a stranger or naked or sick or in prison, and did not minister to thee?" (45) Then he will answer them, "Truly, I say to you, as you did it not to one of the least of these, you did it not to me." *And they will go away into eternal punishment, but the righteous into eternal life.* (italics added)

James 3:20 tells us that faith apart from works is dead. Between the rapture and the second coming, those who place their faith in Christ must exercise that faith in love for their neighbors. Those who had faith but did not act upon it will be rejected. Those who rejected Christ will also be rejected. This is the separation of sheep and the goats for those who enter the millennial reign of Christ on this earth in their natural bodies.

Under Old Testament law in Leviticus 16:5–10 and 20–22, there is additional information concerning this event.

> And he shall take from the congregation of the people of Israel two male goats for a sin offering and one ram for a burnt offering. (6) And Aaron shall offer the bull as a sin offering for himself, and shall make atonement for himself and for his house. (7) Then he shall take the two goats, and set them before the LORD at the door of the tent of meeting; (8) and Aaron shall cast lots upon the two goats, one lot for the LORD and the other lot for Azazel. (9) And Aaron shall present the goat on which the lot fell for the LORD, and offer it as a sin offering; (10) but the goat on which the lot fell for Azazel shall be presented alive before the LORD to make atonement over it, that it may be sent away into the wilderness to Azazel. (20) And when he has made an end of atoning for the holy place and the tent of meeting and the altar, he shall present the live goat; (21) and Aaron shall lay both his hands upon the head of the live goat, and confess over him all the iniquities of the people of Israel, and all their transgressions, all their sins; and he shall put them upon the head of the goat, and send him away into the wilderness by the hand of a man who is in readiness. (22) The goat shall bear all their iniquities upon him to a solitary land; and he shall let the goat go in the wilderness.

*Let There Be Light*

The goat used for the sacrificial offering represents those who lay their lives down for the Lord. Matthew 10:39: "He who finds his life will lose it, and he who loses his life for my sake will find it." The Christian is a living sacrifice who has laid his life down on God's altar. The goat that goes into the wilderness carries the sins of the people into desolation. This goat represents the unrepentant, who found their lives in the pleasures of sin. They are cut off from the Lord and his people. The solitary land is a wilderness without God. They will die on the day of the Feast of Atonement, and will enter into the abyss. (It should be noted that the world population will not come to Jerusalem when this judgment takes place. God is omnipresent worldwide.)

The Feast of Tabernacles (or Booths) is the last event that will set the stage for the rule of Christ upon the earth for one thousand years.

Leviticus 23:33–36, 39–43:

> And the LORD said to Moses, (34) "Say to the people of Israel, on the fifteenth day of this seventh month and for seven days is the feast of booths to the LORD. (35) On the first day shall be a holy convocation; you shall do no laborious work. (36) Seven days you shall present offerings by fire to the LORD; it is a solemn assembly; you shall do no laborious work. (39) On the fifteenth day of the seventh month, when you have gathered in the produce of the land, you shall keep the feast of the LORD seven days; on the first day shall be a solemn rest, and on the eighth day shall be a solemn rest. (40) And you shall take on

the first day the fruit of goodly trees, branches of palm trees, and bought of leafy trees and willows of the brook; and you shall rejoice before the LORD your God seven days. (41) You shall keep it as a feast to the LORD seven days in the year; it is a statute for ever throughout your generations; you shall keep it in the seventh month. (42) You will dwell in booths for seven days; all that are native in Israel will dwell in booths, (43) that your generations may know that I made the people of Israel dwells in booths when I brought them out of the land of Egypt: I am the LORD your God."

This feast runs for a total of eight days. The first and last day shall be a solemn rest. There is a symbolic issue in the numbers. God created the earth in six days, and on the seventh day he rested. As noted in Genesis chapter 3, the seventh day of rest was broken with the sin of Adam and Eve. A new day was required to repair the broken relationship between mankind and God. The new day started when Jesus came into the world, was crucified, and resurrected. It was the beginning of the eighth day of creation. It is the day of our Lord. It is a day of redemption and restoration of mankind to restore everything that was lost in the seventh day of creation before the sin of Adam took place. Here, the new believers are to embrace the Word of God, Jesus. It is the Word of God that will produce spiritual and material blessings worldwide in harmony with God the Father. Those who attend this feast are God's harvest after the rapture. The harvest of the world is now complete. It is time to rejoice and celebrate the marriage of the Lamb. Those who God harvested after the rapture are the invited guests to the marriage supper. The bride is composed of all who were raptured and given new glorified bodies, free from their sinful nature.

When God delivered the Jews from Egyptian bondage, God made them dwell in booths for seven days during this feast. The booth is made up of "...branches of palm trees, and boughs of leafy trees, and willows of the brook" (Leviticus 23:40). A booth of this nature was normally used by the guardian of a vineyard or vegetable garden when the fruit was ripe and could be taken by animals or thieves. It is used in the Feast of Tabernacles (Booths) as a ritual to make the people aware that they are the guardians of God's garden, which is the Word of God that produces the fruit of the spirit that brings unity and harmony to life on earth and productivity throughout the world. This goes back to Genesis 2:15 when Adam was placed in God's spiritual garden to till and keep it. The booth is also a symbol for the fact that this earth is only a temporary dwelling place. Our permanent home will be with God in the New Jerusalem of Revelation 21:1–4. With the completion of God's worldwide harvest, God's people (Jew and Gentile) are delivered from bondage to the Devil and the fallen worldwide corruption.

The people in their natural bodies who attend this feast are now the guardians of God's Word. In keeping God's Word, they will maintain their freedom and rest. Throughout this feast, there is communion with God. God and humans can now tabernacle together on earth in peace. The last day of the feast will mark the end of the old ecclesiastical calendar. All form and ritual is completely fulfilled in Christ. From this time forward all nations will continue to feed upon and keep the Word of God through the power of the Holy Spirit. This is due to spiritual rebirth under the sovereign ruling authority of Christ. For one thousand years, justice will be worldwide, and peace will prevail!

When Jesus rules from Jerusalem, many changes will take place. Jerusalem will be the center of life for the world. The people and the place will be holy. The animals will no longer be hostile or carnivorous. Isaiah 65:25: "The wolf and the lamb shall feed together, the lion shall eat straw like the ox; and dust shall be the serpent's food. They shall not hurt or destroy *in all my holy mountain* [the elevated government of God around the world], says the LORD" (italics added). Isaiah 11:6–8: "The wolf shall dwell with the lamb, and the leopard shall lie down with the kid, and the calf and the lion and the fatling together, and a little child shall lead them.

(7) The cow and the bear shall feed; their young shall lie down together; and the lion shall eat straw like the ox. (8) The sucking child shall play over the hole of the asp, and the weaned child shall put his hand on the adder's den."

The second change will be the increase in the life span of humans. Isaiah 65:20: "No more shall there be in it an infant that lives but a few days, or an old man who does not fill out his days, for the child shall die a hundred years old, and the sinner a hundred years old shall be accursed." For those who walk in obedience to Christ, they could live to be more than nine hundred years old, just as in the days before the flood.

The third major change will be peace between nations. There will be no armament programs and expensive defense budgets. Isaiah 2:4: "He shall judge between the nations, and shall decide for many peoples; and they shall beat their sword into plowshares, and their spears into pruning hooks; nation shall not lift up sword against nation, neither shall they learn war any more." The world will know peace under God's rule. When anyone violates this standard, Zechariah 14:17–19 tells us what will happen to those people:

> And if any of the families of the earth do not go up to Jerusalem to worship the King, the LORD of hosts, there will be no rain upon them. (18) And if the family of Egypt do not go up and present themselves, then upon them shall come the plague with which the LORD afflicts the nations that do not go up to keep

the feast of booths. (19) This shall be the punishment to Egypt and the punishment to all the nations that do not go up to keep the feast of booths.

The plague noted in verse 18 is the same in the Battle of Armageddon mentioned in Zechariah 14:12: "And this shall be the plague with which the LORD will smite all the peoples that wage war against Jerusalem: their flesh shall rot while they are still on their feet, their eyes shall rot in their sockets, and their tongues shall rot in their mouths." Judgment and punishment will come swiftly to those who want to come against the Lord. It is the bride of Christ that will oversee the nations as noted in Revelation 20:4:

> Then I saw thrones, and seated on them were those to whom judgment was committed. Also I saw the souls of those who had been beheaded for their testimony to Jesus and for the word of God, and who had not worshiped the beast or its image and had not received its mark on their foreheads or their hands they came to life, and reigned with Christ a thousand years.

When the Feast of Tabernacles (Booths) takes place, there will probably be about one and a half billion people on the earth who will be the wedding guests. There are no figures in Scripture on this issue. It can only approximated by adding up the death toll of the fourth seal, the sixth trumpet, the rapture of the saints, the seven bowls of wrath, Armageddon, and those who die at the Feast of Atonement. With the massive destruction that takes place before the return of Christ, reconstruction will be a major issue. People will marry and raise families in peace and security. Their children and future generations will all be aware of Christ and his sovereignty. Each new person born on earth will need to make a commitment to Jesus and receive spiritual rebirth. The continuation of the sinful nature of the natural body will still be an issue in the lives of these people. While they have the benefit of a godly environment to live under, their freewill choice remains, along with the fallen nature of Adam.

**EVENT: End of the millennium reign of Christ and the release of Satan from the abyss**
**TIME FRAME: From Eternity Present—Creation 6998, Jewish 6783, Western October 10, AD 3022 to Eternity Present—Creation 6999, Jewish 8 Tevet, Western Friday December 31, AD 3024. The last day of this creation**

While peace will reign for one thousand years on earth, the hearts of many people will not embrace Jesus as Lord of their life. At the end of the period, Satan will be loosed to entice the unsaved population into rebellion against God. Revelation 20:7–9: "And when the thousand years are ended,

## Let There Be Light

Satan will be loosed from his prison (8) and will come out to deceive the nations which are at the four corners of the earth, that is, Gog and Magog, to gather them for battle; their numbers is like the sand of the sea. (9) And they marched up over the broad earth and surrounded the camp of the saints and the beloved city..." It should be noted here that this event cannot happen until after the one thousand year period has ended.

Once again, God uses the Devil to separate those who want to live in the light of God from those who want to live in darkness and deception.

Ezekiel 38:1–13:

> The word of the LORD came to me: (2) "Son of man, set your face toward Gog, of the land of Magog, the chief prince of Meshech and Tubal, and prophesy against him (3) and say, Thus says the Lord GOD: Behold, I am against you, O Gog, chief prince of Meshech and Tubal; (4) and I will turn you about, and put hooks into your jaws, and I will bring you forth, and all your army, horses and horsemen, all of them clothed in full armor, a great company, all of them with buckler and shield, wielding swords; (5) Persia, Cush, and Put are with them, all of them with shield and helmet; (6) Gomer and all his hordes; Bethtogarmah from the uttermost parts of the north with all his hordes—many peoples are with you. (7) Be ready and keep ready, you and all the hosts that are assembled about you, and be a guard for them. (8) After many days you will be mustered; *in the latter years you will go against the land that is restored from war*, the land where people were gathered from many nations upon the mountains of Israel, which had been a continual waste; *its people were brought out from the nations and now dwell securely, all of them*. (9) You will advance, coming on like a storm, you will

be like a cloud covering the land you and all your hordes, and many peoples with you." Thus says the Lord GOD: (10) "On that day thoughts will come into your mind, and you will devise an evil scheme (11) and say, *I will go up against the land of unwalled villages; I will fall upon the quiet people who dwell securely, all of them dwelling without walls, and having no bars or gates*; (12) to seize spoil and carry off plunder; to assail the waste places which are now inhabited, and the people who were gathered from the nations, who have gotten cattle and goods, who dwell at the center of the earth. (13) Sheba and Dedan and the merchants of Tarshish and all its villages will say to you, 'Have you come to seize spoil? Have you assembled your hosts to carry off plunder, to carry away silver and gold, to take away cattle and goods, to seize great spoil?'" (italics added)

Gog is a fallen angel that was given authority as a prince, a ruler in darkness directed by Lucifer, over the territory near Russia where the sons of Japheth settled after the flood of Noah. When he is released from the abyss, he will gather the countries of his area, Persia, and those countries to the south of Israel. The thoughts and desires of these people who are not born again will be turned to the work of Satan. Because the people have not committed their hearts to the Lord, they will be fertile ground for the Devil to plant his seeds. Jerusalem will hold the wealth of the world, spiritually and materially, under the rule of God. The villages surrounding her will be without walls and armament. The purpose of their attack will be to gather great material wealth, power, and prestige to rule over others. The style and plans of the Devil never change.

Before the attack upon Jerusalem ever begins, God exercises judgment upon them.

Ezekiel 38:21–23:

> I will summon every kind of terror against Gog, says the Lord GOD; every man's sword will be against his brother. (22) With pestilence and bloodshed I will enter into judgment with him; and I will reign upon him and his hordes and the many peoples that are with him, torrential rains and hailstones, fire and brimstone. (23) So I will show my greatness and my holiness and make myself known in the eyes of many nations. Then they will know that I am the LORD.

Revelation 20:9–10 adds clarity to this event:

> And they marched up over the broad earth and surrounded the camp of the saints and the beloved city; but fire came down from heaven and consumed them, (10) and the devil who had deceived them was thrown into the lake of the fire and sulphur where the beast and the false prophet were, *and they will be tormented day and night for ever and ever*. (italics added)

With this final battle, the Devil and all the fallen angelic creatures are thrown into the lake of fire. Demonic deception and destruction are finished forever!

It should be noted here that Ezekiel chapter 38 regarding Gog encompasses two separate prophetic events. In verses 38:1–16, the prophecy deals with the end of the millennial reign of Christ. In verses 38:17–25, the prophecy deals with the last half of Daniel's Seventieth Week and the return of Jesus to this earth for the Battle of Armageddon.

After the final battle and judgment of Satan, there is a short period left on earth until the end. 2 Peter 3:8–13 sums up the end of this creation:

> But do not ignore this one fact, beloved, that with the Lord one day is as a thousand years, and a thousand years as one day. (9) The Lord is not slow about his promise as some count slowness, but is forbearing toward you, not wishing that any should perish, but that all should reach repentance. (10) *But the day of the Lord will come like a thief, and then the heavens will pass away with a loud noise, and the elements will be dissolved with fire, and the earth and the works that are upon it will be burned up.*
>
> (11) Since all these things are thus to be dissolved, what sort of persons ought you to be in lives of holiness and godliness, (12) waiting for and hastening the coming of the day of God, because of which the heavens will be kindled and dissolved, and the elements will melt with fire! (13) *But according to his promise we wait for new heavens and a new earth in which righteousness dwells.* (italics added)

**EVENT: The last day of this creation and God's educational program**

**TIME FRAME: Eternity Present—Creation 6999, Jewish 8 Tevet 6785, Western Friday December 31, AD 3024**

**POINTS TO BE REMEMBER**

1. The last three feasts of the Jewish religious calendar mark the entrance into the thousand year reign of Christ

over this world. They deal with everyone who is alive after Armageddon takes place upon the earth.

2. The first feast is the Feast of Trumpets. It is a day of solemn rest and reflection on your commitment to Jesus for all that he has done for you and your willingness to be under his authority. If you are not afflicted with true sorrow for your sins and a commitment to follow Jesus on that day, you will not enter into the new time period. If you received the mark of the beast, you are doomed for destruction. Your decision was made at that time.

3. The second feast is the Feast of Atonement. It is the day when Jesus will judge every individual on earth to determine their acceptance or rejection. Those who are rejected will die on that day and enter into the abyss. Those who are accepted will be part of God's kingdom on earth.

4. The third feast is the Feast of Tabernacles (or Booths). It is the official entrance into the millennial reign of Jesus. It begins with the marriage supper of Jesus with his bride on earth. The marriage took place in heaven. Every person from the time of Adam that walked with God and remained

faithful to the time of the rapture of the saints will make up his bride. Those who were martyred for their faith after the rapture who did not take the mark of the beast will also become part of the bride.

## SUMMERY OF THE FIFTH STAGE OF GOD'S EDUCATIONAL PROGRAM

God the Father, God the Son, and God the Holy Spirit will have complete rule over the entire earth. There will be no wars among the nations or false gods to be worshiped. There will be no demonic activity to tempt people into sin or take up residence within them. The animal population will be tame. It will be a safe and secure environment to live in. The only obstacle to perfect peace will be the fallen sinful nature inherent in the lives of the people that entered into this time period in their natural bodies. The sinful nature can only be overcome through the work of the Holy Spirit dwelling within the people who committed their lives to Jesus and their continual submission to the Lord. Each person born during this thousand year period must make a free will decision to commit their life to Jesus as their Lord and be led by him. There will be those who enjoy the benefits of living in a healthy, safe, protective environment, and they will have a clear understanding of who God is, but they will not invite Jesus into their life. Since the sinful nature of man directs us to rise above others and rule over them, it will cause personal conflicts. But they will not go beyond a low level of sinful activity because of the sovereign control of God. Yet there will still be some harm and suffering as a result.

At the end of the thousand year reign of Jesus, Lucifer and the fallen angels will be released from the abyss. They will enter into the lives of those who never received spiritual rebirth. They will be directed by the Devil to rise up and overthrow Jerusalem. But when they surround Jerusalem, the Lord will bring down fire from heaven and destroy them. At that point, Lucifer and all of the fallen angels will be thrown into the lake of fire forever!

So what will all creation learn from seven thousand years of good and evil upon our earth? Without God's sovereign ruling control over every aspect of life in perfect wisdom, power, holiness, and love in and through his created beings that have free will choice and limited ability, everyone will clearly see that we will destroy ourselves and one another through our ignorance and selfish desires. By being separated from God in a fallen spiritual condition, there is no end to the depth of degradation, misery, poverty, and suffering in life that we can come too in our bondage to sin. Unless God redeems us from sin and removes our sinful nature, we are lost to eternal damnation in the depth of our individual depravity and despair. God has revealed it to us and has given us a free will choice.

## CHAPTER 23

# THE FINAL JUDGMENT

**EVENT:** The great white throne judgment
**TIME FRAME:** Eternity Future

**INTRODUCTION NARRATIVE:** *At the end of the one thousand year reign of peace worldwide under the control of Jesus, the Devil and his angels will be released from the abyss. They will gather those who were never born again by the Spirit of God during this time period. They will be drawn together by the Devil as an army and will go to Jerusalem to conquer the city and acquire great wealth. But fire will come down from heaven and destroy them before the battle begins. Then the Devil and his angels will be thrown into the lake of fire forever!*

*At the end of the seven thousand years of our creation, God will destroy our heaven and earth along with the angelic heaven. Then everyone who has not been thrown into the lake of fire will appear before the throne of God for the final judgment to take place. The holy angels and those who were part of the bride of Christ will not be part of this judgment. The judgment will only be for those who entered the millennium reign of Jesus in their natural bodies and those who were born during that time period, along with everyone that entered the abyss from the time of the fall of Adam. Anyone who was not born again by the Spirit of God will be thrown into the lake of fire. Then God will create a new heaven and a new earth, and the new city of Jerusalem will come down from God's heaven onto the new earth. The education program will be complete, and we will have returned to the position of Genesis 1:1 with two heavens and one earth and no darkness, forever!*

Revelation 20:11–15:

> Then I saw a great white throne and him who sat upon it; from his presence earth and sky fled away, and no place was found for them. (12) And I saw the dead, great and small, standing before the throne, and books were opened. Also another book was opened, which is the book of life. And the dead were judged by what was written in the books, by what they had done. (13) And the sea [the sea of humanity] gave up the dead in it, Death

and Hades gave up the dead in them, and all were judged by what they had done. (14) Then Death and Hades were thrown into the lake of fire. This is the second death, the lake of fire; (15) and if any one's name was not found written in the book of life, he was thrown into the lake of fire.

Everyone, apart from the bride of Christ, will now stand before God's throne of judgment. That is everyone who lived from the time of Adam to the end of the earth that never walked with God, and those who accepted Christ after the rapture of the saints. This engulfs a period of seven-thousand years. Everything that everyone has ever done is recorded on the soul. When God sees us, we are open books to him. Everything is exposed. Only those who received the light of God and acted upon it through faith during the time period in which they lived have all their sins forgiven. Their names are recorded in God's Book of Life. Their judgment comes upon the *good works* done after salvation. Besides eternal life, they are rewarded for their maturity and service. Those who rejected the light of God will go into eternal damnation, the lake of fire, and will suffer each to the degree of sin they committed.

When the sea gives up its dead, it is a reference to the sea of humanity, not the ocean. The dead are those who were alive at the end of Eternity Present but had never made Jesus Lord of their life (2 Peter 3:10, "the Lord comes as a thief").

Those who belong to Jesus are not given up. They continue with the Lord. "Death and Hades" is a reference to those who died physical while on earth and went to hell (the abyss) to await this final judgment. Everyone who does not belong to Christ will be thrown into the lake of fire. It is their eternal place of torment. This event is the second death. To stand before God is to know him. John 17:3 tells us that this is eternal life. Man was separated from God on earth through sin, which was death to him (separation from God). Standing in God's presence a person has life. Then he departs into the lake of fire, separated from God again. This is why it is called the second death.

When standing before God, you will know the absolute holiness, purity, and love of God. From that position before God, you will clearly see every aspect of the evil that was conducted throughout your life with no true repentance unto God. The clarity of your evil conduct will never depart from your awareness for one moment throughout Eternity Future and what is has cost you. There is no love or comfort, or the joys of life in fellowship and accomplishment in eternal damnation, only the weeping and mashing of teeth because no one cares about anyone else. Life on earth was all about me, not God or others, unless I could make use of them for what I wanted, contrary to the will of God.

Death and Hades also go into the lake of fire. This means that the only separation from God in all creation will be those who are in the lake of fire. It also means that this is the only place where hell can exist. The rest of creation will be pure and holy. There will be no more mixture of the kingdom of Light and the kingdom of Darkness operating side by side. And the best is yet to come!

**EVENT: The new heavens and the new earth**
**TIME FRAME: Eternity Future**

In Revelation 21, we have a view of what God has planned for those who love him. Verses 1–4:

> Then I saw *a new heaven and a new earth*; for *the first heaven and the first earth had passed away*, and the sea was no more. (2) And I saw the holy city, new Jerusalem, coming down out of heaven from God, prepared as a bride adorned for her husband; (3) and I heard a loud voice from the throne saying, "Behold, the dwelling of God is with men. He will dwell with them, and they shall be his people, and God himself will be with them; (4) he will wipe away every tear from their eyes, and *death shall be no more, neither shall there be mourning nor crying nor pain any more, for the former things have passed away*." (italics added)

With the passing away of our heaven and earth along with the first angelic heaven (2 Peter 3:10), we will return to the original state of Genesis 1:1 before the fall of Lucifer. There will be two heavens and a new earth (the heaven of God's throne plus the heaven around the new earth). The statement, "the sea was no more," refers to humanity as we know it on this earth. After the judgment, everyone who belongs to God will be like angels (Mark 12:25). The new Jerusalem, which God is preparing for us now in the third heaven, will come down to the new earth. God and humans (in angelic form), along with the angels that never sinned, will dwell together. The sorrow, pain, and suffering of today will be no more!

In 2 Peter 3:10 it states: "...the *heavens* will pass away with a loud noise..." (italics added). The term "heavens" is plural. Then in 2 Peter 3:13 it states: "But according to his promise we wait for new *heavens* and a new earth in which righteousness dwells" (italics added). The term "heavens" is again plural. But in Revelation 21:1 John states: "Then I saw a new *heaven* and a new earth..." (italics added). The term heaven is singular. Revelation 21:5 states: "And he who sat upon the throne said, 'Behold, I make all things new.'" There are only three heavens listed in Scripture. Peter tells us that the "heavens" and the earth are destroyed. This means that two heavens are terminated, and everyone from those two dimensions will go to the third dimension, which is the throne of God for judgment day. Then God will create one new heaven and one new earth. So we now have two heavens and one earth. Yet Peter states that there will be "new heavens" when only one new heaven is created. Is Peter in error or is there a different context to his statement? I believe Peter's context is in reference to God's statement: "Behold, I make all things new." With the completion of God's seven thousand year educational program, everything has changed for the good of those who love God. There is a new maturity in God's relationship with all of his children because of his education program! A simple example of this on earth deals with parents raising children. Children must be disciplined during their maturing process. But when they have become adults, hopefully in righteousness, the relationship between parents and children changes. I believe that this is what Peter was referring to in what will be a new, glorious, enhanced relationship between God and his children within the *two heavens*.

Revelation 21:5–8 states:

> And he who sat upon the throne said, "Behold, I make all things new." Also he said, "Write this, for these words are trustworthy and true." (6) And he said to me, "It is done! I am the Alpha and the Omega, the beginning and the end. To the thirsty I will give from the fountain of the water of life without payment. (7) He who conquers shall have this heritage, and I will be his God and he shall be my son. (8) *But as for the cowardly, the faithless,*

*the polluted, as for murderers, fornicators, sorcerers, idolaters, and all liars, their lot shall be in the lake that burns with fire and sulphur, which is the second death."* (italics added)

God does not destroy everything and start new things. He transforms the past and makes everything "new." Each of us will be molded into the perfect child of God that he desired us to be from the beginning. Whatever God begins God finishes. The "fountain of water of life" is the knowledge, truth, understanding, and wisdom of God that keeps our life in balance with him. It flows from Christ into our lives today, and it will continue in the life that is to come. This is our heritage *if* we keep our faith in Jesus. For those who are cowardly, faithless, and vile, their heritage will be the lake of fire. Faith in Christ will produce tremendous dividends! The exhortation of Revelation 21:5–8 is for today and the future.

In Revelation 21:9–21 we have a description of the new city we will occupy if we are faithful:

> Then came one of the seven angels who had the seven bowls full of the seven last plagues, and spoke to me, saying, "Come, I will show you the Bride, the wife of the Lamb." (10) And in the Spirit he carried me away to a great, high mountain, and showed me the holy city Jerusalem coming down out of heaven from God, (11) having the glory of God, its radiance like a most rare jewel, like a jasper, clear as crystal. (12) it had a great, high wall, with twelve gates, and at the gates twelve angels, and on the gates the names of the twelve tribes of the sons of Israel were inscribed; (13) on the east three gates, on the north three gates, on the south three gates, and on the west three gates. (14) And the wall of the city had twelve foundations, and on them

the twelve names of the twelve apostles of the Lamb. (15) And he who talked to me had a measuring rod of gold to measure the city and its gates and walls. (16) The city lies foursquare, its length the same as its breadth; and he measured the city with his rod, twelve thousand stadia; its length and breadth and height are equal. (17) He also measured its wall, a hundred and forty-four cubits by a man's measure, that is, an angel's. (18) The wall was built of jasper, while the city was pure gold, clear as glass. (19) The foundations of the wall of the city were adorned with every jewel; the first was jasper, the second sapphire, the third agate, the fourth emerald, (20) the fifth onyx, the sixth carnelian, the seventh chrysolite, the eighth beryl, the ninth topaz, the tenth chrysoprase, the eleventh jacinth, the twelfth amethyst. (21) And the twelve gates were twelve pearls, each of the gates made of a single pearl, and the street of the city was pure gold, transparent as glass.

The bride, the wife of the Lamb in verse 9, is the city of God that will be filled with the people of God. Then the Son of God can manifest his love in and through them. That was God's desire from the very beginning of his creation, a loving relationship with free willed beings he created. What we see in these verses is the fulfillment of that desire. The city is like a rare jewel. There are no trashed neighborhoods. It is clear as crystal. There are no shades of darkness or defects. Everything is bright and pure.

The exterior wall is a symbol of God's eternal protection of his people. The twelve gates with the names of the twelve tribes of Israel symbolize God's government to the world as a standard of righteousness through his chosen people, the Jews, the entryway into God's kingdom. The twelve foundations of the walls with the names of the apostles are symbolic of the foundation work laid through the preaching and teaching of the gospel of Christ. Christ was the fulfillment of the laws that we were not able to keep. Through spiritual rebirth and power of the Holy Spirit, our lives are transformed. The foundation of the wall is a symbol of the support of our eternal protection. The New Covenant of grace united Jew and Gentile in Christ and separated those who would perish.

The measuring road of gold is a symbol of the divine standard of God's measurement of all things. The layout of the city is foursquare. It renders a statement of equal access for all who would come from every direction. The city is fifteen hundred miles square. That covers an area larger than the landmass given to the Jews by God on our planet earth. The city is "pure gold, clear as glass." Everything in God's kingdom is clear and transparent because there is nothing to hide. Embedded in the foundations are a variety of jewels. They are symbolic of the authority and gifts of God placed in those who served God on earth. The "single pearl" of each gate speaks of the "pearl of great value" in Matthew 14:45–46, the church. Even the street (pathway of life) is gold (the divine nature of God) and transparent as glass (the way of life is clear). In this city, everyone walks on holy ground. Nothing is dirty, polluted, confusing, deceptive, or false.

Revelation 21:22–27 presents our relationship with God:

> *And I saw no temple in the city, for its temple is the Lord God the Almighty and the Lamb.* (23) And the city has no need of sun or moon to shine upon it, for the glory of God is its light, and its lamp is the Lamb. (24) By its light shall the nations walk; and the kings of the earth shall bring their glory into it, (25) and its gates shall never be shut by day—and there shall be no night there; (26) they shall bring into it the glory and the honor of the nations. (27) But nothing unclean shall enter it, nor anyone who practices abomination or falsehood, but only those who are written in the Lamb's book of life. (italics added)

In the New World, there is no separation between God and his people. No temple is needed. There will be no sun or moon, only continuous light. Our standard of time will be different. It appears that we will not have to rest our bodies. Unlimited energy will be ours forever. There will be absolute clarity in everything we do. There will be no confusion of mind or heart in our goals or purpose. Living will be a daily joy in freedom instead of an effort brought on through fallen flesh. The redeemed from all the nations of today's world shall be there. I believe the term "kings of the earth" is a reference to everyone who learned to walk with God and was victorious over the fallen worldly system through the power and authority of the Word of God given to us through the Holy Spirit. Since there is no night in the New World, the gates of the city will never close.

Revelation 22:1-5:

> Then he showed me the river of the water of life, bright as crystal, flowing from the throne of God and of the Lamb (2) through the middle of the street of the city; also, on either side of the river, the tree of life with its twelve kinds of fruit, yielding its fruit each month; and the leaves of the tree were for the healing of the nations. (3) There shall no more be anything accursed, but the throne of God and of the Lamb shall be in it, and his servants shall worship him; (4) they shall see his face, and his name shall be on their foreheads. (5) And night shall be no more; they need no light of lamp or sun, for the Lord God will be their light, and they shall reign for ever and ever.

The river and the tree of life are literal in form and spiritual in substance. They represent God's spiritual system. The tree produces twelve kinds of fruit. According to Galatians 5:22, there are nine different fruits of the Spirit. Considering this difference of three fruits, I can only assume that the quality and character of life in that dimension are going to be higher and great than we can experience here on our earth.

To gain insight concerning the leaves of the tree used in the healing of the nations, we need to look at the process of the tree. It is a symbolic presentation of the life flow of God through his people.

## Let There Be Light

Matthew 12:33–37:

> Either make the tree good, and its fruit good; or make the tree bad, and its fruit bad; for the tree is known by its fruit. (34) You brood of vipers! How can you speak good, when you are evil? For out of the abundance of the heart the mouth speaks. (35) The good man out of his good treasure brings forth good, and the evil man out of his evil treasure brings forth evil. (36) I tell you, on the day of judgment men will render account for every careless word they utter; (37) for by your words you will be justified, and by your words you will be condemned.

The heart of humans is composed of two elements. The first is free will. The ability of having free will gives us the freedom of choice to determine the purpose of our life. The second attribute of the heart of people is the ability to reason. These two functions determine what our life will be about, either good or evil or a mix of the two. Whatever you commit your heart to will produce the fruit of your life!

The leaf of the tree combines the light of the sun with the minerals and water from the soil as it is drawn up through the tree trunk. The process is called photosynthesis. The result of this work is fruit on the tree!

John 15:4–8:

> Abide in me, and I in you. As the branch cannot bear fruit by itself, unless it abides in the vine, neither can you, unless you abide in me. (5) I am the vine, you are the branches. He who abides in me, and I in him, he it is that bears much fruit, *for apart from me you can do nothing*. (6) If a man does not abide in me, he is cast forth as a branch and withers; and the branches are gathered, thrown into the fire and burned. (7) If you abide

in me, and my words abide in you, ask whatever you will, and it shall be done for you. (8) By this my Father is glorified, that you bear much fruit, and so prove to be my disciples. (italics added)

When a person commits their heart to follow Jesus, the light of God starts to fill the soul, and the evil contained in that life begins to be expelled. When God says that the "leaves of the tree are for the healing of the nations," God is referring to his divine system of life. The leaf is a symbol of the heart of a person. In God's perfect kingdom, there is no darkens to defile the works of God's children in either their natural or spiritual order. Because of faithful hearts committed to God, only pure light will exist, and the nations will be healed, completely! Everything will be conducted in harmony with God in love, peace, and joy. The education program of seven thousand years with the mix of good and evil will prove forever that obedience to God is the only way to live life!

The *river of life* is *crystal clear*. Most of our education process comes through our five senses operating in the natural order. In our fallen state and with a polluted environment, what we perceive is not always the truth. In the new world we will perceive the true condition in everything. The flow of God will be involved in every aspect of life. The picture presented with the Tree of Life on both sides of the river is a completely balanced life. Our perspective will not be one-sided or skewed in either the material or spiritual part of our being.

Revelation 22:6–7 confirms that all the events and issues spoken of will happen. "And he said to me, 'These words are trustworthy and true. And the Lord, the God of the spirits of the prophets, has sent his angel to show his servants what must soon take place. (7) And behold, I am coming soon.' Blessed is he who keeps the words of the prophecy of this book." What may appear to some as "pie in the sky in the sweet by and by" is unfolding at this very hour. This generation will not pass away before the return of Jesus to our earth!

In Revelation 22:10–16, the exhortation continues:

> And he said to me, "Do not seal up the words of the prophecy of this book, for the time is near. (11) Let the evildoer still do evil, and the filthy still by filthy, and the righteous still do right, and the holy still be holy. (12) Behold, I am coming soon, bringing my recompense, to repay everyone for what he has done. (13) I am the Alpha and Omega, the first and the last, the beginning and the end. (14) Blessed are those who wash their robes that they may have the right to the tree of life and that they may enter the city by the gates. (15) Outside are the dogs and sorcerers and fornicators and murderers and idolaters, and everyone who loves and practices falsehood. (16) I Jesus have sent my angel to you with this testimony for the churches. I am the root and the offspring of David, the bright morning star."

God gives us a stern warning about our future. God will allow evil and filth to continue as a free will choice. Those who do right and are holy unto the Lord should continue. When Jesus returns, he will repay and reward each of us according to our deeds. The Word of God (Jesus) was at the beginning of creation and that same Word of God will continue after this creation. Those who wash themselves in the blood of Jesus (life of God) will have the right to live in the new world. All others will find themselves in the lake of fire. Jesus is the descendant of King David, the promised Messiah. He is the light of the world, the bright morning star.

In Revelation 22:17, there is one final call to everyone. "The Spirit and the Bride say, 'Come.' And let him who hears say, 'Come.' And let him who is thirsty come, let him who desires take the water of life without price." God does not want anyone to perish. He does not take pleasure in destruction but in bringing life to everyone. If you have read and believed the contents of this material and have never made a commitment to Jesus, now is the time! Simply say to Jesus in prayer: "Lord Jesus, I'm a sinner. Forgive me and come into my life. I now commit my life to you for your control and guidance!" To seal this commitment, go tell another

Christian what you have done. Spend time in prayer daily and study God's Word. You now belong to him!

There is a final warning to all, saved and unsaved. Revelation 22:18–19: "I warn everyone who hears the words of the prophecy of this book: if anyone adds to them, God will add to him the plagues described in this book, (19) and if anyone takes away from the words of the book of this prophecy, God will take away his share in the tree of life and in the holy city, which are described in this book." The *book* is not just Revelation, but the entire Word of God from Genesis through Revelation. Do not doubt God, seek to know him and understand his ways and his Word. It will prove to be a harvest of great blessings!

Let there be light in your life! Jesus is coming very soon. The grace of the Lord be with you!

## POINTS TO REMEMBER

1. At the end of the seven thousand years, this earth and heaven, along with the angelic heaven, will be destroyed.

2. The entire angelic realm (minus Lucifer, his angels, the Antichrist, and False Prophet), the bride of Christ, and all of

mankind that lived upon the earth from Adam to the time of the earth's destruction will stand before the throne of God. God will pass final judgment on every human that was not part of the bride of Christ. Those who refused to walk with God according to the light that was given to them during the time period that they lived will be thrown into the lake of fire. Those who embraced the light will remain in God's presence forever.

3. The condition of death and hell will be thrown into the lake of fire. Death, spiritual and physical, will no longer be allowed in God's creation. It will only exist in the lake of fire.

4. After God's judgment, God creates a new heaven and a new earth for all of God's angels and the redeemed of mankind in new glorified bodies to dwell together forever. Now we have returned to the position of Genesis 1:1, two heavens and one earth in a pure and holy state.

5. God dwells, once again with his created beings in perfect harmony of love, peace, joy, and productivity forever. All of God's created beings now clearly understand, due to the seven thousand year educational program, why we cannot live outside of God's sovereign control over his creation!

Let There Be Light

# TIME TABLE OF EVENTS FROM GENESIS THROUGH REVELATION

| Creation Year | Jewish Date | Western Date | Event |
|---|---|---|---|
| Eternity Past | | | Angelic creation |
| Eternity Past | | | Rebellion of Lucifer |
| Eternity Past | | | Proclamation of God, "Let there be light" |
| Eternity Present | | Day One | Separation of light and darkness |
| Eternity Present | | Day Two | Creation of a new heaven |
| Eternity Present | | Day Three | Angelic earth placed into the new heaven |
| 0 | | Day Four Jan 1, 3977 BC | Reassignment of angels; creation of sun, moon, and stars; beginning of our astrological time system |
| 0 | | Day Five | Creation of fish, birds, animals, and creeping things |
| 0 | | Day Six | Creation of man and woman |
| 0 | | Day Seven | God rested from his work and blessed the new creation |
| 0 | | 3977 BC | Adam and Eve sinned and are removed from Eden |

| | | | |
|---|---|---|---|
| 5 (?) | | 3972 BC (?) | First male child, Cain, is born |
| 36 (?) | | 3941 BC (?) | Cain kills Abel |
| 130 | | 3847 BC | Enoch is born |
| 216 | Tishri 1, 1 | 9-1-3761 BC | Beginning of the Jewish calendar and correlation of the three calendars |
| 1536 | 1130 | 2441 BC | Degeneration of life on earth, spiritually |
| 1656 | 1440 | 2321 BC | The flood of Noah |
| 1948 | 1732 | 2029 BC | Birth of Abram (Abraham) |
| 2453 | Nisan 15, 2237 | Mar 27, 1524 BC | Exodus of the Jews from Egypt |
| 2493 | Nisan 11, 2277 | Mar 13, 1484 BC | Entrance into the Promised Land |
| 2498 | 2282 | 1479 BC | Rest in the Promised Land |
| 3014 | 2798 | 963 BC | Kingdom of Israel is divided: ten tribes, two tribes |
| 3256 | 3040 | 721 BC | Assyrian conquest of Israel |
| 3371 | 3155 | 606 BC | Babylonian conquest of Judah |
| 3388 | 3173 | 588 BC | Babylonian destruction of Jerusalem |
| 3439 | 3223 | 538 BC | Media-Persian Empire conquest of Babylon |

| 3441 | 3225 | 536 BC | Jews return to Jerusalem to rebuild temple |
| --- | --- | --- | --- |
| 3520 | Nisan 1, 3304 | Mar 21, 457 BC | Proclamation of Artaxerxes to rebuild Jerusalem (beginning of Daniel's Seventy Weeks of years) |
| 3642 | 3426 | 335 BC | Alexander the Great invades Persia |
| 3914 | 3698 | 63 BC | Pompey takes Jerusalem |
| 3971 | Tishri 15, 3755 | Oct 10, 7 BC | Jesus is born |
| 4001 | 3785 | AD 25 | Jesus' ministry begins |
| 4003 | Nisan 1, 3787 | Mar 25, AD 27 | Daniel's Seventy Weeks stops with one week left |
| 4003 | Nisan 10, 3787 | Apr 3, AD 27 | Jesus rides into Jerusalem |
| 4003 | Nisan 14, 3787 | Apr 7, AD 27 | Jesus is crucified |
| 4003 | Nisan 18, 3787 | Apr 10, AD 27 | Jesus comes out of the tomb |
| 4046 | Av 9, 3830 | Aug 2, AD 70 | Roman destruction of Jerusalem and temple |
| 5924 | Iyyar 5, 5708 | May 14, AD 1948 | Jews return to Israel as a nation |
| 5962 | 5746 | Jul 5, AD 1986 | Beginning of the great tribulation period |
| 5990 | Iyyar 14, 5774 | May 14, AD 2014 | Opening of the sixth seal |

| | | | |
|---|---|---|---|
| 5990 | Iyyar 21, 5774 | May 21, AD 2014 | Beginning of Daniel's Seventieth Week |
| 5993 | 5778 | AD 2017 | Seventh trumpet of the seventh seal—rapture (prior to Nov 19, 2017, middle of the Seventieth Week) |
| 5993 | Heshvan 19, 5778 | Nov 8, AD 2017 | Antichrist crowned leader over Islamic nations |
| 5993 | Kislev 1, 5778 | Nov 19, AD 2017 | Overthrow of Jerusalem by ten Islamic nations |
| 5997 | Iyyar 19, 5781 | May 1, AD 2021 | Seventh bowl of wrath |
| 5997 | Sivan 9, 5781 | May 20, AD 2021 | Jesus returns to the Mt. of Olives, last day of Daniel's Seventieth Week |
| 5997 | Tammuz 24, 5781 | Jul 4, AD 2021 | Battle of Armageddon |
| 5998 | Tishri 1, 5783 | Sep 26, AD 2022 | Begin Jewish New Year (Feast of Trumpets) |
| 5998 | Tishri 10, 5783 | Oct 5, AD 2022 | Feast of Atonement (judgment day) |
| 5998 | Tishri 15, 5783 | Oct 10, AD 2022 | Feast of Tabernacles, entrance into the millennial reign of Jesus on earth |
| 6998 | 6783 | Oct 10, AD 3022 | End of one thousand year reign of Christ, the Devil is released |

| 7000 | Tevet 9, 6785 | Jan 1, AD 3025 | Beginning of Eternity Future with destruction of this creation, the great white throne judgment, and the creation of the new heaven and earth |

# Endnotes

1. Time as we know it did not being until the fourth day of our creation. The term "day" in its original context was not dealing with our literal time system. It was dealing with events that took place. Each new "day" consisted of new events added to the development of our creation. When God blessed everything on the seventh day and he rested from his work, it was a positional day that encompassed time. That would not change year in and year out unless something changed in the relationship to God's governing position in holiness over the established events which he had blessed. To say that each day of creation consisted of a 24 hour time period is foolishness. Time as we know it started on the fourth day of our creation, but it was not a controlling factor to the completion date of our creation! How long it took is not given to us. But based upon the complete picture, it could have been hours, days, weeks, months, or a combination of all, in the events that made up each day for a total of seven days. It certainly didn't take long for God to bless the seventh day. Also, the seventh day would not have ended to this day if sin had not impacted the condition. Whatever length of time it took for God to create our creation, it was very short!

# Let There Be Light

2. There is no time reference in Scripture of how long Adam and Eve were in the Garden of Eden before the temptation took place and the fall of mankind.

3. We do not have a specific date in Scripture so this date is an estimate at the time of birth for Adam and Eve's first male child.

4. This is an estimated time.

5. The term "grandson" is not used in Scripture. Every descendent down the line is called a "son." Also, Leviticus 18:8 states, "You shall not uncover the nakedness of your father's wife; it is your father's nakedness." The clothing of man was a symbolic covering by God for the spiritual sin of mankind that placed him outside of God's holy protective covering. Outside of that protective covering, man is subjected to demonic control and possession. The closer man walks with God in his fallen state, the more fruitful his life will be upon this earth. Through a person's continual act of faith in God, they are accepted by God, but life will be a continual battle until mankind's complete redemption of body, soul, and spirit. At that point, our sin nature will be gone forever along with our battle against evil. To see the nakedness of a person means that their sin is exposed.

6. This month marks the beginning of their religious calendar that runs for a period of seven months, within their regular calendar of twelve months. It begins six months before the end of the year, and concludes at the end of the first month of the following year. It is a symbolic picture in form and ritual of the precise steps that God will perform in the spiritual realm of this creation concerning his plan for our redemption from sin.

7. Ten is a symbol of the law that Christ will fulfill.

8. The lamb is a symbol of Jesus. All of us will partake of his life.

9. Jesus will go to the cross at 9:00 a.m. on the 14th and will die at 3:00 p.m. There are two evenings in the Jewish day: the evening of the day's end at 3:00 p.m., and the evening at 6:00 p.m., which is the beginning of a new day when it starts getting dark.

10. When we partake of the life of Jesus, his blood is upon us, our body, where we live.

11. This is a fiery death to our self-will, so the will of God can be exercised through us.

12. This is to be a sinless act.

13. There must be true repentance with sorrow concerning our sins.

14. Our salvation cannot be watered down. It is a serious issue with God.

15. The act of repentance must be complete. Nothing is left over.

16. We must leave a life of sin and bondage behind us.

17. The Lord passes from life to death, so that we may pass from death into his eternal life.

18. While the Holy Spirit was already given to dwell within man to give God's enlightenment to us, now the Holy Spirit will come upon us with power and spiritual gifts. With spir-

itual rebirth through the Holy Spirit, the kingdom of God enters into us, and we enter into the kingdom. We are now in Christ! With the baptism of the Holy Spirit, the power of God comes upon us, and we become participating members of the body of Christ in performing the works of God on earth using God's spiritual gifts.

19. Verse 20 shall take place with the opening of the sixth seal in Revelation 6:12–17 on May 14, AD 2014, which is Jewish Iyyar 14, 5774, beginning at 10:16 p.m. UTC over Jerusalem.

20. It should be clearly understand that the "church" is not a building or denomination. The church is the sum total of all believers who have accepted Jesus as their Lord and Savior and are under his control, individually and collectively. Individually, in our daily activities, we follow the leading of the Holy Spirit. Collectively, when we gather together in groups to worship the Lord and grow in our relationship with Jesus through the help of those individuals that Jesus has raised up with special gifting. The apostles, prophets, evangelists, pastors, and teachers that help us are to be under the leading of the Holy Spirit, and they are accountable to Jesus and to the people that they serve. Jesus runs the church individually and collectively, and there are chastisements and disciplinary actions rendered individually and collective when Christians walk in disobedience. We are also called the "body of Christ." The "body" has one head, and each member has different functions. When church leaders think that they can run the church without the leading of the Lord through the power of the Holy Spirit, they enter a path of folly and futility.

21. This event will begin May 14, AD 2014, at 10:16 p.m. over Jerusalem with the opening of the sixth seal in Revelation 6:12–17.

22. This event will take place sometime shortly before the end of the first three and a half years of the final seven year period of Daniel's Seventieth Week that begins after the opening of the sixth seal.

23. God-given perception.

24. This is the Antichrist who will proclaim that he is God.

25. The holy place is not dealing with a physical temple. Since the resurrection of Jesus, man is the temple of God and man's heart is the holy place. That is why it is stated in parentheses, "let the reader understand." At this point, the Antichrist is standing, which means he is presenting himself to be God; he has not yet taken his seat in man's heart as God.

26. Jesus is speaking to the Christian population living in Judea, not the Jews. The Jews, as a nation, will not have the revelation of Christ until the rapture takes place.

27. When Jesus returns for his saints, it will be a major worldwide event that everyone will know about. There will be no secret arrival!

28. Where ever the body of Christ is around the world, they will fly like eagles to meet the Lord in the air.

29. It is clearly defined here that the great tribulation is in process and the Antichrist is involved.

30. This is the opening of the sixth seal as defined in Revelation 6:12–13.

31. This marks the beginning of Daniel's Seventieth Week on the eighth day after the seven days of darkness, from the sixth seal opening. From the "sign" that is presented, a multitude around the world will be made aware that Jesus is the Son of God and is the true Messiah. There will be great sorrow and weeping in the lives of the people because of their sinful state, relative to the holiness of Jesus.

32. In verse (30) from the sign of the Son of man in heaven to his coming on the clouds for the rapture, there is a time separation just short of forty-two months.

33. This is the rapture!

34. The first beast represents the Babylonian Empire.

35. The second beast represents the Media-Persian Empire.

36. The third beast represents the Grecian Empire.

37. The fourth beast is the Roman Empire that is different from the rest, because there is a transformation that takes place in the territorial boundaries down through the ages to this present time. It began as a heathen nation and oversaw the crucifixion of Jesus in AD 27. But within 300 years after the resurrection of Jesus, Christianity became the leading religion of the nation. Then in AD 626 Mohammed developed the religion of Islam. Today these two religions dominate the territory of the old Roman Empire.

38. It is different because it is a religious order of nations.

39. The little horn represents the Antichrist that will come on the scene after the ten nations have joined together. He will take over three of the nations and he will become their

awaited messiah. The saints will be raptured just before he takes authority over all ten nations and rules for the last half, forty-two months, of Daniel's Seventieth Week.

40. This refers to the rapture of the saints before the seven bowls of wrath occur, because we are the ones that give sacrifice and offering to the Lord.

41. With the opening of the seventh seal and the trumpet judgments, there are no fixed dates that we can pinpoint specific starting points and completion dates. However, there are in sequential order and will take place from the beginning of the final seven year countdown being May 21, AD 2014, to November 19, at noon, AD 2017, which is the exact middle of Daniel's final Seventieth Week of prophecy, a total of three and one-half years.

42. There are six nations controlled by the Devil that have taken Israel captive throughout history. They are the Egyptian, Assyrian, Babylonian, Media-Persian, Grecian, and Roman Empires. The seventh head or empire, not yet formed, will consist of ten Islamic countries joined together and will dominate the world for forty-two months.

43. For this forty-two month period all creation will see the results of planet earth being totally dominated by evil. Sacrifice and offering as we know it, rendered to the true God, will not be allowed.

44. The seven bowls of wrath that are poured upon the earth during the last forty-two months of Daniel's Seventieth Week are in sequential order. Only the seventh bowl can be pinpointed to a date of May 1, AD 2021.

CPSIA information can be obtained at www.ICGtesting.com
Printed in the USA
BVOW072202110312

284857BV00001B/2/P